# TWO | PATHS

## ALSO BY JOHN KASICH

*Courage Is Contagious: Ordinary People Doing
Extraordinary Things to Change the Face of America*

*Stand for Something: The Battle for America's Soul*

*Every Other Monday: Twenty Years of Life,
Lunch, Faith, and Friendship*

# TWO | PATHS

*America Divided or United*

# JOHN KASICH

with

## DANIEL PAISNER

A THOMAS DUNNE BOOK ☙ ST. MARTIN'S PRESS   NEW YORK

THOMAS DUNNE BOOKS.
An imprint of St. Martin's Press.

TWO PATHS. Copyright © 2017 by John Kasich. All rights reserved. Printed in the United States of America. No part of this book may be used or reproduced in any manner whatsoever without written permission except in the case of brief quotations embodied in critical articles or reviews. For information, address St. Martin's Press, 175 Fifth Avenue, New York, N.Y. 10010.

The Library of Congress Cataloging-in-Publication Data is available upon request.

ISBN 978-1-250-13846-0 (hardcover)
ISBN 978-1-250-13847-7 (e-book)

Our books may be purchased in bulk for promotional, educational, or business use. Please contact your local bookseller or the Macmillan Corporate and Premium Sales Department at 1-800-221-7945, extension 5442, or by e-mail at MacmillanSpecialMarkets@macmillan.com.

First published in the United States by Thomas Dunne Books, St. Martin's Press

First Edition: April 2017

10  9  8  7  6  5  4  3  2  1

*To Karen, Emma, and Reese, always . . .*

*And to everyone who's ever helped me in my career*
*and given me the chance to be a leader . . .*

Man's mind, once stretched by a new idea, never regains its original dimensions.

—OLIVER WENDELL HOLMES

# CONTENTS

# TWO | PATHS

# SEPTEMBER 18, 2015

# Mackinac Island, Michigan

The day started like any other. We were in Los Angeles, headed to Chicago, where we would catch a charter flight to Mackinac Island, Michigan, for the Mackinac Republican Leadership Conference.

Business as usual—or, at least, what passed for business as usual on the campaign trail.

It was just a couple months after I'd announced my candidacy, yet we'd very quickly fallen into a routine. Our itineraries would change one day to the next, but there were predictable markers along the way. There was always someplace I needed to be . . . some important, must-attend event on the calendar, some extra few hours we desperately needed to squeeze into our days to accomplish everything we'd set out to do, and my team was merely trying to move heaven and earth and maybe even part the skies a little bit to get me to this tiny resort island on Lake Huron. Trouble was, Mackinac Island wasn't the easiest place to get to—tough to leave, too, if you talked to the locals, but you had to get to the island first. We had to charter a small plane to take us there from

Chicago—about an hour-long flight in the best of circumstances, only these weren't exactly the best of circumstances.

Understand, when you run for president, you tend to hear the phrase "flying into weather" a whole lot more than you do at any other time in your life. But you're also inclined to tune it out. You tell yourself you've got no choice but to keep pushing ever onward. You're moving about constantly—"up in the air" in every sense— and it starts to feel like you've got to keep to the schedule no matter what. Of course, that's never actually the case. The schedule is sacrosanct—but only until it isn't. You can always reschedule, or skip an event, or make some other arrangement, but in the middle of a national campaign, these never feel like good options. You want to make doubly sure to honor your commitments and hit all the right notes, make all the right stops, so you learn to trust that the professional drivers and pilots you hire to ferry you around the country will get you where you need to be—on time and in one piece. You leave yourself no choice but to trust in this, because you know the other folks running for president are flying into weather of their own and you don't want to be caught short.

You do what you set out to do.

That's kind of what happened here. We'd set it up so we were to be met at the Mackinac Island Airport by Michigan legislator Tom Leonard and his wife, Jenell, who would accompany our team in a horse-drawn carriage to the island's signature resort, the Grand Hotel. Tom's support was key, we all believed, and it meant a great deal that he and his wife were to come out to meet us like this. And the horse-drawn carriage wasn't for some photo op. That's just the way you get around on the island, where there are no motorized vehicles other than a fire truck and an ambulance. It's one of those "land that time forgot" kind of places, a bucolic throwback to another era, where people "dress" for dinner (and for breakfast and lunch, too!)—and here it was looking like more than half the candidates for the Republican nomination were planning to make an appearance over the run of the conference.

This buggy ride with the Leonards was just the first meeting on my calendar. There were also one-on-one interviews with Jake Tapper of CNN, Chuck Todd of NBC, and local reporters from Detroit and Chicago; a visit with a former ambassador; a private meeting with Michigan governor Rick Snyder. Oh, and I was also expected to give a speech at the conference luncheon and meet afterward with area executives and potential donors, so there was a whole lot riding on this visit. So when my campaign manager, Beth Hansen, was hightailing it from Columbus to Tiffin, Ohio, just south of Toledo, she wasn't too worried about the urgent calls she kept getting from the charter service we'd hired to fly us to the island, telling her there was a line of thunderstorms coming in that they wanted to avoid. I mean, yeah, she was worried, but like me, she trusted the pilots to make the determination on whether it was safe to fly—and here they were telling her that we were in good shape, provided we take off on time.

It was just a little weather, right? No big thing.

The plan was for Beth to hitch a ride from Tiffin to Chicago, where she would meet our flight from LAX and join us for the short trip to Mackinac Island. But that was now Plan B. John Weaver, my campaign adviser, had been with us in Los Angeles, and the original plan had been for him to join us for this leg to the Upper Peninsula, but he had to beg off at the last moment, so a seat had opened up for Beth, a Michigan native who had been the political director of the Michigan Republican Party. Beth knew the lay of the land, and a lot of the people we'd be meeting at the conference; it made all kinds of sense for her to now accompany us, so she hurried to Tiffin for the ride-along to Chicago.

By the time Beth met up with us in Chicago, she could see the reports of those terrible thunderstorms on the airport television monitors. My whole team could see them. Meanwhile, I was busy grilling the pilots. Flying into weather was one thing, but I always made doubly sure that the skies were safe, and one of the ways I did this was to take the pilots' measure. I thought that if I talked to them, I'd get a good read on the situation. There's a reason the airlines track such storms so closely, and I wanted to understand what the pilots were seeing, what they were expecting. Beth told me later that she saw I had my back to the monitors in the airport, and she knew that if I turned around and saw all the weather alerts, I would not have let us take off, even if the pilots gave us the green light. She's probably right on this, but I never did turn around. I was too busy looking out the window at the darkening skies and taking in the confident looks on the faces of the serious pilots. They flew in and out of these types of storms all the time—to them, the weather was concerning but not any more concerning than, say, crossing a busy street, so we climbed into the small plane we'd chartered and prepared to take off before our weather window closed.

My poor assistant, Alex Thomas, was consigned to an odd jump seat: it doubled as a toilet—that's how jammed in we were. The close quarters didn't do a whole lot to help us relax. The pilots, they seemed fine, but all this talk about the approaching thunderstorms had us passengers a little on edge, so as we buckled in and got ready for takeoff, we were a little quieter than usual.

Almost as soon as we were up at altitude, we started getting slapped around pretty good. It felt as if we were in a clothes dryer, on tumble. We were all experienced flyers; we'd flown through our share of turbulence and stomach drops and flash moments of worry on airplanes. But this flight was so far beyond any of that. It was crazy, terrifying—and it just went on and on and on, with no letup.

Got to admit, I was uncomfortable—and angry. I hated that we'd made the decision to fly through this storm, even though we'd come to that decision in a reasonable manner. If you sat on the ground until your flight path was completely clear and calm, you'd never get anywhere. There are always bumps along the way; the idea is to check the satellite forecast and know what you're getting into—and here we all thought we were in good shape.

Yet, here we were, getting slapped around.

Usually, when I flew with this group, there was an awful lot of talking. We'd watch movies. We'd laugh. We'd strategize. But on this flight to Mackinac Island, no one said a word—except, every few minutes, I'd holler to the pilots to ask them what was going on up there. Those pilots were all business, no nonsense, and I don't think they appreciated hearing from me in the middle of those thunderstorms, but I had it in my head that those guys couldn't see a blessed thing, that they'd lose a sense of the horizon, that we'd be propelled right out of our seats.

Afterward, some of the others on board told me they thought we'd crash. I never felt that way because I kept hearing from Pat Kellum, the Ohio State trooper who was traveling with us on my security detail, that we were going to be just fine. But we were deep into panic mode—privately, separately, each of us was running through all the worst-case scenarios in our heads.

Let me tell you, folks—it was bad. And it was relentless. There was just no letup. And it's not like we could climb a couple thousand feet and find a smoother ride; we were in this thing the rest of the way. This was our "weather window"—another phrase you hear all the time when you're running for office.

At one point, my trusted political adviser Doug Preisse leaned over to Alex Thomas and asked if there was any booze on board. Doug had been traveling with me since I announced my candidacy, and he never missed a chance to let me know how much he hated flying. We were all white-knuckling it on this flight, but Doug's knuckles were undoubtedly the whitest, and he thought a drink might help calm his nerves.

Much as I loved to argue with him, I couldn't argue with him on this one.

Alex found a half bottle of Crown Royal and a couple of paper cups. I don't usually drink whiskey, but I poured myself a shot, and as I threw it back, I thought, Okay, Lord, we've had just about enough. Knock it off. We get it. We shouldn't have taken off. Bad idea. We should do a better job establishing our priorities.

I fell into silent prayer, to see if there was maybe some way I could talk Him out of whatever it was He had in mind.

Alex, Doug, our communications director Chris Schrimpf— they were all pretty much braced for impact, thinking their numbers were up. Me? I was uncomfortable, uneasy, but I never thought our plane was going down. I never got that far in my thinking. Why? Because if you let yourself think like that, you'll never board another plane in your life. So, I was worried but not panicked; daunted but not defeated.

That half bottle of Crown Royal didn't last very long, I'll say that. And the whiskey didn't do too much to calm us down, but by some miracle of faith and expertise and instrumentation, our pilots managed to land the plane safely at Mackinac Island. As we touched down, you could see the color return to the faces of our traveling party. (I can't imagine how I must have looked to them— not good, I'm betting.) Nobody'd gotten sick, but we were all soaked in sweat and dread and the absolute certainty that we'd just dodged some kind of bullet. One of the things I kept thinking about now that we were safely on the tarmac was all those politicians who'd lost their lives on small planes, desperate to keep to their schedules, chasing their runaway campaigns. I didn't want be remembered that way. We'd been at this thing only a couple of months, and in that time our message of hope and civility had really started to connect with voters across the country. It was important—but so was our safety.

I turned to Beth and said, "Never again."

Meaning, this was the last time we'd fly a small charter plane into anything resembling a storm.

Meaning, nothing was so important that it couldn't be rescheduled.

Meaning, we'd stop paying attention to what all the other candidates were doing and just worry about our own campaign.

And then the strangest thing happened. As we stepped from the plane, the skies cleared. The weather turned from treacherous and terrible to quite pleasant. The ground was wet, and as we made our way to Tom and Jenell Leonard waiting with the horse-drawn carriage, there was the fresh scent of recent rain all around. And it was quiet! Really, it was a lovely evening, and as we pulled away from the airport, I was struck by the incongruity of the moment. We'd gone from a full hour of absolute terror to complete silence. Remember, there were no cars. The typical hustle and bustle of daily living was nowhere apparent on Mackinac Island—part of the appeal of the place, I was realizing. The frenzy of a presidential campaign, where you run around the country chasing momentum, had been put on pause. It was as if that horrible flight had never happened, as if a switch had been flipped and we were set down on this picture-postcard island, where we would now catch our breaths and gather our wits. We'd be able to be back at it soon enough.

It was almost jarring—to be hurtling through the sky in the

middle of a heinous storm one moment, and in the next moment to be rolling down quiet streets in a horse-drawn carriage to a grand hotel that once boasted the longest covered porch in America.

Such is the life of a presidential candidate, I guessed—and yet, as we left the airport, I took the time to wonder what the heck I was doing there.

# 1.

# "What Moose, Daddy?"

We live in a post-truth environment.

That's a term I heard throughout the 2016 presidential campaign, long before anyone was talking about "alternative facts," and it set me off. One of the reasons it bothered me, I think, was because it's true. And I have to think that one of the reasons the expression has caught on the way it has—the *Oxford English Dictionary* named "post-truth" the "international word of the year"— is because it points out a fault in our culture. It suggests that in politics, in government, in our national dialogue, the truth is no longer relevant.

These days, the space between truth and half-truths and utter falsehoods is almost unrecognizable. What's most concerning is the way these post-truths have seeped into the back-and-forth that now passes for political discourse. Too many of our politicians and elected officials have taken to saying whatever they want to in order to make their point, and it doesn't seem to matter if what they're saying is even close to true. What matters, apparently, is how such false or misleading statements make American voters *feel,* and how so-called or would-be leaders can fool us into believing that they themselves stand a little taller than they actually do.

*What people believe prevails over the truth.*

That's a line from Sophocles, and he was on to something, I guess. In matters of the heart, or faith, or personal relationships, I suppose there's value in this view. We're human beings, after all. We're wired in an emotional way. We tend to respond to certain situations with our guts instead of our heads. I get that. The ancient Greeks, they got that, too. But in a political campaign, I believe we should place the truth above all else. I don't care what party you belong to or what office you're seeking—you owe it to your constituents, to the people you're looking to serve, to get it right. If you say something is so, then it ought to be so.

You know, before I was elected to the Ohio Senate, there was a push to build a bridge in my district. My constituents were all for it, and wanted some assurances from me that this was something I could get done after I was elected. So, I went to then-Governor Jim Rhodes and asked him about it. I said, "Is this something we're going to be able to do for these people?"

He said, "Just tell them you'll get it for them, and we'll see what happens."

That was the way of things in politics, I was learning, and I didn't like it. So, I stood against it. I didn't like it then, and I don't like it now. From the very beginning, when I gave people my word, I meant to keep it.

This disconnect reminds me of the guy in that great Beatles song, "Nowhere Man," who just sees what he wants to see. I guess Lennon and McCartney were on to something as well, recognizing that at times we can all turn a blind eye to what troubles or confuses us. This, too, is our nature. But in a presidential election cycle, I don't think we have that luxury. Wishful thinking doesn't cut it. We can't pick and choose among half-truths and utter falsehoods and grab only at the ones that reinforce our preconceived notions or stoke our shared fears. We can't live in our own reality—not if we hope to come together and attempt to solve the very real problems facing this great country. We owe it to ourselves, and to each other, to understand the world as it appears before us, not as we might remember it or hope it will be again.

There's a disconnect in America now, and it troubles me. Perhaps it troubles you. Maybe that's one of the reasons you picked up this book—because, like me, you've become frustrated at the tone of our national conversation. How did this happen? When did this happen? And *what* are we going to do about it? We've got to do *something,* because it's a worrisome and dangerous thing when we allow the post-truths that marked the 2016 presidential campaign to permeate our culture and (mis)inform our shared thinking, when we allow the truth to become beside the point.

*The truth shall set you free.*

Ah, now *that's* a line from John 8:32, and I have to think he was on to something most of all, something we would all do well to keep in mind as we move forward. I think most of us can understand the impulse to hide our heads in the sand and look away from looming trouble. But our leaders shouldn't prey on that impulse. In fact, they should help us recognize it, overcome it, and confront our troubles head-on. Because the truth, even a painful truth, is absolute.

There is no path forward without it.

## THE SUM OF OUR FEARS

As we wake up to the reality that we live in a polarized nation, with a deeply divided electorate and a new president who seemed at times during the campaign to embrace that polarization—who against all odds and prognostications found a way to cross that deep divide and win the White House, who took the time from his presumably busy schedule to tweak his "enemies" with a "Happy New Year" message on Twitter—we must pause to reflect. It's time to consider how the post-truth environment we live in might have created the extraordinary circumstances that set in motion one of the most extraordinary elections in our history—and to understand what we can do to restore reason and decency and calm to our national conversation.

I've spent a great deal of time thinking about the tears in the fabric of our society, and praying about them, and talking them through with some of the best political minds in the country, and what I've come to realize is that there are no easy ways to explain the uneasiness of the American people. However, there are signposts we might have seen leading up to and running all the way through the last election, if we were paying good and close attention. The most telling of these signs—glaring, obvious signs—is that people are hurting. There's a sense out there in America's heartland, and all over the world, that we are no longer in control of our own lives. Whether it's job insecurity, or rising student debt, or endless worries over how to pay for health care and prescription drugs, people have good reason to feel at a loss. And in some cases, this sense that our lives are out of our control can lead to hopelessness, especially when we look up to find that our troubles don't seem to trouble a very select few. For the folks who live at the upper reaches of society, the so-called elites and 1 percenters, these worries are simply not relevant—truths to be bent into post-truths, or spun into alternative facts, or even set aside. Everything appears to be going great for the folks at the very top, and those who are struggling can only look on and become angry at the disparity.

And you don't have to dig too, too deep beneath that anger to find an underlying fear, and when politicians set out to stoke that fear, to build on it—well, that's when you find yourself living in the kind of uncertain landscape we saw during the 2016 campaign. That's when people start to feel alone, as if their lives are happening *to* them instead of them directing their lives. Granted, they might start to feel that way on their own, as the circumstances of their lives conspire against them, but when they're *made* to feel that way by someone or a group of *someones* out to exploit those feelings of anger and fear, that's when they begin to think that there's no one looking out for them, that they're being left behind.

Nowadays, when someone extends a kindness, it's almost not to be believed. The way we pay such kindnesses forward can really brighten our days—like the time just after the election when I went to my local Verizon store to see about a problem with my cell phone. The problem, regrettably, was that I'd just taken up swimming, and I'd dropped my phone in the pool. It was totally my fault, and I told the store manager what had happened. I was in the store a good long while, until they finally got it all sorted out and set me up with a new phone.

I said, "What do I owe you?"

The store manager smiled and said, "There's no charge. We made you wait so long, so there's no charge."

Of course, I'd fully expected to have to pay for my boneheaded move at the pool, so this kindness took me completely by surprise.

I said, "That's so nice of you, but it's really not necessary. It was my fault."

And the store manager said, "Oh, that's nothing," and then proceeded to tell me the story of another customer who'd just been in the store who'd had a problem with *her* phone, and who'd burst into tears when she was told there'd be no charge. Through her tears, the customer said, "Nobody treats people like this anymore."

No, they don't. *We* don't. Not as much as we should, at least. Not as much as we used to. We've simply fallen out of the habit of caring for one another, most especially in our cities and suburbs. The days of neighbor helping neighbor seem to be gone. Most of us go about our lives with our heads down, eyes to the ground and focused on the road ahead, instead of with our heads held high, eyes up and open to the world around us. There are way too many of us moving about in our own little bubbles, doing what we need to do to get by, and this, too, contributes to that sense of anger, and to the fear at its core. And you can just imagine what happens to all these emotions when politicians start telling you that someone else is the cause of your worries. When they start pointing fingers and encouraging you to blame our leaders and our institutions and perhaps even other groups of people for the difficulties you're facing. You're likely to become even angrier, even more afraid, and to start looking for ways to express that anger and fear.

There's no denying that a great many Americans have missed out on the economic recovery of the past decade—if, indeed, that's what it was. The stock market might be up, and the dollar might be strong, but more and more people are being left behind. More and more people are seeing their jobs downsized, or moved overseas. They're unable to trade the skill set they've developed and honed their entire adult lives for another set that might open up a new career opportunity. They're stuck, and as the pace of our lives gets crazier and faster, as we become more and more connected to one another through social media, with instant access to every conceivable bit and byte of information, some folks are undoubtedly finding themselves feeling more disconnected than ever before. Time-worn anchors such as family and community are no longer in place to keep us grounded—here again, *especially* in our cities and suburbs—leading many good, hardworking people to feel that they've got no support system to help them through whatever crisis they might be facing.

That said, there are a great many of our rural communities where the church remains an anchor, a beacon; where the union hall offers a sense of stability and certainty; where people come together to support one another in times of trial. We find ways to keep connected, no matter where we live, but my point here is that such connections don't run as deep as they do in our memories. They don't find us as often as they should.

Think back to the Great Depression, when our families and communities were stronger than they seem to be today. People were hurting, then as now, and many were afraid, then as now. But in all the histories I've read of that period, all the documentaries I've seen, I can find no traces of the anger that bubbled forth from the electorate during the last presidential campaign. Back during the Depression, people worked together to get through the hard times. That's an oversimplification of events, I realize, but there's a point to be made in general terms. Today, it feels to a lot of folks that they're going it alone, that they've got no place to turn. Again, I'm generalizing, but I hope you take my point: When you're feeling desperate and isolated, it becomes easy to start throwing around blame; and when you start throwing around blame, it's inevitable that we start to turn on one another.

Yes, we're struck by the random-acts-of-kindness stories that still seem to find us—only, now they're an anomaly instead of the order of the day. I'm thinking of stories like that of Linda Wilson-Allen, the San Francisco bus driver who treats her job like a calling, and considers her bus route her ministry. Her story was featured on the front page of the *San Francisco Chronicle* during the last weeks of the 2016 campaign, and as I read it I wondered just how this had become front-page news. Don't misunderstand me, it was a good and blessed thing, the way this woman approached her work each morning with a song in her heart. She learned the names of her regular commuters, was known to keep the bus waiting if one of them was running late, and would even step down from the driver's seat to help a passenger struggling with grocery bags. In the article, it said that this woman was such a joyful presence in the lives of her passengers that some of them would let a bus go by if the doors opened up and they saw that Linda Wilson-Allen wasn't behind the wheel. But as I read the article, which was pointed out to me by my friend Tom Barrett, I started to wonder when it happened that a simple kindness, even a sustained kindness shared over time, had become so newsworthy.

As a side note, another friend, John Ortberg, reached out to tell me he'd invited Linda Wilson-Allen to speak at the Menlo Park Presbyterian Church in California, where he is the pastor, and that at the end of her talk, members of his congregation lined up to shake her hand. What's remarkable about this is that a lot of the folks lining up to celebrate this woman were high-powered Silicon Valley CEOs, so her example is a great reminder that you don't have to do something *big* to change the world. Sometimes it's the small, daily acts of human kindness that matter most of all—even to the movers and shakers and Silicon Valley CEOs among us.

I'm thinking, too, of a Boston cab driver who picked up another friend of mine when he was vacationing with his family during the summer of 2016. The cabbie heard the family talking about a famous local bakery in the North End that was known for a particular pastry. My friend and his family wanted to try it, they all said, but they were put off by the long lines, stretching around the block. Without a word, the cabbie turned down a side street, switched off the meter, and announced to my friend that he would like to present the family with a gift, as a kind of welcome to his city. Then he raced into the back door of the famous bakery and came out with four of the aforementioned pastries, one for each member the family. When my friend tried to pay the cabbie for his kindness in the form of a generous tip, the cabbie refused—another good and blessed thing, and I share this story here for the way it stands as the exception instead of the rule.

Every time my friend shares that story, he says, people can't get over it, and what they're responding to, I think, is the way it reminds them of the decency and generosity of spirit we used to take for granted. I don't mean to suggest that these aspects of the human character have left us entirely. Not at all. We're all on the receiving end of such kindnesses from time to time—like when we drop our phones in the swimming pool and step sheepishly into our local Verizon store—and many of us find ways to give as good as we get. Lately, though, we tend to see this type of behavior when there's a tragedy, such as a death or an illness. We see it in times of celebration, too—at a wedding or the birth of a child. Mercifully, blessedly, we still find ways to come together when we live at the extremes, in joy and sorrow. We lift each other up. We hold each other close. We're in it together.

But what about those business-as-usual moments, when we're all just getting by? I'm thinking here of that great line often attributed to C. S. Lewis: "Integrity is doing the right thing, even when no one is watching." What about all those times when no one is watching? Then, it can feel like we're off on our own, which I guess is why it's so remarkable when we step onto a city bus driven by someone like Linda Wilson-Allen, or get into a taxi driven by someone like my friend's cabbie.

It was in this context, I believe, that the anger of the 2016 presidential campaign was allowed take hold, that our post-truth environment was allowed to take shape. And when we added feelings of being disconnected and afraid for our futures to this troubling trend of politicians telling us whatever they thought we wanted to hear, whether or not it was the truth, there was no telling how the American people would respond.

## LOOKING AWAY

I can remember a family trip Karen and I took with our twin girls, back when Emma and Reese were about six or seven years old. We were hiking in Montana. Karen was trailing behind with Reese, and Emma and I were up ahead. All of a sudden, a giant moose stepped onto the path in front of us. I suppose this was something I might have anticipated, given that we were hiking in the woods of Montana, but this moose took me completely by surprise. Emma and I stopped dead in our tracks. Emma was probably too young to be afraid, but I was anxious enough for both of us, because this great beast was right in our path—close enough that we could hear him breathing, snorting.

I don't know if you've ever seen a moose, but it's a majestic and terrifying sight. Most people, when they think of a moose, picture a playful cartoon character like Bullwinkle, or the moose on the Moosehead beer label. They think of the stuffed moose head over the fireplace in a ski lodge. You can't really know how imposing and intimidating an adult male moose can appear until you've seen one up close and personal. Really, it's huge—just incredible. This moose probably weighed over one thousand pounds, easy. I actually took time to wonder how he was able to even hold his head up, because the antlers were just enormous.

Mostly, though, I worried what the heck I should do. I was holding Emma's hand—tight, tight, tight—but I didn't want to let on that I was frightened. She was just a little girl, and if she'd picked up on the fact that I was spooked, it would have been all over. And naturally, I couldn't let the moose know that we were frightened, either, because he'd pick up on that; so I didn't want Emma to make any sudden movements. The moose is a very dangerous animal. It might seem to move about at a very lumbering pace, like you'd have all the time in the world to get out of its way if it gave chase, but it can be lightning quick, especially when it feels threatened. And its hooves are razor-sharp—that's how it kills, how it survives in the wild. I knew all these things, in a back-of-the-mind sort of way. It felt as if we were staring down this moose for the longest time, waiting him out. I was careful not to do the wrong thing, careful not to let Emma see that I was so worried.

I started to back up, ever so slowly, holding Emma's hand so tightly she had no choice but to follow. We took baby steps—steps so small you might not have noticed. Soon, we'd put a little distance between ourselves and the moose, and as good luck would have it, he became distracted by a noise in the opposite direction, turned tail, and lumbered back into the forest.

I'm guessing you could've heard my sigh of relief for miles.

Emma and I continued on our way, almost as if nothing had happened. My heart was beating like crazy, but even now that the danger had passed, I didn't want to make a big deal out of it. Still,

I thought it was something we should talk about, so after we'd walked for a while, I said, "Hey, Emma, what'd you think of that moose?"

And she turned to me and said, "What moose, Daddy?"

It hadn't even been five minutes.

I thought that was a remarkable thing, the way she'd blocked it out. Like the moose itself, her response caught me completely by surprise. It's not that she forgot about it over time. No, she put it out of her head *immediately,* as if this close encounter with Bullwinkle had never happened. It was all just too much for her little head to consider, so she'd set it aside.

Now that I think back on this moment, I realize there must be a coping mechanism that allows us to avoid a difficult reality, to step over the moose droppings in our path if we find them too troubling, too difficult to consider. When we're frightened, when we're up against it, when we can't see our way to a workable solution or a hopeful future, we have the ability to create our own facts, to rewrite our own narrative. This is a dangerous thing, wouldn't you agree? It might have been a harmless childhood impulse for Emma to turn away from that fear, but when we see it on the campaign trail, in the media, in the back-and-forth among supposedly informed adults purportedly seeking to advance the public good, we're headed for trouble.

And when we see it in ourselves, when we begin to accept this post-truth environment as the law of the land, we are well and truly doomed. As I've said, there is no path forward unless we are guided by the truth. So, let's be clear on what is abundantly clear. Let's rise above this post-truth environment and accept our world on its face. Let's accept that we live in a time when many Americans are struggling. Let's accept that people are having a tough time paying their mortgages. They don't have the money for the prescription drugs they need to stay healthy. Their jobs are disappearing, or their wages are being slashed. They're worrying over retirement or a disability. Their neighborhoods are deteriorating. They live with the threat of global warming and global terror; or they live in the shadows, struggling with addiction or a deepening depression they cannot afford to have diagnosed or treated. More and more, they're feeling they're all alone. These are very real concerns, ones not to be minimized or ignored, and we cannot rely on someone else to fix all these problems for us. They will not magically right themselves, or disappear.

Here is what I know, as sure as I know anything. Here is what we all know, deep down. The solutions to these problems will not come from a place of hate or polarization. They will not rise up from a well of anger, nor will they emerge from a single, narrow point of view. Throughout the 2016 presidential campaign, I stood onstage at those debates and watched in amazement as some of my counterparts attacked one another, wallowed in the mud, lied, called each other liars, and disparaged each other's character. It was just nuts, and I suppose I could've let it go, but as I took it all in, I kept thinking how important it was for each and every candidate to examine his or her own behavior to make sure that it was worthy of the office they were seeking, and to understand that any path to darkness does not represent what makes America strong.

Once I withdrew from the race, once the way forward appeared blocked and the contested battleground moved from state to state, from sea to shining sea, the hatred and polarization seemed to get worse. I wouldn't have thought such a thing possible, but there it was, now laced with a coarseness that had no place in a presidential campaign—and no precedent.

And now as we move as a nation through the first uneasy days of the Trump administration, a time that has been quickly stamped by the "alternative facts" that flowed freely from White House spokespersons, I'm pushed yet again to consider the weight of the truth against the sleight of hand of deception and denial. As I was trying to make sense of all this, I came across an interesting opinion piece in *Christianity Today*, written by Ed Stetzer. The article suggested that the Trump Administration had gotten off to a bad start with respect to the truth—a concerning thing to Stetzer, a well-known author and pastor.

"Even if the truth doesn't seem favorable to us," he wrote, "we don't have to go looking for an opposing story. We have a hope in something greater."

As I consider these words and look back on this last election cycle, I see that there are lessons to be drawn from my time on the campaign trail, from the campaign itself. Yet those lessons come to light only when we place this presidential race in context. Really, the negative tone of the campaign could not have come at a worse time. Many Americans are being left behind, or maybe they're making it, doing okay, but feeling betrayed by a system or a government that's too big to fail. Maybe they're feeling alone, that their lives are out of their control, that they can't make a difference— not just for themselves, but for their families, their communities.

I spoke to these realities as I traveled the country, but I tried to do so from a place of hopefulness. I looked for ways to remind voters that America was already great, and that its greatness resided in the goodness of its people. This stood in stark contrast to some of my Republican opponents, who seemed content to turn on one another and fire up the electorate in ways that could only reinforce the feeling that the deck was stacked against them. Yet these other candidates failed to consider the resilience of the American people. In their efforts to divide us, I could only hope that my opponents were really unlocking America's secret weapon, uniting us as a country and as a people. I wanted to believe this more and more, as our campaign bus rolled on. I heard it in our town halls, and from folks I'd meet on the street, in the airport, at the local diner. And I would try to honor these feelings and to give them voice as I spoke to the good people who came out to my events and to those I met along the way.

Throughout the campaign, some people on my own team were telling me I should get into it with some of these candidates, but I didn't want to go there. It wasn't right. It wasn't me. If this was what it took to win, then winning wasn't for me. I didn't want to be the candidate who won by trading on people's fears and sinking into the mud. Even more important, at the end of the day, I didn't think this approach would work. Why? Because the nastiness spewing from these other campaigns did not represent the mood of the country. Because the key to winning the support of the American voter was in reminding them not how they might be *less than* or *neglected*, but how they were special, unique. Because I understood that each of us looks for opportunities to matter and to make a difference, and that each of us deserves to be celebrated, not beaten down into believing they are being passed over or left behind.

*Because I refused to take the low road to the highest office in the land.*

That's a line I first heard from my friend John McCain, during his 2008 presidential campaign, but at the time, it didn't really resonate with voters because the low road to which he referred had yet to sink to today's levels. When I reprised it in one of my speeches, it became a kind of rallying cry for my entire campaign, and I echo it here in these opening pages so that we might imagine where the high road can take us.

Imagine for a moment that America's supposed decline will lead the way to our finest hour.

Imagine that we will find a way through the darkness of today and into the light of tomorrow.

Imagine that we will come together to reject those who would prey on our weaknesses and our basic human nature, and instead choose leadership that serves and strengthens this nation, leadership that honors the American people, leadership that helps us look up instead of down, forward instead of back.

Imagine a bottom-up form of government that starts with each of us, where we live as individuals, recognizing that the true power of our democracy rises *up,* from the many, and that it doesn't rain *down* on us at the pleasure of the advantaged few.

Imagine that the future of this country rests with *you* and *me*—that it's on *us* to ensure that we survive and thrive for generations to come, just as we have survived and thrived for centuries.

This is the path I believe in, the America I believe in. It's the path I laid out in the "Two Paths" speech I gave that became one of the signature moments of my campaign (a speech I'll share in its entirety a little later in these pages). Yet, as I write this, there's a giant, hulking moose in that path, and most of us choose not to see it. We need to pay attention to this—not just to the "moose" itself, but to the fact that it has become too easy for people to ignore what is plain to see. Yes, when times are tough, we can borrow a page from my daughter Emma's playbook and tell ourselves that there is no moose. We can look away from our troubles, pretend they aren't there. But when things calm down, as they undoubtedly will, when the scapegoating and unseemliness of the 2016 campaign melt away and we return to the business of government, of setting things right, we've got to spend some time on this. We've got to recognize that the very real problems facing this country cannot be ignored. We cannot be confused or distracted by bitterness and rancor. We cannot allow exclusion to take the place of inclusion. We cannot accept distorted truths and half-baked notions simply because they make us feel good—or because they make us forget for a moment how we *really* feel.

No, when we deny the moose, we kick the can down the road. Okay, so that's a mixed metaphor, but you get what I mean, yes? When we as a people get angrier and angrier, when we grow more and more frightened, when that anger and fear is stoked we drift deeper and deeper into darkness and despair. We leave these worsening troubles to fester and metastasize and block the way forward for our children and grandchildren. At some point there'll be a clearing, and we'll take our children by the hand and guide them past these troubles, ever so slowly, and then we'll look at them and say, "Well, what do you think about *that*?"

## TODAY I SAW HOPE

When I suspended my campaign for president on May 4, 2016, people started telling me I should write a book. In the press (and, to be honest, in and around my own campaign), there was a lot of talk about how I was the last true Republican standing in what had once been a crowded field of presidential hopefuls. This was arguably true, and there was no arguing that I was the last challenger to Donald Trump for the Republican nomination. I was enormously proud of what we accomplished in the campaign, even though we weren't able to take it all the way to the convention. Remember, we started out with relatively no money and virtually no name identification across the country, but somehow we hung in there and managed to make ourselves heard.

Still, I didn't see the fact that we'd outlasted all those other candidates as the takeaway headline. Let's be clear: Senator Ted Cruz had dropped out only the day before, so that "last man standing" designation was extremely short-lived. And let's not forget, I'd *lost*. It wasn't clear to me then what kind of impact we'd made on the race, how our campaign had been a kind of beacon for voters looking for a positive message, a hopeful message—although, of course, I *knew* these things when I was out there campaigning. I felt them in my bones. But I needed to step away from the race in order to fully appreciate the impact we'd had on the people who found something to cling to in our positive message.

I needed to catch my breath on this and think it through, but even with perspective, I didn't think people would be interested in my take on the presidential race. I thought I'd said everything I had to say during the campaign, and the idea of a book didn't seem all that interesting to me. (And, naturally, if the idea of a book isn't all that interesting to the author, you can be sure it won't be all that interesting to the reader.) But I kept hearing from people on this, so I kept thinking about it, and the more I thought about it, the more I came to realize that there had been an important message at the heart of our campaign, and that a book would give me an opportunity to reflect on that message and share it with readers who didn't get a chance to come out to one of our town hall events, or who didn't respond to what I was saying until after I'd thrown in the towel.

So, the idea for this book began to take shape, and as it did, I gathered my thoughts (and the thoughts of some key members of my campaign team) and started to realize that we'd had a really good run. It wasn't the victory we'd hoped for, but in a lot of ways we *did* make a difference, so I guess you could say it was a victory of a kind. We made some meaningful noise—and of course it wasn't *just* noise. Alongside all that venom and vitriol coming from my opponents, and their clarion calls of gloom and doom, there was a sure, strong voice—and it wasn't *my* voice that stood out. No, it was the voice of the American people, desperate to be heard above the din.

What did I hear from the American people, exactly? Well, the message was probably best summed up by Bob Ehrlich, the former governor of Maryland, who joined us one day for an event in Annapolis. I should mention here that this kind of thing happened all the time during the campaign: we'd roll into town, and some local dignitary or politician would come out to offer support, and we'd be happy to have them. Typically, these meetings would be set up by my advance team, although, from time to time, there was a surprise visit. Here in Annapolis, it was arranged that Bob would follow us back onto the bus after our town hall. Once on the bus, he seemed a little shaken. Like me, he was worried about the tone of the debates and the rallies, the negativity that was in the air and all around. Really, it was just remarkable—in the worst way. But our events were different, as I'll try to show in the pages ahead, and as Bob sat down with me that day, he said, "John, today I saw hope."

That's all he said, and I was floored.

You have to realize, this guy had been a congressman. He'd been governor. (He was defeated in 2006 by Martin O'Malley, a Democrat who was also running for president in 2016.) He knew how things were supposed to go in politics, and, in contrast, he could see how they appeared to be going this primary season. He could see the bad behavior, the incendiary language. He'd been troubled by it, as I was. And now here he was, just back from one of our town halls, and he was struck by the joy, the hopefulness. So, when he said those words—"John, today I saw hope"—let me tell you, it meant the world to me.

One of the things Bob saw at that town hall was an impromptu exchange I had with a young boy of about ten. The boy's father had brought him around to meet me before the event, and mentioned that his son was a big baseball fan, so we fell in to talking. It turned out the kid wasn't just a fan; he wanted to grow up to play in the big leagues.

I asked the boy to show me his batting stance. He did, and in his face, I could see that what he was doing seemed to matter a great deal to him: the way he was strutting his stuff in front of this guy he'd never met, a guy who just happened to be running for president of the United States. We finished our encounter, and that would have been that—except that at some point during the town hall I happened to catch this kid's eye, so I called him up and asked him if he'd show everyone his batting stance. I hadn't planned to call on him in this way, but I'm sure glad I did. The people just loved it. Why? Because they could see the determination in the boy's face, to make a good showing. They could see the possibilities in his future, and in this way, perhaps, they could see something of themselves.

*Today I saw hope.*

Looking back, I can't shake thinking we should have put that line on a bumper sticker—but then, if you weren't on the road with our team, if you weren't in attendance at one of our town halls, if you weren't with us pounding the pavement or making phone calls or visiting folks at the local diner or barbershop or community fair, if you hadn't seen this little kid stand up and demonstrate his batting stance as if his career as a ballplayer depended on it, you might have thought it was just a line.

You might have thought, a line like that, it was just politics as usual.

Yet, to Bob Ehrlich, the great message of our campaign was in the mood of the room, the mood of the country. And that message was one of hope—a message I wish to share in the pages ahead.

Not because I'm out to toot my own horn, not because I expect my observations to reflect well on me or my candidacy, not at all. It simply feels to me like I'm meant to shine some meaningful light on the positivity and richness and great good cheer that attached to our little campaign as we traveled the country—a welcome and astonishing thing when you stand it up against the negativity that characterized this election cycle. And please know that by calling it "our little campaign," I don't mean to diminish the hard work and extra efforts of our key staff, of the thousands of volunteers; it's just that none of the pundits or so-called political experts gave us much of a shot when I first announced my candidacy. (And, in the goes-without-saying department, we all know how well those very same pundits and so-called political experts were able to predict the outcome of the general election, right?) We were late to the party. We hadn't raised a ton of money. I didn't have the kind of name recognition you need in order to stand out in a crowded field. We were counted out before we were counted in. In fact, it sometimes felt, on the inside looking out, that we were the little campaign that could—that the best we could do was pick up steam and keep chugging along.

On a deeply personal level, I'd have to say that the most meaningful ray of light to shine my way was an epiphany that found me in the wake of the campaign, as I tried to understand its impact—on me and my family, on the people who threw in with us, and on those who came out to support us. It came to me that most of us find satisfaction when we try to live a life bigger than ourselves. This alone was nothing new. We need to look for ways to make a difference in the lives of others, in the world around us. Yet, sometimes we fall short. In fact, *most* times we fall short. We do the best we can, and sometimes that means we don't do much at all.

But as I caught my breath after the campaign, I started to spend some time thinking about the ways we remember the people we love or admire after they're gone. We remember the times they managed to rise and be their best selves. We remember those moments when those people reach a little further, dig a little deeper, climb a little higher. We don't stand up at someone's funeral and talk about all those days they made breakfast for their kids. We don't talk about what their lives were like when they moved about on autopilot—the mundane, workaday aspects of living and raising a family and punching a clock at work. No, we remember the above-and-beyond moments, the moments of grace, the moments when they made a real difference. There are heroes all around us, but even the best and brightest of our heroes aren't heroic all the time.

It's like that line from that old David Bowie song: "We can be heroes, just for one day."

We all have our moments. Me, I live at the base level, along with everyone else. What I mean by that is that I've established a kind of comfortable baseline, where I spend most of my time. But, every once in a while, we defy our own personal gravity a little bit and do something wonderful, something unexpected, something bigger than we could ever have imagined. And then, when that wonderful thing is done, when that beautiful thing is done, we return to our base level and go about our business.

*This*, to me, was a revelation. *This*, to me, was something I believed I needed to consider, as I reconsidered my campaign.

This was me, after all—and so here it is, at the heart of this book. Something to think about as we rediscover our shared moral compass after the craziest, most directionless presidential election in anyone's memory.

Look, I like to think I'm a pretty good guy. I try to help other people, create opportunities, model good behavior for my daughters—not as much as I should, but I'm working on it. I screw up, same as you. I misstep, same as you. I aspire to do better, same as you. I live with the sin of Adam and Eve. I tend to think at times that life is all about me. Those are not my best moments, and it's only every so often that I'm able to shake free of those feelings. That's how it is with a lot of people who put themselves out there for the greater good. You see it all the time in business, in sports, in public life. For a while, we're able to do things that are a little bigger than we are. For a while, we can go beyond the norm. We can be heroes, just for one day.

None of us is a saint. Yet we can always do just a little better. That's the key. After all, it's the little things we do that make the biggest difference—the small acts of everyday kindness like the ones by that San Francisco bus driver, and the occasional displays of generosity like those demonstrated by that Boston cabbie with his gifts of those famous North End pastries. We'd all do well to borrow a page from the parable of the Good Samaritan, from the Gospel of Luke, which tells the story of a stranger who happened upon a traveler who'd been stripped of his clothing, beaten, and left for dead by the side of the road. Do you remember that story? The Samaritan nursed the traveler back to health, lifted him onto his horse, and led him to a nearby inn where he might rest and recover. He did these things because he believed they needed doing. And it is the simplicity of the kindness that holds the lesson of the story. There was nothing heroic about the way the Samaritan rescued the traveler. There was only compassion—compassion that can be seen as doubly meaningful when we consider that the Samaritans were treated as outcasts.

I'll give you another example, which just happened to take place as I was sitting at home one afternoon writing this book. Specifically, I was mulling over these very thoughts, looking for ways to make this very point, when the doorbell rang. I was working from home that day because we were expecting a visit from the cable guy; my wife, Karen, had some things she had to do outside the house, and the girls were off at school, so I stuck around. After a while, the cable guy showed up and did his thing, and of course he figured out that he was working in the governor's house and we got to talking. It turned out that this fellow had read somewhere that one of Karen's big initiatives as First Lady was to get involved in the fight against human trafficking, and he wanted to know if there was some way he, too, could get involved. At any other time, I might have seen this as merely a casual request, but at this moment, in this context, I thought it was amazing. Here is this guy out on a routine service call, living his life at that same base level as the rest of us, doing his job at that same base level, and out of nowhere he saw an opening in his day-to-day reality, a chance to reach up and beyond and give of himself in ways he probably hadn't even thought of until he walked through our front door and made the connection to a news item he'd seen about Karen. He didn't wake up that morning and task himself with finding a new outlet for his energies, or a new way to fill his free time. He wasn't out looking for a moment bigger than himself; he just happened to run into one, and to recognize it as such, and he stepped to it.

You can find other examples of this everywhere you look. You can see it in the decision of those two Jewish-American sprinters, Marty Glickman and Sam Stoller, who pulled themselves from the $4 \times 100$ relay at the 1936 Berlin Olympics because they refused to run on the Sabbath. They'd trained all their lives for this moment, only to set it aside when their race fell on the Jewish day of rest, and against a backdrop of Hitler's Berlin, they thought it was more important to keep the Sabbath than to compete.

You can see it in the stand of Rosa Parks, the "first lady of civil rights," who refused to give up her bus seat to a white passenger.

You can see it at the corporate level, with companies like John-son & Johnson, who responded to an isolated tampering crisis by removing all bottles of Tylenol from the shelves, quelling public fears at great cost to the company.

You can see it in the pop star who scrolled through her Twitter feed to find a random invitation to the prom from one of her young fans, and who reached out and accepted the invitation, because she knew it would make the kid's day, his year—his childhood, even.

What's that term for the speed needed to break free from Earth's gravitational pull? *Escape velocity*—that's the concept I'm after here. We don't live at the higher level all the time because the stuff of our lives weighs us down. We can't live that high all the time—there's a pull to our worldly possessions, to the mad dash we all make in pursuit of wealth or fame. But if we accept that we all operate at this comfortable baseline level, we must make room in that thinking for the moments of transcendence, when we are able to crank it up, full throttle, and achieve our own personal escape velocity, when we see a thing that needs doing and it occurs to us that we're the ones capable of doing it.

The baseline level—that's where we stumble and fall, that's where we go through the motions. And that's where most of us live, most of the time. But the health of a society can be measured by how often and how meaningfully its people are able to reach that higher plane, to live lives bigger than they are.

I freely admit that I live at the baseline level more often than not, and that's certainly where I was when I decided to run for president this time around. It doesn't make us mean or bad or lazy, that we live this way. It just makes us human. But in the course of traveling the country and telling people to do good, to be good, to celebrate the good of America, I worried that I was starting to sound a little preachy, that I was putting it out there that we all needed to be saints, all the time. That's a big, unattainable ask. About the only saint I've seen in my lifetime is Mother Teresa, and it took twenty years after her death for the Catholic Church to formally canonize her. The rest of us—we go about our lives, pay our bills, love our families, and if we're lucky and self-aware and righteous in our thinking, we find room in our routines for occasional moments of greatness, when we're able to leave a footprint a whole lot bigger than our shoe size.

I suppose it follows that if most of us live at this base level, there must be room in this line of thinking for those who might live in the basement. To be sure, there are negative impulses and influences all around, just as there are these intermittent points of inspiration. The key to living a rich, meaningful life is to seize the "higher purpose" moments that present themselves and avoid the basement-level temptations.

Now, it just so happens that I believe in God. I've dedicated my life to Him, and have come to believe that it's easier to find and embrace these moments if you have a spiritual relationship with your creator. But that's just me. You might worship in a different way, and that's great. Whatever works for you—as long as *something* works for you. Maybe you're a humanist, and the values you hold dear are tied to the common good. That's great, too. But when you believe in something bigger than yourself, when you have a road map you're meant to follow, when you're guided by a transcendent power, it can be a little easier to discover these meaningful opportunities. You're on the lookout for them, even if you're angry or frustrated and not all that interested in living a higher moment because your life is a mess. You're ever mindful that there are better days ahead, and far more likely to take good care of yourself and try to set things right.

What do they tell you to do when you're on an airplane and there's a sudden change in cabin pressure? You're supposed to put the oxygen mask on yourself first and then offer assistance to those around you. What's the first directive for making a water rescue? To make sure you're a strong-enough swimmer and to take extra care that the person who's drowning doesn't drown you. The idea is that we have to take care of ourselves before we can take care of others—not because we *deserve* to go first, but because we need to put ourselves into a position where we can be helpful to those around us. We need to clean up our own messes before we can help others clean up the messes in their lives. And let's keep in mind, for a lot of us, these "messes" are never quite as messy as they seem. Maybe you've got money troubles, or your kids are struggling in school, or your neighborhood has a drug problem, or you're feeling like you're stuck. When you're in that mode, it's hard to think about living a life bigger than you are. And when you're in that mode, you're vulnerable. When somebody comes at you and feeds on that vulnerability by telling you that the reason your life is such a mess is that you've been cheated, or somebody took your stuff, or your voice isn't being heard—that's when it gets harder and harder to rise above your circumstances.

That's when the negative tone that found us during the 2016 presidential campaign can resonate and take hold.

That's when those of us who are feeling weak or disadvantaged or somehow *less than* are inclined to buy in to false promises.

That's when we come upon the giant, hulking moose in our path and pretend it's not there.

## 2.

# Where I Come From

Running for president doesn't just up and happen. It's not like you get out of bed one morning and there's a lightbulb shining overhead with this bright idea that gets you thinking you can convince a vast number of donors and volunteers and delegates and voters to stand with you, and that you can then somehow find a way to harness all that support and give yourself a decent shot at your party's nomination.

At least, it's not like that for *most* of us, and it certainly wasn't like that for me. In fact, the convincing seemed to run the other way around: I had all these friends and advisers telling me that a presidential campaign was something I should be thinking about long before I finally decided to run.

I'd run for president before, in 2000, while completing my ninth and final term as a member of the U.S. House of Representatives from Ohio's Twelfth Congressional District, where I'd served for eighteen years as a member of the House Armed Services Committee and six years as chairman of the House Budget Committee; played a significant role in the passage of welfare reform; and was the chief architect of the Balanced Budget Act of 1997. That first presidential run didn't take me all that far—heck, I was out of the race before the first primary! Still, I'd been encouraged to run by my friends and advisers—some of the same friends and advisers who were on me to run in 2016. I took that 2000 campaign seriously, thinking I could win the Republican nomination—only to learn later that my friends and advisers never thought I had a shot. They wanted me to run just to run, to see what it felt like to run for president—an experience I might file away for later.

When I left Congress, I worked in the private sector as an investment banker, hosted a show on the Fox News channel, wrote a couple of bestselling books, and campaigned for Republican candidates and causes across the country, before deciding in 2009 to run for governor of the great state of Ohio. After winning a second term as governor, by an almost two-to-one margin, I started to think more and more that the approach we'd taken to turning around our state could work just as well in Washington, and that's when I began to give serious thought to what all those folks had been telling me: that I should seek the Republican nomination for president. Like I said, I was helped along in this serious thinking by a great many people, who this time around believed I could make it all the way to the White House.

I took their good counsel to heart.

Don Thibaut has been one of my best friends for many years—he ran my very first campaign—and his good counsel mattered most of all. I was all over the place with this one: I just couldn't seem to decide if a run was right for my family, if it was right for the state of Ohio, if it was right for the Republican Party, and on and on. Whenever I sat down with someone whose opinion I trusted, I'd bend their ear on whether I should run, until finally,

Don came to me and said, "John, enough is enough. I think you should run."

I said, "Why?" I wanted to know what had changed in his thinking that he was now able to express his opinion in such a conclusive way.

He said, "Because if you don't run, you'll drive everybody crazy. If you don't run, you'll probably end up blaming me. So, just go ahead and run."

Basically, he wanted to shut me up—and for the moment, he succeeded. But then I thought about it and realized I needed my good friends to slap some sense into me. It took a harsh response from someone who knew me as well as Don did to get me to see this decision in a new way, and I was grateful for the rush of clarity. Of course, Don was right—it was time to step up to it.

I might not have had the national name recognition of some of the other candidates in the 2016 presidential race, but I certainly had the experience. More to the point, I believed I had the demeanor and the ability to work in a practical, no-nonsense, nonpartisan way to solve some of the problems facing this country. Also, I thought I was uniquely positioned to take on the divisiveness and gridlock that were creating some real issues for us in the Republican Party, in Washington, and across the country.

That's why I ultimately decided to seek the Republican nomination—only, by the time I got around to announcing, there were already fifteen other candidates in the field, and the first debate was just two weeks away. (Former Virginia governor Jim Gilmore would round out the list of GOP hopefuls the following week.) I'll get to all the wheels that were set in motion by this decision, but for now I want to address the magnitude of what it means to seek the office of the president. It's a big, big deal—there's no overstating it. Yet, I suppose there are some folks who never quite get their heads around what it actually means to *be* president of the United States of America. They just don't get that far in their thinking. Or maybe they do and it still never quite feels real. That was never the case for me. I'd spent all that time in Washington, and as governor, I had the experience of being a chief executive of a big state. I knew what the job of president entailed, and I knew I was up to it, so there was no room in my thinking for doubt or for feeling that the office was too big for me or that I was in over my head. Actually, it was just the opposite. I felt I was the person for the job.

I was good and ready.

The reason I felt such a sense of certainty about my ability to serve had only a little to do with my experience and qualifications—those were just a part of it. The "context" I just laid out? That was only a part of it, too. Truth was, my certainty mostly had to do with the way I was raised. It had to do with *how* I grew up and *where* I grew up—all of which had left me thinking that I was made for the role, instead of worrying if I could ever rise to meet the challenge it presented. Let me tell you, the whole time I was running for president, I don't think I had a single "pinch me" moment, that moment when what you're doing doesn't feel quite real.

Granted, I had a few of those moments when I was in Congress, and probably a couple more as governor—those points at which I stopped to wonder how Little Johnny Kasich from McKees Rocks, Pennsylvania, had managed to put two and two together in a way that took him to Washington, or back to the Ohio Statehouse in Columbus. Typically, those moments hit me each time I was *in the moment*—meaning each time I won an election, each time I adjusted to a new role, each time I saw my name stenciled on the glass door to my new office.

A lot of folks believe that those "pinch me" moments are laced with hubris, but the 2016 campaign was not about that. This campaign had more to do with how to set right the pendulum of American government than it did with how the swing of that pendulum might have brushed up against me or my family or my background. This campaign was about the economy, about immigration reform, about health care and taxes and national security and civility, and helping our struggling friends and neighbors step in from the shadows.

It wasn't just about the issues; it was about our souls.

It was about *us*.

## BACK TO McKEES ROCKS

The issues I talked about during the campaign, and the values that shaped my views on those issues, had everything to do with the values I found during childhood. And so, in these opening pages, it makes sense to spend some time considering the boy I was, alongside the leader I hoped to become.

The greatest gift I ever received from my parents was their example. In our house, in our church, in our community, I was taught the importance of faith, humility, accountability, personal responsibility. By watching my parents, I learned what it meant to have integrity, to do the right thing, to care for your family, and to leave the world a better place for your having been there.

McKees Rocks was a blue-collar town outside Pittsburgh, a hardscrabble community where the God's honest truth was just that: God's honest truth. Back when I was growing up there, McKees Rocks was mostly a steel town, mostly middle class, mostly Democratic. It was the kind of place where everyone knew most everyone else. I can still remember the man who lived across the street from us, who used to rise before the sun each morning and climb into his truck and drive away. In him, looking back, I see the hope of America back then. I probably didn't recognize it as such as a small boy, but it's clear to me now. This man would come home late at night, long after the other dads on the street had finished their dinners. He was always dressed in work clothes—and had the look of a man determined to do right by his family. But the memory alone doesn't tell this man's story, because I never knew his full story. I could only imagine that he was a fix-it man who drove from odd job to odd job, doing whatever work he could to get and keep ahead. But he was a proud man; this much was clear. His shirt always looked clean in the morning. His lawn was well kept; the house, in good repair.

My parents had a few good friends, but for the most part, they kept to themselves. They had their work and they had their family; that was their focus. There wasn't time for too much else. They both worked, which wasn't so unusual in our neighborhood. Money was tight, but I don't mean to suggest that we lived in poverty—not at all. I grew up in a nice house, although we certainly weren't rich. My parents scraped for everything we had, and they made sure to give us kids a little extra besides. Every year, we'd go to a Pirates game, usually on Labor Day, because there was always a double-header and you'd get two games for the price of one. We'd sit in the right-field bleachers and count our blessings. To a baseball-mad kid, this was just about the closest thing there was to Heaven on Earth.

When you don't have a whole lot of money, you worry over what you spend it on. Once, I went with my father to the mall and wandered into a bookstore. He was off doing his errands. When I met up with him, I had a package in my hands.

He said, "What's in the package, Johnny?"

I told him I'd bought a book.

He said, "A book? That's what libraries are for."

So, I went back to the bookstore and returned the book.

A big night out for us would be dinner at a local smorgasbord—you know, one of those all-you-can-eat buffets. At those times, my father's message was much the same: "Johnny, don't fill up on the bread. Eat the meat. We can get bread at home."

Another time, when I was home from college, I went to a diner with my mother while we were out doing errands. When the waitress asked what I wanted, I ordered a shrimp cocktail. You could have knocked my mother over with a feather. She looked at me like I was insane. *A shrimp cocktail?* It was beyond her comprehension that I would order something like that, so of course I looked sheepishly at the waitress and changed my order.

What we had we put to meaningful use, and we didn't "waste" our money on air-conditioning or a car with automatic transmission. We lived simply, but we had everything we needed. And we were taught to look out for others less fortunate than ourselves. Everything is relative, right? I used to see my father slip a couple of extra bucks to the man who picked up our trash, and my mother was always generous when she saw someone struggling to make an honest living—like the time she gave the boy running the pony ride concession at the school grounds a few extra quarters.

When I asked why she'd overpaid like that, she said, "He needs the money more than we do, Johnny."

My mother grew up dirt poor. She was the first in her family to graduate high school, and she learned to speak her mind. Her mother was from Yugoslavia and barely spoke English. She lived with us for a while, and it made an impression on me. For my parents to stretch their two modest incomes to feed three hungry kids, pay the bills, and still make room under their roof for my grandmother—well, it's just what you did. You found a way to take care of your family, to do the right thing.

If you want to learn what I'm about and how I came to think I should be speaking out for what I thought was right, I suppose it started with my mother. She used to listen to the radio all the time, and the joke I always tell was that she was a pioneer of talk radio because she used to yell at the radio whenever she heard something she didn't like. Her opinions reflected her personal strength. She would argue about the issues of the day, and she always seemed to be riled up about political corruption or favoritism. She fought for the underdog, and I learned from listening to her to be honest and independent in my thinking. She just couldn't abide a corrupt politician, or a transparent abuse of power, and she wasn't the type to hold her tongue. When something rubbed her the wrong way—an injustice, a travesty—she let you know how she felt.

My parents both worked in the post office—my mother in downtown Pittsburgh, my father in McKees Rocks. My mother used to sort the mail, routing letters by zip code, back before there were computers or scanners to do the same job. She was very clever and came up with all kinds of new ways to do things more efficiently. Meanwhile, my father threw all those letters on his back and carried them up and down the streets. The only way for him to do his job more efficiently, really, was to hightail it from one house to the next. It ended up that he knew everyone on his route, and they came to really love him. He knew them all by name, knew what was going on with their families, and if he saw something that needed looking after, he went ahead and looked after it.

My mother took on more work as we kids got older. Early on, she was around quite a bit, and on most afternoons, she was home waiting for us at the end of the school day. My parents were Democrats, like most folks in town, driven by the ideals of faith and family and common sense. They didn't talk about the war in Vietnam or any of the hot-button issues of the day. They didn't smoke or drink. We went to church on Sundays, but I don't think my mother felt a true calling to faith until she was older. She'd been raised a Catholic, and later on she would become a very devout Christian, but early on, when we kids were little, it was mostly about going to church just like everyone else. It's what you did.

Me, I was drawn to the ritual and wonder of religion. For the longest time, I thought I'd grow up to be a priest, and as soon as I was old enough I became an altar boy—a pretty good one, too, according to our assistant pastor, who took me aside one Sunday and told me he was starting to think I knew the services better than he did. My experiences as an altar boy led directly to a story I've often told over the years, one that might provide a glimpse of my future calling to politics and leadership. What happened was our priest asked me to be a commentator and to lead the congregation one Sunday morning. I had to stand up before everyone and lead the prayers, but I drew the line at singing—that was for sissies, I thought. Still, it was a big deal, and people were a little surprised to see someone so young step into that kind of role.

I took my job seriously, but I think the opportunity was a little too big for me because, at one point, I made a mistake and told everyone to turn to the wrong page in their hymnals. This was pretty confusing, as you might imagine, but all I knew at the time was that people weren't singing as forcefully as I wanted them to. What did I do? I told the organist to stop playing and I chastised the congregation for failing to sing in full voice. I said, "Come on, people. God loves it when the faithful sing, so sing it like you mean it!" Well, this certainly didn't help the situation. The parishioners could only stumble along more loudly, because they didn't want to disappoint the young commentator at the pulpit. Trouble was, they had no idea what they were meant to be singing because I'd sent them to the wrong page in their hymnals. They were good sports about it, though, and it wasn't until later that one of the church elders came up to me and explained all the confusion. "We love to sing, young man," he said. "But could you give us the right page next time?"

## EARN YOUR OWN WAY

The great message of my growing up was to think big. We might have lived a small, simple life, but it was a good life, and out of that, I learned that all things are possible. My parents always told me I could be anything I wanted to be. In a million years, they would never have guessed I'd become a politician. Politics wasn't viewed as an honorable profession in our town, but now that I think back on it, my choice of career should not have come as such a great surprise. My parents were good people. They worked hard for everything they had, never had their hands out, never wanted to be beholden to anyone for anything, always went out of their way to help others in need—so, maybe it follows that if you raise three kids with that type of role modeling, one of them might just feel a calling to a life of public service. Plus, they'd heard me talk about wanting to become a lawyer. They knew I used to visit the courthouse and listen to the lawyers argue; I'd come home fascinated about what I'd seen and heard. And they'd seen me in church, where I had the opportunity to speak publicly and gain experience and confidence, so all these pieces were falling into place.

There's another story I've told a few times that I want to revisit here. It has to do with my father's sense of right and wrong and with baseball, one of the great passions of my childhood. I was a little on the scrawny side as a kid, the kind of scrappy boy who doesn't always stand out straightaway. One year, when I was trying out for Little League, I didn't stand out at all, and when the teams were announced, I learned that my name wasn't on any of the lists. "Crestfallen" doesn't even begin to describe how it left me feeling. But it wasn't just the disappointment of not making a team that got to me. As I looked up and down the lineup of the kids who'd made the team, I noticed that some of them were just as scrawny as I was—and, just being honest, I thought I had them beat. This would have been a simple life lesson if that was all it was, a frustration, but there was something else going on. (Even I, at eleven years old, could see that.) A lot of the kids who'd made the team, it turned out, had some type of connection, some type of pull. Maybe their fathers were friendly with the coaches or the team sponsors or the guy who ran the league. Whatever it was, quite a few of these kids had had a leg up—so I naturally looked to get a leg up of my own. I figured that if anyone had deep connections in and around McKees Rocks, it was my father. He delivered all the mail. He had a good relationship with everyone. He knew the coaches, the league officials. So, I went to him one night after dinner and told him what was going on.

I said, "I don't think it's fair, what's happening on those Little League teams."

He said, "What's happening, Johnny?"

"I'm just as good a ballplayer as a lot of the kids. Better than some of them, I think. But I can't get a spot and all these other kids are playing."

He said, "And why do you think that is?" He knew the answer, but he wanted to hear me say it. He wanted to know if I had seen that the fix was in.

I said, "It's connections. Everybody's got connections. Isn't there someone you can talk to, maybe get me on a team?"

I might as well have asked him to bribe my teacher to give me a good grade. My father wasn't the sort of man who would ask anybody to bend the rules or extend a favor just so his son could play baseball, and I should have known that. But I put the request to him anyway, and he said, "Johnny, this is something you're going to have to figure out for yourself. You're going to have to earn your way onto one of those teams."

It was a hard lesson, but even then, I knew my father was right. I didn't like it, but I couldn't fight it. All I could do was hold my head high and keep playing ball—by myself, for a while, because, as it appeared, I was a kid without a team. Still, I practiced, playing catch against the wall as often as I could, and I continued to root like crazy for my Pittsburgh Pirates, and imagine myself onto *that* team. And wouldn't you know it? A couple of weeks into the season, someone broke his leg, and a spot opened up for me on one of the teams. One of the coaches had seen me play and thought I was pretty good, so the spot went to me.

I was thrilled to finally get my chance. My father was thrilled, too—probably because he knew how much I wanted to play. Probably, too, because he knew how easy it would have been for him to make a call, maybe ask someone for a favor so I could play.

That's always the way of it: when you look to take the easy way around, you start looking for shortcuts. My father knew that if he had put his hand out on this issue, he would have owed someone a favor in return—and I would have received the message that I'd gotten my spot for reasons other than merit (although, frankly, in those low moments, when I was a kid without a team, I don't think I would have minded all that much).

Each time I share this story, I'm reminded of what it means to do the right thing, to live a principled life, to keep throwing that baseball against that wall until it finally bounces back into your glove, right in the sweet spot.

I wish I could say I went on to tear up the league once I got my chance, but the truth was I did only okay. I held my own. At least nobody watched me play and wondered how it was that I'd even made the team, and that was an important takeaway for me: the simple feeling of satisfaction that comes your way when you accomplish something on your own.

I belonged, at long last, and that was something.

My parents both had it tough growing up. My father was a child of immigrants. His father worked as a coal miner in western Pennsylvania, a job that eventually claimed him when he died of black lung disease. Still, my grandfather never believed he was entitled to anything beyond this backbreaking, life-threatening work, and perhaps as a result, my father was determined to build a better life for his children. The way he went about it was to work hard and to move through life with his eyes on the road ahead. He wasn't about to ask for any kind of special treatment, whether it was something as trivial (to him!) as his son making a Little League team or as significant as a new job opportunity. Whatever came his way he earned on his own—and his children would learn to do the same.

One of the other great messages I took in from my parents was to speak up. Maybe that came from my mother talking back to the radio and never being afraid to share her strong opinions. Whatever it was, the message took, and I was never the type to let an injustice pass unnoticed. Even a *perceived* injustice was up for discussion. I can remember being outraged when a play I was in didn't receive the kind of attention by the local newspaper I'd thought it deserved. Yes, I happened to have the lead that year, but I like to think I would have kicked up the same kind of dust if I hadn't had a vested interest. I thought it was dispiriting and disloyal to the young people of our town that the high school seniors should have put in all this effort on the school play, and for the event to pass with hardly a word in the local newspaper. Oh, there was a brief account, deep inside the paper, nowhere near the front page, but to my mind at least, the cast and crew had been mostly overlooked. So, I went to school the next day and told my teacher how corrupt things were in our town, and how the school ought to be doing more to encourage the students in our extracurricular pursuits.

I was on the side of right, and I said what I thought needed to be said.

(The play that year? *Rally 'Round the Flag, Boys!* with me in the Paul Newman role. Alas, nobody would mistake me for Paul Newman. Looking at it objectively, his eyes were much bluer than mine, but I had it on good authority that we had the same piercing stare.)

Another time, I went to a school board meeting after there'd been a racial incident at our high school. People were duly concerned, but I didn't like that the administration was so late to address the tensions in our community, so I grabbed the microphone and said, "You guys just pay attention when there's a crisis, but why aren't you engaged on this issue all the time?"

I don't think I accomplished anything beyond saying what needed to be said, but my father must've heard about it from some of the people on his route, because when he came home from work the next day, he said, "Johnny, what did you do down there?"

It was always understood that all three of us kids would go on to college. That was just a given. When I was growing up, that meant the University of Pittsburgh, the great cathedral of learning—at least as far as everyone in McKees Rocks was concerned. Pitt made sense to me. I could have commuted to classes and saved a bunch of money on expenses and in-state tuition. Every time we drove past the campus, my mother or father would point the campus out to me and say something like "Someday, Johnny" or "That's where you're headed, Johnny." They set it up as this great goal, a path to opportunity, and it certainly was, but by the time I graduated high school, I had my heart set on Ohio State University—or, *the* Ohio State University, as Buckeyes are now fond of saying.

The way it worked out, a child of one of my mother's coworkers had started school at Ohio State, and my mother happened to mention it, so I drove out there with my father one weekend and felt immediately at home. I was drawn to the energy of the place. There were forty-eight thousand students on campus when I started there in 1970, and it just seemed so incredibly exciting, to be living and studying among such a large group of inquisitive young people, in such a dynamic environment.

So, that's where I went, and it was during the first couple of weeks of my freshman year that I found myself in the office of Ohio State's then-president, Novice Fawcett—another story I told on the campaign trail and will share again here.

I'd made the appointment with him to talk about a matter of school policy, and let me tell you, it wasn't easy getting on the man's calendar. I had to talk my way past a secretary who guarded his schedule as if it held state secrets.

President Fawcett was an imposing, impressive figure, about a half foot taller than me. When I walked into his office, he was sitting behind an enormous desk surrounded by big wooden chairs and the kind of artwork I'd seen only in museums. I suppose a lot of first-year students would have been intimidated at the sight of such a big man, in such a big job, but that's not how I was wired. I just saw him as a regular guy who happened to be in charge of the whole school, and I thought I could learn something from him, so I started asking a lot of questions. This was still just a few weeks into my freshman year, and I hadn't yet settled on a course of study, though, at the time, I was thinking I'd probably wind up being a lawyer.

Now, I was a curious young man—"curious" as in interested in the world around me, but also as in odd, not quite like the other students, which might have explained what I was doing in President Fawcett's office in the first place. You see, even then I was the sort of person who wasn't shy about asking questions and making things happen. If I was struck by what you were doing, I'd ask you about it. As it happened, my curiosity got the better of me that day in President Fawcett's office, and I started pressing him on what the job of a university president actually entailed. I wanted to know what his days were like, what his responsibilities were. I was struck by the size of his office, the size of his job, and I had a genuine interest in the choices people make when they set off on a career. For some reason, President Fawcett indulged me in this. It was clear from the way he spoke that he really enjoyed his job, and enjoyed talking about it. He told me what it was like to raise money for Ohio State, what it was like to deal with the school's trustees and administrators, what it was like to interact with students and alumni—and then, at some point, he mentioned that he was headed to Washington, D.C., the following week to meet with President Nixon.

Well, I thought that was just about the coolest thing in the world. It was October 1970, and looking back, I can see that the

D.C. trip was merely a photo op for him, but President Fawcett said he thought the visit might enhance the university's profile in an arena outside big-time college football. I could only agree with him of course, and then I did what any overeager college freshman in just that situation would have done: I asked if I could join him.

Up until that moment, President Fawcett had responded to each and every question with great good cheer, but this was a bold ask—even I could see that, though it hadn't stopped me from making it. As for President Fawcett, the question caught him by surprise, I think, and his good humor all but disappeared. He just looked at me flatly and said, "No."

Still, I was determined. I said, "Well, if I can't go with you to meet President Nixon, can you at least deliver a letter to him from me?" I wasn't about to let this opportunity slip away—though it was really no opportunity at all, not as far as I was concerned. Still, I saw it as my chance to win an audience with the president of the United States, even in this once-removed way.

President Fawcett shrugged and said, "I guess so." Underneath the shrug, he was probably thinking, What in the world is up with this young man?

## MY FIRST TRIP TO WASHINGTON

When I got back to my dorm room that day, I sat down and wrote a three-page letter to President Nixon. I don't know that I was motivated by anything other than the prospect of communicating with a U.S. president, even in this roundabout way. I signed off on the letter with a postscript. "P.S.," I wrote. "If you'd like to discuss this letter further, please don't hesitate to contact me."

I truly believed that President Fawcett would make good on

his promise and deliver the letter to the White House. And I truly believed President Nixon would take time out of his busy schedule to read it and consider my request to continue our conversation in Washington. (I'd written that I was prepared to pass up a trip to the Rose Bowl that year if it presented a conflict, so he could see that I was serious about wanting to visit.)

I was not disappointed.

A couple weeks later, I opened my mailbox to find a letter from the "Office of the President of the United States." I was crazy with excitement—and, frankly, a little shocked. Still, if I'm being honest, I have to say that part of me was expecting to hear back. My thinking was: You get a letter from someone, you sit down to write a reply; that's just common courtesy, right? What really surprised me, though, was what I found inside. When I tore open the envelope, I saw that it held an invitation to come to Washington, D.C., to continue the conversation with the president.

I raced to the dormitory phone and called home. I was bursting with this news, but I also needed money to pay for plane fare to Washington, so it was a strategic phone call as well as a celebratory one. When my mother answered, I gave it to her straight: "Mom," I said, "I'm going to have to fly to Washington to meet with the president of the United States, in the Oval Office."

You know, as if things like this were just an everyday thing for us Kasichs.

My poor mother. She must've thought I had a screw loose, because the next thing I heard was her calling into the next room for my father. "Honey," I could hear her yelling through the receiver, "pick up the phone. Something's wrong with Johnny."

What was wrong with Johnny was that I was wound up. I mean, this was the president of the United States! And I was headed to the Oval Office *to meet with him*. One on one. At eighteen years old! How cool was *that*? I didn't have any kind of agenda. I wasn't out to press my views on President Nixon. I was simply thrilled to be granted an audience, to be presented with a front-row seat/backstage pass to the inner workings of the White House.

As for President Nixon's agenda in agreeing to meet with me— well, I can only imagine now that there was something in my letter that made him think of me as a typical college student, and that meeting me was one way to keep connected to what was happening on American college campuses. Remember, this was just a few months after the shooting deaths of four student protesters at Kent State University by National Guardsmen, and now here was this young man from another school in Ohio reaching out to him in this way. I have to think he'd been looking for opportunities to engage with students in the wake of that national tragedy, one that had led to student demonstrations and strikes all across the country. I'm only speculating here, of course, but I've often wondered what it was about my appeal to that appealed to him, if you will, and this seems to me as good an explanation as any.

The letter said that I would hear back from the president's office to schedule a time for our meeting, and sure enough, within a couple weeks, I got a call from a White House secretary. Let me set the scene, because the call itself paints an incongruous picture, and reinforces how unlikely it was that someone like me would even be on the radar of someone like President Nixon.

I had fifteen "roommates" living in my dorm room suite that year, and we all shared this one phone, so when the call came in, the guy who picked it up just assumed it was my mother. I was in the shower at the time, so he poked his head into the bathroom and said, "Hey, Kasich, it's your mother on the line." I raced out to the phone thinking I was answering a call from my mother, and that's the picture I made when I started talking to the White House secretary. It's amazing how these big moments can catch you un-aware, right? Here I was, just stepping out of the shower, answer-ing the most remarkable phone call of my young life.

A week or so later, I was waiting in the reception area just out-side the Oval Office, listening to some Nixon staffers brief me on what to expect in my meeting. Someone mentioned that I would have five minutes with the president, and I thought, Are you kid-ding me? I'd come all the way to Washington. There's no way I was just going to shake the president's hand and leave. We had things to talk about.

Let me tell you, it was an awe-inspiring moment, probably the first "pinch me" moment of my young life. And the thing of it is, I don't remember feeling intimidated at all by the situation. Re-spectful, yes. Intimidated, no. To be in the White House, seated across from the president of the United States, walking around that office, with all those symbols of our great democracy decorat-ing the walls, the floors, the desk—I could really feel the weight of history in that room.

I don't know what it was about me or my personality that had left me thinking I was in a position to speak to the president with-out feeling overwhelmed or out of my element—I guess that was my McKees Rocks upbringing on full display.

Well, if I thought Novice Fawcett's office at Ohio State was grand and imposing, the Oval Office was all that and more. Pres-ident Nixon wasn't nearly as tall as President Fawcett, but of course the "weight" of his office was far greater. And yet, here again, I don't recall feeling anxious or intimidated in any way. President Nixon might have been the leader of the free world, but he put his pants on the same way I did each morning, so I was comfortable talking with him. That said, a part of me also recognized that the moment was so much bigger than I was, so much more impactful than anything I'd ever experienced. Still, I didn't let any of that get in the way, and we fell in to talking. Those first five minutes fairly flew by—the next five, too. I wish I could remember what we talked about exactly, but the point here is that we talked, and talked. The president really seemed to be listening to what I had to say.

Eventually, a staffer came in to end our visit, and as I thanked the president for making the time to meet with me, I caught sight of a clock: I'd been in the Oval Office for *twenty minutes*—not all the time in the world, but an astonishing amount of time for a college freshman. And enough time, in my mind, to enable me to return to Columbus with my head held high, thinking I'd made some kind of impression.

And here's the kicker: At eighteen years old, I spent more time alone in the Oval Office with the president of the United States than I would in nine terms as a U.S. congressman. The easy joke here, which I tell on myself at every opportunity, is that I should've quit while I was ahead.

## THE START OF SOMETHING

Something was lit inside me that day in Washington. I wouldn't call it a fire, because it was subtler than that. I wouldn't call it a hunger to lead or bring about change, though those impulses were in there somewhere, waiting to be put into play. But when I got back to campus, I did start to think more and more about a career in government. I still had plans to become a lawyer, but I felt that politics was consistent with that. Then, during my sophomore year, I applied to work as a White House intern—not because I wanted to change the world, but because it seemed like the natural next step, an outgrowth of my White House visit. I didn't get the job, but my résumé was passed along to someone at the National Institutes of Health, and I wound up with a summer job at the National Library of Medicine. That's how it goes for a lot of us, when we set out on a career path: one thing leads to another, and then you look up one day and realize that the path has somehow taken you where you were meant to be all along.

Anyway, I was thrilled at the prospect of the library job. I took a Greyhound bus to Washington at the end of the term and rented a room for the summer in a fraternity house. The job wasn't all that interesting—there was a lot of busywork, as I recall—but it had gotten me to Washington. And I still had time for fun; most weekends, a group of us would hitchhike to the ocean. On one of those weekends, we were picked up by a guy named Claude Desautels, who'd been a special assistant to President Kennedy. He pulled up in this grand Cadillac and started telling us all these wonderful stories about working for JFK and, later, LBJ. I was fascinated. When I got out of the car, I asked him if I could take him to lunch—as you can probably tell by now, I wasn't shy about asking people in positions of authority to give of their time. He gave me his phone number, and I went to his office to meet with him soon after that. Turned out he'd made a reservation at a pretty fancy restaurant. I took a look at the menu and said, "I don't have enough money to pay for this." He just burst out laughing.

Claude Desautels became a mentor to me, and said I should start thinking about a job for the following summer. For whatever reason, he went out of his way for me, took a liking to me. He told me to apply to all these congressional offices, so I sent out about 250 résumés over the next couple weeks. I didn't get called for a single interview. I was disappointed of course, but what I'd learned during my short time in Washington was that, in a lot of ways, it operated like a small town. Interns, assistants, young staffers—everybody seemed to know one another, so snagging a lot of these entry-level jobs came down to whom you knew. This put me on the outside looking in, because I didn't know too many people—but I did know Claude Desautels. So I went to work for him the following summer. At the time, he was a lobbyist and had a lot of close ties among Democrats. One of the big projects we worked on that summer was an early Alaskan pipeline initiative, which put me in a position to immerse myself in an issue and meet a lot of congressmen.

It was a busy, heady time—so busy, in fact, that my "summer" job stretched into the fall. I was learning a lot, and in no rush to get back to school, so I made arrangements to take off the next quarter. (At the time, Ohio State's academic calendar was divided into quarters, not semesters.) My parents weren't sure what I was up to, missing out on school like that, so I had my old friend Dr. Fawcett call home and tell them I was doing just fine. After that, they still weren't sure what I was up to, but they could only assume that if the university president was reaching out on my behalf, what I was up to was all right.

I finally graduated college in December 1974. By that time, I'd already been accepted to law school at Temple University for the following fall; that meant I needed to find a job. Once again, I sent out a bunch of letters and résumés—and once again, nobody would hire me. It seemed to me I'd been rejected by every business in Columbus, and I was down about it, but I kept pounding the pavement, sending out résumés, making calls. One afternoon, I walked past the Ohio Statehouse and thought again about what it would be like to work in a government job. Then I thought back to all those folks who'd ignored me down in Washington.

I didn't think anything would come of it, but I went inside anyway, just to see what I could see. I was met in the lobby by a man named Salty Lewis—another happenstance connection that would push me further along the path I was meant to follow.

We struck up a conversation—I learned that Salty Lewis worked for the Legislative Reference Bureau—and soon I was fat in the middle of another one of those moments: you know, the ones where I have the temerity to ask an authority figure for a job or a meeting.

"Sir," I said. "I'm about to go to law school in September, but I need a job to tide me over until then."

"I'll hire you," Salty Lewis said.

And just like that, he put me to work writing resolutions and commendations for Ohio residents. It wasn't much, but it was something, and a week or so later it led to something else. I came in for work one morning, and Salty mentioned that there was an opening in the legislative internship program; he suggested I apply. I guess it was another one of those "right place, right time" situations, or my moment to shine, because I walked away with the job.

The very first person I met on my very first day in the program was my friend Bob Blair—we're still great friends to this day. Bob and I were the only two aides for all those senators, so we worked very closely together, and early on in our friendship we had an opportunity to campaign together for Ronald Reagan when he first ran for president, in 1976. The opportunity came about because one of the state senators I was working for, a guy named Donald "Buz" Lukens, was a big Reagan supporter. So Bob and I would go out—on some nights until midnight!—collecting signatures to make sure California governor Ronald Reagan got on the ballot. Then, during the Republican National Convention in Kansas City,

Senator Lukens called and said, "We could use a little help out here, John."

I dropped whatever I was doing and made my way to Kansas City for the front-row seat that was being offered to me. Here again, I had no agenda. Again, I wasn't motivated by any high or pious ideals. I believed in Reagan's message, and it was a thrill to go to work for him, but it was just an opportunity, one thing leading to another. And when I got to Kansas City, this one opportunity led to an even bigger opportunity, one I could have never seen coming.

Senator Lukens had instructed me to meet him in a certain trailer outside the convention center, which served as a kind of command center. When I got there, I announced myself, saying I was there at the instruction of Senator Lukens of Ohio. The trailer was filled with a lot of powerful, important people—all the key organizers of the Reagan campaign. I didn't know who all these people were at the time, but I learned soon enough: Lyn Nofziger, who'd been Governor Reagan's press secretary; John Sears, who'd run Reagan's presidential bid during the primaries; Charlie Black, who'd go on to play a central role in Reagan's 1980 and 1984 campaigns and eventually serve as a key campaign adviser to George H. W. Bush and John McCain (and to me). There were all these heavy hitters in that trailer—and me.

One of the heavy hitters turned to me and said, "We're short one of our organizers. Could you run five states for Governor Reagan?"

They could have asked me to split an atom and I would have found a way to make it happen. I had no idea what it meant to run five states, but of course I said, "Absolutely!"

Out of nowhere, it was now my job to try to whip votes among the party delegates in North Dakota, South Dakota, Montana,

Iowa, and Minnesota, which put me on the convention floor hag-gling with all these delegates. If you remember, the 1976 Republi-can National Convention was America's most recent contested convention, and it was a wild scene. I had no idea what I was doing at first, but I was a quick study, and at some point, I even found myself in a car, driving with Governor Reagan to a couple of events, even *introducing* him at a couple of events. It was an un-believable experience. (Talk about a "pinch me" moment, right?) I was there for only a week, and I don't think I slept more than a couple of hours each night; they had me running all over the place.

Then, when it was all over, when it was clear that President Ford would get the nomination, they had us up to the top floor of the Alameda Hotel for a kind of consolation/concession gather-ing. Governor Reagan was there of course. His top advisers were there. And I was like Forrest Gump, standing in the background behind all these big, important people who would go on to accom-plish all these big, important things. It was surreal.

The talk around the room was that the convention was lost but the fight was not over. It was all very uplifting. A lot of people were crying. Even then, Governor Reagan was able to inspire tre-mendous loyalty. People really believed in him, saw something in him. And here I was, implausibly, right in the middle of this his-toric scene—again, not feeling the least bit intimidated, but at the same time humbled and excited to be in on such an event as this.

I was pretty full of myself when I got back to Columbus. My head was so big with what had happened in Kansas City that Bob Blair didn't want to hear from me, but he was really the only per-son I could talk to about it, and I talked his ear off. I got over the experience soon enough, and one of the ways I got over it was to start thinking more seriously about my own political career. There was something galvanizing in seeing how politics worked at the very highest level—so much so that I found myself imagining what it would be like to run for office myself. It was something I could see myself doing: working to bring about change.

After a while, I decided to put off law school for the time being. And a while after that, I made the decision to run for office. I'll never forget the day I told Bob Blair. We were at McDonald's, which was about the only thing we could afford on our salaries, when I turned to him and said, "I'm going to run for state senate."

He was sipping a full cup of soda at the time, and he dropped it right to the floor. It was like one of those double takes in a movie; there was soda everywhere! It was just about the last thing he expected to hear from me, but there it was, and to this day I don't know that there was any one thing that pushed me to want to run. It must have been all that time at our kitchen table, listening to my mother tell me I could do anything, become anything; listening to my father tell me I needed to find a way to figure things out on my own; watching the two of them do whatever they could to help others. Or maybe it came from working in the legislature, looking on at all those politicians doing their thing, or attempting to do their thing, and thinking, I can do a better job of this than these guys. Or maybe it had to do with that unlikely meeting with President Nixon in the Oval Office, or the chance to work for Ronald Reagan in such a thrilling way at the Republican National Convention.

Basically, I was just following my instincts. I was young, but I don't think I was arrogant; rather, I thought that my determination to succeed and to work for the good of others would serve me well in office, and that it was time for me to reach for a new opportunity.

One of the reasons Bob dropped his soda that day was because he realized I was going to run against an incumbent state senator named Robert O'Shaughnessy, a household name in the district and a man with deep ties in the community and a long family history in the state legislature. There weren't a whole lot of people on the Republican side of the aisle looking to run against O'Shaughnessy. Actually, that's a bit of an overstatement. There wasn't a *single credible candidate* looking to run against him— that is, other than *me,* and here you have to stop for a moment and consider what it meant to be a credible candidate.

The one hitch to my plan was that, in order to make a credible run, I'd have to leave my job as an aide. I was married at the time, and my first wife worked as a schoolteacher, so at least there'd be some money coming in. Still, I had no staff, no office, no base of support, no idea how to go out and raise money to fund even a bare-bones campaign. Still, I decided to go for it, and since I had almost two years to ramp up, I started in the slow lane, making phone calls, knocking on doors, getting my message out to the voters of Ohio's Fifteenth District in whatever way I could. Even so, at twenty-five years old, I found it tough to get anyone to take me seriously. I remember going to a county picnic during this time and trying to introduce myself to the county chairman. The guy just turned on his heels and walked away from me.

I can't say I blamed him; I looked about twelve years old.

At first, I had no idea what I was doing. At one point, my wife and I moved out of the district and didn't even know it. I realized my mistake almost immediately and moved right back, but I mention it here to illustrate how inexperienced I was politically. After a while, though, I started to figure things out. This clarity seemed to come around the time Don Thibaut signed on to run my campaign, and from that point forward we figured it out to together. Before I started my campaign, I created a group called the Citizens Committee on Energy, which talked about solar and wind and related environmental issues. It turned out to be a meaningful platform, a way to get my name in the newspaper. The committee also served a dual purpose—it forced me to figure out if I could get people together on an issue. I'd invite various energy experts to seminars, and then I'd invite the media. I figured this was a good way to build some credibility.

Somewhere in there it occurred to me that if I was passing myself off as the chairman of this committee, I ought to be duly elected, so a few of my friends I'd put on the "board" of the Citizens Committee on Energy shrugged their shoulders and elected me.

We were out there talking about important stuff, and offering up salient information, but try as we might, we just couldn't get folks to come out to our events. I remember one conference we put together in German Village when the temperature outside was about one hundred degrees, and I realized as we were about to start our presentation that there were more people on the panel than in the audience. Still, we could always count on someone from the local paper to show up or, at the very least, run a press release or a photo.

And in this way, little by little, I made my presence known.


## RUNNING ON FULL

In the beginning, nobody gave me a shot in my run for the legislature. The Fifteenth District back then had more than 300,000 people, so there was a lot of ground to cover. Still, that didn't stop me from covering it—on foot, for the most part, going door to door, doing what I could to introduce myself to voters and build a grassroots campaign. Making it up as I went along—like the time I pulled out the phone book and started thumbing through the listings for all the phone numbers beginning with the 888 exchange and cold-calling every household in Worthington, Ohio.

It's tough to build a grassroots campaign when folks don't know who you are—a problem I would face again when I ran for president. Still, I kept at it. After a while, I got the attention of some influential people in the Republican Party who decided to help me, which was a great good thing because, by this point, a couple other "credible" candidates were considering challenging for the nomination.

Early on, I had to make an impression on Republicans in the district—and not just *any* Republicans, mind you, but the ones in a position to decide whom to run for the state senate seat. My boldest move probably was getting my hands on the list of all the Republicans who were on the central committee that would ultimately nominate the party's candidate. The move was bold because nobody had ever done it before, but to me it was the obvious play. There were about one hundred people on that list, and I drove to every single one of their homes. I'd call first and make an appointment, but I thought it was essential that I meet these people face-to-face and tell them who I was and what I had in mind. Once I got the nomination, I knew I'd have to win over Democratic voters as well, but I didn't see this as a problem. Even then, I was able to get along with everybody, no matter our differences. Even some people who knew me and worked with me seemed to have no idea of my political affiliation. For example, Claude Desautels, who gave me my first job in Washington, very generously made a contribution to my campaign, but when he found out I was running as a Republican, he demanded his money back.

That first state senate race was run on a shoestring. It was just me and Don Thibaut. After a while we had a few volunteers, and after another while we had a few *more* volunteers, and then a few more after that. Really, by the time it was all over, we'd assembled a great group of supporters who worked tirelessly to help get the word out about my campaign. We would have been nowhere without their extra efforts. But we had no money. Strike that—we had a little money. How much? Well, here's a story to give you some idea.

I was driving myself to an event in Worthington, Ohio, when I was pulled over for speeding. When the police officer came to the window to ask for my license and registration, I took the time to tell him who I was and why I was in such a hurry. Basically, I went into my whole campaign pitch—thinking that police officers were voters, too, and here I had a captive audience. Then I reached into my pocket and pulled out a quarter, which I showed to him with my license and registration, pointing out that if he gave me a ticket, it might just put an end to my campaign. I pulled out my empty pockets for emphasis and said, "This is all I've got, officer."

I don't know if I earned that cop's vote, but on this day at least I think I earned his respect, because he let me off with just a warning—and my campaign lived to fight another day.

Don Thibaut was a tremendous campaign manager. He put out newsletters, he recruited volunteers, he had a strategy. He helped me work my way through the screening committee of the Republican Party, and then on to the full central committee that voted to give me their recommendation for the nomination. He was all over it.

As Election Day was drawing near, we found ourselves with enough money to film a commercial, which we'd never expected to be in a position to do. (In all, we spent about $78,000 on that campaign—compared to the seven figures some candidates spend today.) Our plan was to go to the Ohio Senate floor and film the commercial there. We had it all worked out in our heads. But the Republicans were in the minority back then, and when we got to the statehouse to film the commercial, the senators in charge moved to block us. One of them came out and said, "You can't film here."

We knew we were within our rights, and we said as much, but these senators wouldn't budge, so I took them to court—here, again, the obvious play, the only move we thought we had left. When the judge sided with us, we made plans to film the commercial a second time, but the Democrats went and appealed the decision, so we were right back where we started. This all happened over the course of two or three weeks, and during that time we wound up getting a ton of publicity out of this fight over this one little television spot, calling way more attention to my campaign than the ad itself could ever have generated. Looking back, I believe this blatant show of partisanship tilted things our way. The move to block me didn't come directly from O'Shaughnessy, but it was the dumbest move of the Democratic campaign, and it backfired on him. Because out of that pettiness, I started lining up support from quite a few Republican mayors in our suburban towns.

In the end, we gave Robert O'Shaughnessy the fight of his life, and I won the election with over 56 percent of the vote, becoming the youngest state senator in Ohio history. It was a huge upset— and no one was more upset than Robert O'Shaughnessy, who all along seemed to have no idea how hard I'd been working to unseat him.

That's the thing about running a grassroots campaign. It's a lot like running your own business, and there I was, a start-up, taking a dogged, determined, entrepreneurial approach to campaigning, while my opponent was probably taking his reelection for granted.

I might have started as a lone-wolf, long-shot candidate. I was just a kid, really. Nobody thought I could win this thing—and the truth was, I didn't really have any idea what I was doing. I just went at it, hard. I pounded the pavement, knocked on doors, made hundreds and hundreds of phone calls. Then Don Thibaut signed on, and then the volunteers.

I remember thinking on the night of the election how profoundly grateful I was to all those good, selfless people who'd helped out with the campaign. I've thought about these same folks every time I've run for office in the years since. Some of them have stuck around all these years, and some haven't, but even though some of the faces have changed, and people's roles, each campaign takes me back to that first Election Night victory. I felt this gratitude most keenly during the 2016 presidential primaries, probably because the stakes were so much greater—then again, even though I was running for president, a part of me still felt like a twenty-six-year-old kid going through the same experience, as if for the very first time.

Sometimes I catch myself wondering if the folks who worked on my first campaign were surprised how far I went in my political career. I suspect some of them were, and maybe that's why they threw in with me. I suspect others have been surprised to see me still at it, to have seen me making a serious run at the Republican presidential nomination. And then I catch myself hoping like crazy that none of them ever gets to thinking they backed the wrong horse, because, really, one of the goals of my political career all along has been to make doubly sure that none of the people who helped me out in the very beginning would ever regret their decision to do so. I was determined to give them a good return on their investment, and I like to think I've come through on my end of the deal.

## OH, TO BE A YOUNG IDEALIST

As a rookie state senator, I was on the outside looking in. You see, in defeating Robert O'Shaughnessy, I'd also defeated the senate president's best friend, so the Ohio Democrats decided I should be punished for it. For two years they basically ignored me—to the leadership, it was as if I didn't exist. Of course, it's not like I did *nothing* for those two years. I'd made some campaign promises I intended to keep. I had my committee assignments, and I was able to be involved in a going-through-the-motions sort of way, but none of my ideas were taken seriously.

It sometimes felt like I wasn't even there.

That said, I don't mean to give the impression that *all* I did during my first two years in the legislature was twiddle my thumbs. From time to time, I managed to put forward a good idea, and when that happened, we'd find a way to get it through in the other body and move it forward in this sidelong way.

All I could do was all I could do.

Then, two years later, we won the majority, and my world was changed overnight—or, at least my day-to-day world. Those first two years, the Democrats ran everything. Then, all of a sudden, I was the chairman of the Health Committee, and I had to start working with my colleagues in the House. That's when I learned how to get along with people on the other side of the aisle. That's when I was finally given the room I needed to do my job and become the kind of elected official my supporters expected me to be. Yet, as much as I might have wanted to, I couldn't hold a grudge over the way I'd been treated during my first two years in the legislature. I couldn't give as good as I'd gotten. Why? Plain and simple: I hadn't gotten into politics to serve the Republican Party.

From the very beginning, I've told people the Republican Party was my vehicle, not my master, and I realized that, as chairman of the Health Committee, I now had the job to try to accomplish something. It wouldn't do to shut out my Democratic colleagues just because they'd shut *me* out. I never understood that type of thinking. Why go into politics if you're not going to try to get something done? It made no sense.

It fell to me in my new role to try to get all these proposals through the Senate, and then to turn around and try to get them through the House, so I believed I had no choice but to find a way to work with everybody. I might have said some smart-alecky things to the folks who made my life so miserable those first two years, but even though I hadn't been treated fairly, I didn't turn the tables on the people who'd shut me out. What would have been the point of *that*? I remember passing a balanced budget amendment in the Senate, and then working like crazy to get it through the House— but then, as now, that was anathema to Democrats, so in the end it didn't happen.

Still, I kept pressing, looking for ways we could work together. This wasn't a game to me. I wasn't there to punish the other side. I was there to get stuff done.

And what did I get for all that? Well, my own party started criticizing me. They said I was "irresponsible" for not supporting a tax increase, when I'd run on the promise that I wouldn't raise taxes, a promise I was determined to honor. This was no easy task. Our own Republican governor, Jim Rhodes, was supporting the tax increase, and he was just furious with me, but instead of falling into line and voting for it, I huddled with Don Thibaut and tried to figure out how to close the gap on this shortfall in revenues that left everyone in the legislature thinking a tax increase was the only solution. I'd write my own budget, if that's what it took. So, we looked at *all* the operations of government. I found it fascinating. And then all these people I didn't know started coming into my office, whispering to me all these things they thought might be helpful.

Ultimately, Don and I found a way to close the gap, and I presented my budget on the Senate floor—and it got killed. But, so what? I was happy with what I'd done. I hadn't merely refused to vote for a tax hike. I'd put my own ideas out there. I'd offered an alternative. And in the process, I learned that the key to the kingdom in government was to understand *all* the workings of government, a lesson I took with me all the way to Congress, where I started writing my own federal budgets.

Back in the legislature, this kind of thing just wasn't done—at least, not by a twenty-something kid who didn't seem to understand his place in the workings of state government. My own Republican colleagues were really angry at me, yelling at me, criticizing me publicly—it tells you a lot about the Republican Party and my loyalty to it, right? But I wasn't there to serve those Republicans. I was there to carry out my duties and honor the promises I'd made to voters during my campaign, and because of that, some people wouldn't even talk to me. They probably regarded me as a self-righteous—that is, if they regarded me at all.

My relationship with Governor Rhodes didn't exactly get off to a rousing start. Soon after I was sworn in, I was called to a meeting in his office with a group of legislators, whereupon the governor announced an initiative to raise school taxes. His plan, he said, was to shift the vote away from the people who lived in the district and to place it with the school board, a system we had in place in Pennsylvania when I was growing up. I didn't think that was fair to the taxpayers. We were seated in a semicircle, with the governor at the center, and everybody just kind of sat there, not saying anything. Finally, I spoke up. I said, "Governor, I just have to make this clear. I could never support this plan."

I'll never forget the look on this man's face: he was so aggravated with me that I thought steam might start coming out of his ears. We never did approve his measure, but at the time, I was one of the few voices of dissent in the room. I just didn't want to sit there and use my silence to indicate any kind of approval for an approach that I thought was all wrong.

Another time, I was invited to a dinner with members of a delegation from Franklin County, which was to be attended by a group of local judges. When I got the invitation, I was young and naïve enough to think it was just a nice dinner, a chance for all of us to get together in a social setting, but very quickly I realized that the judges had an agenda. They were seeking a pay raise and were using the dinner to build support for the idea. Once again, none of the other legislators said anything; they were too busy enjoying their nice dinner. But I put down my fork and spoke up about it. I said, "I'm sorry, but I can't vote all of you a pay raise if I don't vote all the other state employees a pay raise."

I was on the wrong side of this issue, it turned out—the judges were woefully underpaid and deserving of a raise—but I had my back up. As ever, people were terribly angry at me. It was as if I'd set off an explosion on my side of the restaurant. One of the judges even stood and stared me down and said, "Young man, don't you ever show up in my courtroom."

It was really nasty, and I couldn't have been made to feel more uncomfortable, but the very next day, I got a call from this very same judge; he said he wanted to take me to lunch. Somehow, out of all that, he took a shine to me, and we ended up becoming very good friends. I think he realized that I was young and altruistic, but he appreciated my conviction. And I appreciated his willingness to look past my youthful enthusiasm.

My feeling was that I needed to continue keeping my campaign promises, never more so than when my own party voted itself a token pay raise and I refused to accept it, at a time in my life when I really could have used the money. You have to realize, a $17,500 state senator's salary didn't stretch very far, even in 1979, and a bump to $22,500 would have made a world of difference to me, but I sent the money back. I still had to pay taxes on that extra $5,000, because there was no mechanism in place for me to prevent the state from issuing a check for the full amount. Still, I didn't think it was right for the legislature to vote for a pay raise. It was self-serving. Sure, we were underpaid, but a lot of people in Ohio were hurting. More to the point, many of my colleagues had campaigned on the promise not to raise taxes, so I couldn't endorse it. Voting against it wasn't enough, in my opinion.

This got a lot of attention, my returning the money the way I did. It set me up as a kind of maverick who wasn't afraid to go against his own party, but that wasn't why I did it. No, I did it on principle, because it felt like the right thing to do. Here again, people thought I was nuts—my parents, especially. My father said, "What are you gonna do next year, Johnny?"

I hadn't thought that far ahead, but when next year rolled around, I refused the increase a second time. After all, I'd made a promise that the legislature should not raise their pay, because I believed we needed to have a part-time legislature, and I was determined to keep my promises. Little did I know that each year, I'd have to keep refusing the same pay raise. It got to where the money I'd first refused added up to $15,000, and money that I had to pay in taxes was for money I never actually "earned." It *was* a little bit nuts, wasn't it? It was also, after a while, a little bit beside the point. Nobody seemed to care or even notice. As far as I was concerned, at least, the point had been made. And what point was that, exactly? Well, I like to think I'd put it out there that I was not like any other politician the good people of Ohio had ever seen. That I may have been young, but I was willing and able to stand my ground, and that to stand for what I believed was right and good and true.

Little did I know just then how far that stand might take me.

# 3.

# Running in Place

Before we get too far away from the 2016 presidential campaign, I want to circle back to all those wheels that were set in motion by my decision to seek the nomination. There were a lot of moving parts to consider, as I began my second term as governor, and here I think it helps to acknowledge the state of our state. Ohio was doing well. There had been a significant turnaround since I took office in 2011. We had a terrific team in place, and we were able to work with good Republican leadership in the legislature to get our state back on its feet.

At the same time, you had the Republican field falling into place—in fits and starts at first, but in an orchestrated way soon enough. Rick Perry had seemed to be eyeing the 2016 race since he suspended his 2012 campaign. Jeb Bush, Chris Christie, Marco Rubio—these guys were all finding reasons to move about the country to raise money and to raise their national profiles. And in this environment, when you're the governor of Ohio (a governor who has run for president before), you're inevitably asked if you're considering a run. But I honestly wasn't thinking about it. For the longest time, I wasn't thinking about it. I had been focused on winning a second term, which was certainly not a given. You have to realize, Ohioans voted for Obama twice, and they elected Sherrod Brown to the U.S. Senate. I'd been elected to my first term as governor by only a slim margin over the incumbent Democrat, Ted Strickland, so I had been careful not to get ahead of myself.

When I took office in 2011, our budget was a mess. We were $8 billion in the hole. We'd lost 350,000 jobs. And there was the grand sum of $0.89 in the state's rainy-day fund. Eighty-nine cents! It was slow going, at first. We had a tough time changing the way our state went about its business—mostly because there was a culture of spending in place that we were trying to transform. By our second budget, we were moving aggressively in the area of tax reform, and by the midpoint in that first term, I believe that even Ohio Democrats had to look on admiringly at the progress we were making. We were creating jobs, balancing the budget, rebuilding our resources, reinvigorating our programs and initiatives. Sure, we had to step on some toes and go against a lot of special interest groups that were used to getting their way, but there was no real call among the Democratic base to run me out of office. It was a new day all around the state. Things were looking up.

Just how high was up? Well, that rainy-day fund was now showing a surplus of $1.5 billion.

Still, I could not take my reelection for granted. This was Ohio, after all. This was politics, after all. Anything could happen. So, I followed the advice of the late Ohio congressman Chalmers Wylie, whose campaign strategy was always to run like you're 20 points behind. The first time I heard that, it struck me as sound advice, so I always tried to live by it. Meanwhile, reporters were asking me all the time if I was thinking of running for president.

Potential donors, they were asking, too. So were people on the street. But I had no time to think about a presidential run. I was too busy running for governor as if I were trailing by 20 points in the polls. Oh, and by the way, at the same time, I was trying to run the great state of Ohio.

It turned out we won a second term by an overwhelming margin, but that margin wasn't really reflected in the polls until late in the game, and it was by no means a given. For the longest time, it was looking like a tight race, but we wound up carrying eighty-six of Ohio's eighty-eight counties, including Cuyahoga County, where it's notoriously hard for a downstate Republican. It was enormously gratifying to be returned to office for a second term in such a resounding way.

That left me with the task of reflecting on my first term and looking ahead to my second term as I prepared my inaugural remarks. I took great pains to make sure to jump-start things on just the right note. I should mention here that I like to write my own speeches. Every now and then, I'm able to collect my thoughts in a way that gets to the heart of my thinking, the heart of my *heart*. And here I wasn't so sure I'd hit all the right notes. The speech I had in my head was not at all traditional, and I remember being a little nervous about it—so nervous, in fact, that I reminded my friends to clap, even if they didn't like it. Fortunately, the people seemed to respond to the speech I delivered at my second inauguration, which was held on January 12, 2015. I called the speech "Toward a New Ohio," and I'd like to quote from it here, at length, because the ideas expressed in this address became the cornerstone of my presidential campaign. I guess you never know what your thinking is until you give it voice—and then, with perspective, hear it back as if for the first time.

I began with the usual perfunctory remarks. I honored the

solemnity of the occasion. I thanked the people who deserved to be thanked. I acknowledged the dignitaries in attendance. I detailed some of the accomplishments of our administration and highlighted several of the more exciting programs and initiatives taking place across the state.

Then I got into it. I don't think I realized it at the time, because I had yet to frame my thinking in this way—about how we all live at a kind of base level—but I suppose in this moment I was extending my reach a little bit. I was writing about what it meant to live life on a higher plane.

> Remember, your life and your mission is important to the world. Our world, our nation, our state, your community—they are all made up of people just like you, and these places are only as strong and good as you decide to make them. We are all part of a great mosaic. Our commitment, our efforts, our character—these are what make America great. America didn't achieve what it has achieved because of government. America has always been about the character, tenacity, goodness of its people. Our nation is as strong as we choose to be, as *you* choose to be.

> What are you doing to build a strong community, a stronger Ohio, a stronger nation? What are you doing to build on the work of those who came before us and those who made the ultimate sacrifice? I know you agree that there are values that are important to live by and cultivate, that your contribution—your legacy—matters. Join me in acting today, wherever you are.

> Here in Ohio we know that these values matter and that they can change people: personal responsibility, empathy, teamwork, family, and faith. We're seeing it, but there's more to do.

We are creating pathways so you can put these values to work in your community, through efforts such as our teen anti-drug use initiative, Start Talking; our student mentoring effort, Community Connectors; our initiative to help the disabled find meaningful work, Employment First; and with our work to reduce infant mortality.

These are all opportunities for us to roll up our sleeves and practice what we believe and what we know works. These are opportunities to give of ourselves and help someone else find their way. Some of the toughest problems facing our society can only be solved if we help turn on the light in someone else's life. Not only can it make two lives brighter, but it can shine a light on the way forward for all of us.

We have been our greatest—as individuals and a nation—when we have had the courage to let go of ourselves and feel the pull of a greater power, a power that calls us to work together to heal the world. When we resist that pull and focus on self, that's when we fail—individually and as a nation. That's not our history and we cannot let it be our future.

Our future together will be as strong and prosperous and joyous as we choose to make it. We can't rest in pursuit of that better future, nor become complacent. Yes, it's work, but when we get started and see what we can achieve together, a fire takes hold and we never want to let it go out. Haven't the past four years started to teach us that? When we begin to make progress together, we don't want to rest. We become energized. We relish the constant churn and forward motion we are making together.

This is the path forward for us. It is the path I choose and try to walk every day, and it is the path that I will chart for the next four years as governor of our state.

I will continue to nurture a climate in which the dignity of hard work is respected and pays off, and entrepreneurs can create and innovate. I will continue to build a system for people to learn and grow throughout their lives and reach their God-given potential. I will continue to make sure we are able to catch each other if we fall and help those who struggle live with the dignity and grace deserving a child of God. I will continue to put people and their freedoms over government, because government is for us and by us, not the other way around. And I will go about all of this work by embracing change and innovation and by working every day to bring us together. I will work to the best of my ability to tear down the barriers that divide us and show us that we are stronger together.

And when my work is done I hope Ohioans are more than just better off. I hope we have a better way, that we have a new way of seeing our shared work together. I hope I will have helped Ohioans see how much good can be achieved when we laugh at the impossible and instead just go for it.

## BALANCING THE BUDGET (AND OTHER PRIORITIES)

With the gubernatorial election behind us, I found myself thinking more and more about taking on additional issues. I don't mean to suggest that the business of Ohio was anything less than a priority for me, but we had strong people and programs in place; we were on a sure and steady course; our base level was looking pretty darn good. So, I turned my attention to what I thought was the single biggest stumbling block to real national progress: the glaring absence of a balanced budget provision in the U.S. Constitution. As you might know, I was one of the architects of the Balanced Budget Act of 1997, and it was on my watch as chairman of the House Budget Committee that we balanced the federal budget for the first time since 1969. But that was then, and this was now, and all you had to do was look at a calendar and see that, in 2015, we were as far removed from a balanced federal budget as we'd been in 1997.

I thought we should try to do something about that.

What to do, exactly? Well, we'd been kicking around the idea of a balanced budget tour for a while, toward the end of my first term. Note that this was not a new issue for me; it was something I'd been passionate about since I ran for the state senate as a young man. Note, too, that when I say "we" I'm referring to my core advisers and top aides—many of the key people I'd assembled to help run my campaign for governor and serve in my administration. And note that when I mention a "tour," I'm talking about taking my message on the road and offering up my two cents on the significance of a balanced budget amendment to the U.S. Constitution and meeting with legislators to discuss the various ways we might move forward on it.

Given my experience in Washington, we all believed I was in a good position to advance this issue, but in the run-up to the 2014 elections, I didn't want to lose my focus, so we set the notion aside. Winning a second term as governor was paramount, but now that my second term was in hand, the time felt right to bring the idea back to front and center, to extend my reach a little bit—this on the dual theory that what was good for the nation was good for the state of Ohio, and that what had worked in Ohio with our balanced budget initiatives would work across the country.

The plan, at first, was to travel to targeted states to push the issue. At the time, twenty-four states had passed resolutions supporting a balanced budget amendment, which meant we needed ten more to call for a constitutional convention. Ultimately, we'd need thirty-eight states to approve the change for the amendment to pass, so we had some work to do, and it felt to our core group that we were the ones to do it.

Privately, some of my advisers worried that an effort like this might appear as a kind of exploratory campaign for a possible presidential run in 2016. But I didn't share their concerns. This was an issue that had been central to my time in Washington and was now at the heart of our turnaround in Ohio. I was out to engage American voters and state lawmakers on this one all-important issue, not to gauge *their* interest in *me*. I'd made it clear throughout the gubernatorial race that I wasn't thinking about running for president. I wasn't being coy; a run didn't feel right to me just then. It was in the air, but it wasn't in my heart. I'd always told people, back when I was first considering a run for governor, that I wouldn't run unless and until I felt a calling to do so. Ultimately, I did. And in 2015, I found myself telling people the same thing: I wouldn't run for president unless and until I felt a calling, and at this early juncture, I felt no such thing. To be sure, a balanced budget tour would be one way to gauge *my* interest in traveling the country to talk about big-picture issues, a good and necessary thing to know if I were ever to seriously consider entering the presidential field. If I didn't have the enthusiasm or the fortitude for *that*—well, a run for the White House wouldn't have made a whole lot of sense.

At this point, I had no idea what kind of reception I'd receive outside Ohio. It had been some time since I "campaigned" outside the state, not counting the efforts I'd make every now and then for Republican Party candidates who reached out for my support. Just prior to my second inauguration, however, I'd traveled to Phoenix to see what measures would have to be put in place to win a budget amendment in Arizona. That first trip was meant to be a one-shot deal, but out of that visit we received a half dozen or so invitations from legislators in other states. I'd fully intended to keep the focus on a balanced budget, but once I get going in front of a crowd, there can be no telling where the conversation might take me. (Remember, in our house growing up, I was taught to speak my mind—and apparently, I had a lot to say.) Still, people seemed to really respond to the simple idea at the heart of our message: if our states are prohibited from spending more money than they take in, our federal government should be bound by the same ideal. It's common sense, right? But sometimes it takes a concerted effort and a clear, strong voice to get people to see what's right in front of them, so I decided to take on the issue, because nothing was more important to the future of this country—or, by extension, to Ohioans.

The concerted effort would come through a nonprofit advocacy group called Balanced Budget Forever, together with some key members of my team who agreed to donate their time to this issue, in an after-hours way. The clear, strong voice would have to come from me, and I thought I was up to the task. If people knew me at all, outside Ohio, they knew me as a fiscal conservative in Washington. I was familiar with the material. I knew the drill. And together we all thought we could call some serious attention to the balanced budget issue.

We set our sights on a six-state tour to start: South Dakota, North Dakota, Montana, Wyoming, Utah, and Idaho. Our first stop was in Pierre, South Dakota, where I addressed a group of lawmakers at an American Legion post. "Who the heck thinks we should keep spending without any regard to the consequences?" I asked. "I don't care if you're a Republican, a Democrat, or a Martian. This is not what we should be doing as a nation. It's irresponsible."

That "I don't care if you're a Republican, a Democrat, or a Martian" line got a lot of attention, and we were off and running. And while I was out there, campaigning for this balanced budget amendment, a snapshot of the 2016 presidential race started to come into focus. I suppose, given the timing, it was inevitable that the press would start to think of me as a national candidate, but that really wasn't the case then. I know that might sound like a line, but that's truly where my head was during this time. That calling I was waiting on? I was still waiting on it. So, while I was campaigning for budget reform, there were some who heard in that the drumbeat of a presidential campaign—but that drumbeat wasn't coming from me.

Meanwhile, there were preparatory moves I had to make for when and if I announced my candidacy. Perhaps the most essential (and most time consuming) of these had to do with getting ready for the debate stage. Before I ever decided to run for president, I had to do a certain amount of homework to make sure not only that I was *good and ready* to lead this country, but also that I could demonstrate as much within the constraints of a presidential debate. So, for a few weeks leading up to my decision to seek the Republican nomination, my friends and advisers put me through my paces.

Just in case.

We'd meet two or three times a week, usually for an hour or two, in sessions led by my longtime friend and adviser Bob Klaffky, who would go on to play a crucial role in my campaign. Each time we met, Bob would have me answer a couple dozen questions grouped in four segments. We'd gone through a similar drill when I ran for governor, so I knew the routine. I would answer his questions without interruption, then we'd pause for comments from the friends and advisers we'd recruited to sit in. They'd offer suggestions on how to improve my answers, how I could make my arguments more forcefully, how to better appeal to voters. If Bob planned to ask a specific policy question, he'd make sure to have relevant policy experts on hand to weigh in, and we went back and forth in this way for several weeks.

We continued the practice deep into the campaign, including once the debates were under way, but what's interesting to me here is that we jump-started the effort before I was fully committed to running. Here I was, being prepped to go up against a Republican field that was already taking shape without me. I was already comfortable in front of a camera, after years of practice. Before running for governor, I'd spent my post-Washington career giving speeches all across the country. I'd even hosted my own television show. So, I thought I was doing okay on the public speaking front—yet, it took going through these motions in just this way to get me to feel that I could do a good and credible job of it in a debate setting.

In this way, and in so many others, the pieces were all in place for me to announce my candidacy. Now all I had to do was figure out what I was going to do.

## "WELL, I GUESS I'M GOING TO HAVE TO RUN"

Think back for a moment to the first few months of 2015. The landscape of likely and unlikely Republican candidates for president looked nothing like it would a year or so later, once primary season was under way. Early on, the "elephant in the room" candidate, the guy almost every Republican strategist had tabbed as the de facto front-runner, was former Florida governor Jeb Bush. The talk in GOP circles was that he'd already raised $100 million and lined up all this strategic support. By most objective measures, he was all the way out in front, and I had it in mind to steer clear. Probably, I was a little gun-shy. When I'd run against Jeb's brother in 2000, it felt as if W. had big-footed the entire field. He commanded the bulk of media attention, raised the most money, took all the air out of the room. That's how it went with the Bush family and Republican politics going all the way back to the early 1980s; they wielded a lot of influence, and the name recognition was just through the roof. It's tough to compete against a political dynasty, and here the perception was that Jeb would be tough to beat. I didn't think I had it in me to go up against that kind of juggernaut a second time, not when I already had what I sincerely thought was the best job in government.

What could be better than running the great state of Ohio? Still, there was something about the Jeb Bush candidacy that seemed to leave the door open—not just for someone like me, who wasn't even thinking of a presidential run, but for other candidates: say, Wisconsin governor Scott Walker, who also started to win some attention during this period that political insiders referred to as the "credentials caucus." That's when candidates and would-be candidates and might-never-be candidates crisscross the country harvesting relationships with donors and voters and pundits and campaign strategists and basically dip their toes in the waters of a presidential run. For a while in there, even 2012 Republican presidential nominee Mitt Romney was said to be considering another run at the White House, and his numbers ran pretty high in preliminary polling.

Still and all, Jeb Bush kept polling at the top of the field, and he was being touted by the media (and his own campaign) as a kind of presumptive nominee, so he was commanding a good chunk of the presidential conversation during the first months of 2015. If there was any momentum to be found back then, you can bet the Bush camp was out there looking for it—and doing what they could to make it their own. Recall that every time a potential candidate emerged from the sidelines, such as former Arkansas governor Mike Huckabee or Kentucky senator Rand Paul, his chances were weighed against Jeb Bush's, and whenever my team got me to sit still and consider what a presidential run might look like, the former Florida governor dominated the discussion.

When we talked about how much money I'd need to raise, someone would invariably mention how much the Bush campaign had raised—and of course we'd have no answer to that.

When we talked about the kind of name recognition I could count on, someone would bring up the Bush dynasty—and of course we'd have no answer to that.

When we talked about how late it was in this presidential election cycle, someone would point to the running start the Bush team enjoyed—and of course we'd have no answer to that.

So, there were all these negatives lining up against me, and all these plusses in the Bush column, but we kept at it, pressing the issue on the balanced budget amendment. The only times I thought seriously about running for president during this period were when a reporter put the question to me directly, which happened more and more as we traveled from state to state. I had no plans to run, I'd always say. But then someone on my team would take the opportunity to engage me on the prospect of a presidential run, and in those moments, I honestly didn't know which way I was leaning, or if any of these clear negatives lining up against me were enough to count me out. Here again, I allow that this might sound disingenuous, but this was my mind-set. I still hadn't felt any kind of calling to run for president, hadn't thought through what it might mean for my family, for the state of Ohio, for the Republican Party. I mean, I'd thought about *all* these things, but not in any kind of systematic or thorough-going way, and I suppose I'd been putting off doing so. Why? Because I'd yet to find a compelling reason to do so. Because my heart wasn't in it just yet.

It's not that I was having it both ways, traveling the country while contemplating a run for national office. We were actually getting a good reception from a lot of the legislators I met with, and people were coming out in support of our balanced budget initiative. That all started to change, however, toward the end of March, when I traveled to New Hampshire to participate in the Politics and Eggs breakfast forum in New Hampshire. The trip had nothing to do with our balanced budget tour—in fact, the initiative had already passed in New Hampshire—but we put it on the schedule just the same. I still wasn't thinking of myself as a presidential candidate, but by this point I'd been asked if I was running so many times that I felt I had no choice but to think about it long and hard. My own people were encouraging me to consider a run, and if a run was indeed in the cards, they said, I needed to do the Politics and Eggs forum.

Do you know about this event? Since the late 1970s, it's been a must-stop on the campaign trail for almost every major-party presidential candidate. It's got its own quirky traditions, including, charmingly, the signing of decorative wooden eggs, which are collected and kept on display. (Trust me on this, I've been asked to sign a lot of things during my time in politics—baseballs, T-shirts, plaster casts—but a wooden egg offers just about the strangest canvas. It's almost impossible to get a legible signature on that thing!) For some candidates, the event is seen as an important launching pad as they look ahead to the New Hampshire primary; for others, it offers them a platform before an informed audience, a place to try on the idea of a presidential run; for me, it was yet another way to test the temperature a little bit, engage in a larger conversation on issues of national interest, and see if maybe the fire in the belly I'd been waiting on could somehow be ignited.

While in New Hampshire, I had dinner with former senator John Sununu. John and I went back a long way—we'd served together in Congress. I had his ear, and he had mine, and here he took me aside and told me in no uncertain terms that I should run for president. And it's not like I even asked for his opinion. He just came right out and gave it to me. He said, "Bush can't win here in New Hampshire."

I'd been hearing whispers saying the same thing all across the country: For whatever reason, people weren't excited about Jeb's candidacy. Despite his pedigree, despite his platform, despite all the money he may or may not have raised, he just wasn't moving voters the way you need to move voters at the front end of a presidential campaign. But to hear it here in New Hampshire, where the Bush name was like gold, and from a leading voice such as John Sununu—well, I've got to say, my ears pricked up a little bit. When I got back home to Ohio, I sat down with my wife, Karen, and we talked it through. She was a good sport about it—as she always is, about most of my political decisions. Like me, she was of two minds. She worried how a presidential run would impact our little family. At the time, our twin daughters were finishing their freshman year in high school, and if you've got teenage children, you know that there are enough distractions and highs and lows and tense emotions running through your house without throwing a national campaign into the mix. But we thought we could handle that—*we* meaning the four of us together.

Forget about the rigors and uncertainties of the campaign itself—Karen pushed me to consider what it would mean to us Kasichs, if things went our way, to have to pack up and move to Washington. That was the endgame in all this, yes? You don't run for president just to run for president. No, you're in it to win it, and in this regard the timing was less than ideal, we both agreed. The girls would be in the thick of their junior year on Election Day, and if we were blessed enough to make it all the way to the White House, they'd have to leave behind their friends, their teams, their clubs, their teachers, at a crucial moment in their high school careers.

But we thought we could handle *that* too. Indeed, I started to realize how much the country would have loved Karen and the girls. I may have been biased in this, but I don't think so. My wife has the elegance of a Jackie Kennedy, and a personality that everyone loves, and as we talked about it, I knew she'd just light up the national stage, with Emma and Reese at our side.

Karen helped me look on the plus side. She told me that in her (hardly impartial) opinion, there was no one better equipped to point this country in a positive direction and set right the American pendulum. She told me she'd never seen such a stalemate in Washington, where party politics seemed to have brought the business of government to a standstill. She reminded me that I was well and truly qualified to serve as president of the United States, and that I'd had a history of working in a bipartisan way to get folks to work together for the common good. And she emboldened me to think I was up to the task. I needed to hear all this, let me tell you, and I needed to hear it from Karen, whose good counsel is at the center of everything I do.

One of the things I kept thinking about, as I was weighing the pros and cons of a presidential run, was a visit I made to the Oval Office as I was leaving Congress. There was a White House event on the debt relief issue, and I found myself in the Oval Office with a bunch of staffers and a photographer. President Clinton wasn't around, but we were in his office, and someone suggested I sit in his chair, at his desk. But I couldn't do that—didn't even consider it. Why? Because that's a right you have to earn. It would have been disrespectful, I thought, to *play* at being the president of the United States—unless it was the president of the United States himself inviting me to sit in his chair. So, I declined, and it was only now, over fifteen years later, that I started to think that I had the right to sit in that chair. I'd still have to earn it, but maybe I was finally ready to do that.

At long last.

It was around this time that I had that conversation with my friend Don Thibaut, the one where he basically told me I was driving him crazy and that I should just shut up and run. But that just shows how all over the place I was in my thinking. I was talking to everyone I knew and trusted in my political life, in my personal life—in my spiritual life, even.

You want to know who else I count on to help me see things clearly? Someone who held an important place in *all* aspects of my life: my great friend Ron Hartman, whom we all call Rondo. I'd known Rondo since I was in the state senate, so we went back a long way. Over the years, he's become one of my closest and most trusted advisers. He's the one who drove me to Pittsburgh to sort through my parents' affairs after they were killed in a car crash—that's how close we were. We'd been in the same Bible study group for almost thirty years, so we connected on matters of faith, too, but I valued his opinion on just about everything—from politics to business to what he thought of the latest Justin Bieber video. Rondo's a lawyer by trade, but he's plugged into almost everything. Plus, he's got a keen entrepreneurial streak I came to count on as he helped me to assess the risks and rewards of almost every move I'd made in my career.

One night after I got back from New Hampshire, Karen and I had Rondo over for pizza—he's a real fixture in our household, so this alone was nothing unusual—and the talk turned to the presidential campaign. He could see I was struggling. He could see that the "calling" that had pushed me to run for governor hadn't happened for me on the presidency, but he was the one who suggested that the calling would find me along the way. "Don't give up on that calling just yet," he said. "It'll come."

Rondo remembers that we were sitting in my living room. I had my feet up on the couch. We were just talking, talking, talking—trying to look at every eventuality. Finally, he just turned to me and said, "So what are you gonna do?"

I said, "I don't know. What do you think I should do?"

He thought about this for a while, and the question kind of hung there, waiting for an answer, until finally I just answered it myself.

I said, "Well, I guess I'm going to have to run."

And that was it—my big pronouncement. No fire in the belly. No drumroll. No parting of the skies. I'd just looked at the race every which way and decided I needed to be a part of it. That's all. As it happened, by the time I could assemble a team and get around to making a formal announcement, the presidential field would grow to include Senators Ted Cruz, Marco Rubio, Rand Paul, and Lindsey Graham; former senator Rick Santorum; Governors Chris Christie and Scott Walker; former governors Jeb Bush, Rick Perry, George Pataki, Mike Huckabee, and Bobby Jindal; Carly Fiorina, the former CEO of Hewlett-Packard; and Dr. Ben Carson, the noted pediatric neurosurgeon.

Oh, and somewhere in that mix was the most surprising candidate of all: real estate mogul Donald Trump, a man whose outsize personality and formidable media presence would come to dominate the race in ways that no one in the political establishment could possibly have predicted.

# 4.

# Finding My Way

I've come to a realization about politics and politicians: no one really remembers you once you leave office.

Of course, this is not entirely true, but it is somewhat true, and even if you disagree with me on this, I believe it's a point worth considering. Sure, we pay tribute to our retiring elected officials, on a sliding scale that reflects the size of their office and the weight of their accomplishments. We build monuments to our former presidents and name schools and airports in their honor. At the state and local level, there are plaques in public squares and on park benches to commemorate the good service of former mayors and clerks and town councilpersons. But ask any mayor or clerk or town councilperson if the world looks on them differently once they've left office, and they'll tell you that the stares and double takes that were once meant for them are soon enough directed elsewhere, that the doors that had once opened wide for them have slowly but surely been closed.

My friends and I used to joke that there's no reason to have a phone once you leave Congress. Why? Because no one will ever take your call, and no one will call you. Only, it wasn't really a joke. The year before I left Congress, I was invited to forty Christmas parties; the year after I left, I was invited to two, and one of those was my *own* party, so it doesn't really count. What's the lesson? When you're in office, you face agonizing decisions, and you worry over them—worry over who's going to be mad, who's going to blame you if things don't work out—but you should just go ahead and do the right thing and vote your conscience because nobody's really considering you in the equation.

We shouldn't seek public office just to make sure that the movers and shakers in our community accept our phone calls and invite us to their parties. We shouldn't do it to build our brand or sell more books. We shouldn't devote our lives to public service to be recognized for that devotion—and be assured; we shouldn't do it for the money. (What money?) So, what's in it for us politicians?

Before I attempt to answer that, I want to reach back to another childhood memory that I believe will inform this discussion. I want to go back to all those times I went to Forbes Field to root for my beloved Pirates. Most days, I'd wear a Pirates jersey to the ballpark, with the number twenty-one on the back, to honor my favorite baseball player, Roberto Clemente. I was not alone in this. All through the stands were other kids wearing their own Pirates jerseys: Mazeroski, Haddix, Groat. Adults, too. Some of us were even in full uniform—a practice you see in ballparks today, perhaps even to a greater degree. But we don't typically go to political rallies dressed as our favorite politicians. If we see someone wearing a Richard Nixon or Ronald Reagan mask, chances are they'll be wearing it ironically. As we leaned toward Halloween 2016 (which also happened to have us leaning toward Election Day 2016), there were Trump and Clinton costumes all over the place, but I had to think that most people dressed as a given candidate to make a statement in some way about the other candidate.

There's a key difference here, I think. As kids, we want to emulate our favorite ballplayer, our favorite pop star, our favorite actor or actress. We want to be like them. And if we're not dressing like them exactly, we're borrowing their gestures, their figures of speech, their sense of style. I don't think there's the same impulse at play when it comes to our elected officials—not in twenty-first-century America. When I wore my Clemente jersey to the stadium all those years ago, there was a certain element of buy-in, a part of me that secretly hoped the Pirates would be shorthanded and I'd be called on to help fill out their ranks. I imagine I was not alone in this, too. I can remember making this promise to myself up in the stands: if I got up to bat, I'd swing away. I wouldn't play it safe. I'd dig in at the plate and go for it, swing for the fences. And I think in a lot of ways that's how I've conducted myself in office. Look at my record and you'll see that I've never taken the easy way around, or the path of least resistance, not if I thought that what was best for my constituents was to move forward in a headlong, headstrong way. That's why, as a rookie legislator, I wrote my own budget. That's why I refused that $5,000 pay raise.

I chose a different way, but I don't mean to dismiss or diminish the politicians who play it safe. A lot of them—they're out there doing what they think is right, and part of that is doing what they think they need to do to return to office. They want to keep their jobs, so all those doors will remain open to them. That's just human nature, right? But when keeping your job becomes your focus, it might mean you're more inclined to take the easy path and bend to the pressure of public interest groups or donors or whatever forces are lined up to try to influence you. It's the political equivalent of the sacrifice bunt in baseball—that's one way to look at it. It's giving yourself up at the plate and playing it safe, and I suppose that's part of the reason we don't go to inaugural ceremonies dressed as the politician who's being sworn in to office.

It all comes down to this: If there's nothing *heroic* about how you approach your time in office, you can't expect to be held up as any kind of hero to your nation's young people. We might appreciate these good people—and let's not forget, most of them *are* good people—but we don't celebrate them the same way we do our childhood heroes.

So, what's in it for us politicians? Well, I can only speak from personal experience. I can only tell you why *I* sought elected office in the first place, and in my case, it had to do with speaking out for what I thought was right. It had to do with how I was raised. It had to do with McKees Rocks, with my mother and the great example she set for doing what's right and standing up for the little guy; and with my father's example of taking a genuine interest in the people of his community. It's just how I was wired, I guess—and at twenty-four years old, fresh out of college, a law school education on the back burner for the time being, I found an outlet for that wiring in the work I was doing as a political aide. It was a little bit thrilling, to be in on the workings of our government. The sense of purpose, the sense of moment—it was all right there. That's why I decided to run for the State Senate—and in 1982, at the ripe old age of twenty-nine at the start of my campaign, that's one of the main reasons I decided to run for Congress from Ohio's Twelfth Congressional District. I wasn't looking for a pay raise or better seats at the ball game. I wasn't looking for a plaque or a dinner in my honor. I'd just realized, after four years in the legislature, that, in Washington, I could have a bigger impact on the ways we lived and worked and took care of each other; that I could work toward an even greater good.

I was pushed along in this thinking by a bit of partisan redistricting back home. I could have sought another term in the legislature, but I would have had to run against Ted Gray, a veteran state senator who had been a real mentor to me. This put me in a tough spot. I didn't want to run against Ted. He'd been enormously generous, helping show me the ropes as a young legislator, and I considered him a friend. So, I weighed my options and decided on that congressional run, which meant I'd face a potentially tough primary fight as a sitting state senator and then, I hoped, win the Republican nomination to oppose the incumbent Democrat, Bob Shamansky.

My parents were thrilled that I was so passionate about politics, but at the same time they didn't really know what a political life might look like over the long haul. They'd never known anybody in politics, so it was all unfamiliar to them, and I suppose they were holding out hope that I might reconsider law school at some point. But they were my biggest supporters as I set off on this road—and with that full support, I campaigned the same way I'd run for state senate.

This time around, we had a deeper, more experienced team. We were able to raise a little more money. And we were once again tireless, relentless. If we canvassed one neighborhood street and missed a bunch of houses because people weren't home, we went back at a later hour and tried those houses again. I called one poor guy so often that he finally picked up the phone and said, "Young man, if you promise to stop calling me, you can have my vote."

I guess we knocked on just enough doors and made just enough calls, because I wound up winning the Republican nomination and beating Bob Shamansky in the general election, which sent me to Capitol Hill at the age of thirty—a bright-eyed, iron-willed, not-yet-jaded kid with the idea that legislators could and should work together to seek common ground. Those were the marching orders I gave to myself as I headed off to Washington—to seize this opportunity to find bipartisan solutions to some of the challenges facing the good people in my home district, and the good people of this great nation. My idea was to dig in and go for it, the same way I would have if I'd gotten my chance at Forbes Field.

I planned to swing away.

## CLIMBING CAPITOL HILL

My nine terms in the U.S. House of Representatives spanned a period of tumultuous change on Capitol Hill, and I want to mention briefly a few key moments from those eighteen years so that, once again, I can place them in meaningful context. Some of these moments became the cornerstones of my 2016 presidential campaign, and I highlight them here as further background for readers for whom my story might be new.

My first committee assignment as a young congressman was on the House Armed Services Committee, where I quickly became immersed in some of the lingering Cold War tensions between the United States and the Soviet Union. Remember, this was during Ronald Reagan's first term in office, when we had a very different relationship with the Soviets. I was involved in the drafting of the so-called Goldwater-Nichols Act, which brought about sweeping changes to the U.S. Department of Defense. We were enormously proud of that effort, because it streamlined the military chain of command, increased the powers of the chairman of the Joint Chiefs of Staff, and encouraged all branches of the service to work together and win together. It also signaled the ability of leaders of both parties to collaborate on potentially divisive issues, offering a kind of template for how legislators could work together on a matter of vital national interest.

Perhaps the biggest headline I made on the House Armed Services Committee was my focus on excess spending. Like most Republicans, I'd always been strong on defense, but once in Congress, I started paying particular attention to some of the runaway costs in our federal budget. The one didn't always go hand in hand with the other, I was realizing. However, this realization put me in conflict with some of my colleagues on both sides of the aisle, who came to see me as part of a group they viewed as "cheap hawks." No matter where I saw wasteful spending, I believed it needed to be eliminated, even in our military, but Republicans weren't supposed to think in this way, so my position set some people off. My thinking was this: Just because you're out to curb some of the ridiculous costs doesn't mean you're out to weaken the nation's defense. The Pentagon budget was bloated; yet only a few people were speaking out against it. The talk all over Washington was about the need for cuts in our social welfare and entitlement programs, while there was an unspoken agreement that we were not supposed to be critical of our defense spending. We gave those guys at the Pentagon an awful lot of rope—and an awful lot of money. That was what the American people seemed to want, but I believed we needed to shine a light on waste or corruption or excess wherever we could find it—even on matters of national security—so I set about doing that.

Remember, this was the era of the military-issued hammers and the screwdrivers that cost U.S. taxpayers tens of thousands of dollars. I wasn't the first person to speak out on the need to reform Pentagon procurement practices, but once I saw how much we were spending on toilet seats and wrenches, I got my back up. I started looking long and hard at how to trim this type of spending, in a line-by-line way. This wasn't exactly a strategy for winning friends as a young congressman, but I didn't much care. Once, at a budget meeting in Newt Gingrich's office, one of my congressional colleagues went so far as to call me a traitor, but I chose to wear the term as a badge of honor, because I thought as chairman of the Budget Committee, I was duty-bound to keep an eye on excess spending, even if it meant ruffling the feathers of some hawkish Republicans. As a matter of fact, I turned the other cheek on this guy immediately. I just smiled and said, "You'll regret what you just said to me. You'll be lying in bed tonight, and you'll want to call and apologize. But let me save you the trouble. I forgive you. I'm not mad. You just don't know any better."

These people weren't used to sarcasm or civility, and there wasn't a whole lot of room in their worldview for a sense of humor. And in my defense (not that I needed defending), I wasn't being snarky or disingenuous, I don't think. I was only trying to gently remind this person, and everyone else at that meeting, that we should be above petty name-calling and personal attacks. We were all just doing what we thought was our job, in the best way we knew.

I used to spend a lot of time in Rep. Bill Nichols's office, worrying over those hammers and screwdrivers. Nichols was a Democratic congressman from Alabama, and he took a liking to me—and the feeling was mutual. He went out of his way to encourage me, to give me the benefit of his experience and perspective, and I was endlessly grateful for his friendship and guidance. He was almost like a father to me—so much so that I was privileged to offer one of the eulogies when he died of a heart attack in 1988.

Bill Nichols was military all the way. He'd served in World

War II, and had his leg blown off in a minefield, so he didn't approach the issue at hand lightly. He used to sit behind his desk, with his glasses down over his nose. Every once in a while he'd look up from whatever budget or document I'd prepared for his review, in which I'd highlighted all the wasteful spending, and say something like "Son, your momma don't have more at home like you, does she?"

Young congressmen weren't in the habit of taking on the defense lobby, but I had a job to do. I didn't care that I was making enemies, as long as I was fighting the good fight. The voters back home hadn't sent me to Washington to make friends; they sent me to look after their interests and do what I thought was right. Winning the support of my Republican colleagues never concerned me, even then. That doesn't mean it's not a concerning thing. Oh, it is, absolutely, but only in a general and pervasive sense. The quid pro quo at all levels of government is one of my central concerns for the future of our country, especially as it relates to donors and special interests; it was just a nonissue as it applied to me back when I was in Congress. My thinking was we had all been sent to Washington to be watchdogs over the American good, so it was on me to hold my nose and cry foul when I smelled something rotten, even if it wasn't smart politics for me to do so. It wasn't about me or my political future; it was about doing what was right, and then coming back the next day and doing it all over again.

The best example of this came in the fight over the B-2, which was supposed to be an essential weapon in our Cold War arsenal. I didn't quite see it that way. I couldn't justify or even understand the projected long-term cost of a single plane (nearly two billion dollars). It wasn't *just* that the program didn't make financial sense; it didn't make strategic sense, either. Why spend all that money for a bunch of planes capable of dropping multiple nuclear bombs over the Soviet Union when one bomb would certainly get the message across? It was the very definition of overkill.

What did I do? I held my nose and spoke out about it. Loudly, without any thought of the fallout that might come my way as a result. I joined with Ron Dellums, a liberal California Democrat, and together we set about trying to pare back the B-2 proposal, and perhaps redirect some of those monies to the development of standoff weapons, which we believed would be more strategically effective as well as more cost-effective. We were never out to kill the proposal entirely; in response to an initial proposal of 132 bombers, we proposed a more modest plan of just 13, a baker's dozen. Everybody was against us at first, although over time we were able to bring a bunch of thoughtful Democrats and Republicans to our side of the issue, but it took about a decade for our arguments to win any kind of meaningful support. Meanwhile, it should be noted that throughout most of those ten or so years, Ron Dellums and I were called out on this. Still, we were able to build an unusual coalition of support—starting with Ron Dellums and me, an unlikely pairing on any other issue, even though we saw this one the same way. In response to our efforts, the projected squadron was later cut to 75 B-2 bombers, and at that point I got a call from the Pentagon, asking whether we would agree to a compromise of 20 bombers. So, that's where we landed on this issue—an incredible win, and the first time in anyone's memory that a major weapons program had been so dramatically curtailed for budgeting reasons.

Other formative experiences found me away from Washington— such as the first time I traveled to the Soviet Union as a member of the Armed Services Committee, a trip organized by Les Aspin, chairman of the committee. While we were over there, we made a

side trip to East Berlin, not long before the Berlin Wall came
down. We toured an intercontinental ballistic missile silo and visited with soldiers. I even had a gun pointed at me by an East German soldier as I stepped off the bus in East Berlin. What stayed
with me, then and still, was how closely we were monitored, at all
times. We were warned to be careful about everything we did and
said. I actually went out for a run one morning in Red Square and
discovered all these KGB guys trying to keep up with me, in their
heavy coats.

It would have made a funny picture if it hadn't been so troubling. The Soviet Union felt like a big prison. We ate good food
and drank good vodka, but there was a darkness to my time there—
it was not a happy place. In fact, we'd all heard stories about how
grateful we'd be to finally leave the Soviet Union, and I've got to
tell you, when our plane took off for home, everyone in the cabin
broke into spontaneous applause. No one was cheering louder than
I was, and as I settled in for the flight home I was reminded yet
again how important America was to the future of the free world.

I went back to Berlin several years later, with my wife, Karen,
after the German reunification, and it was a very emotional experience, for both of us, I think. I cried as we toured the site of
the wall, thinking of the suffering and the struggle of all those
people, for all those years. I could close my eyes and picture the
barbed wire and the guards and the oppressive scene I remembered from my first visit to East Berlin—the tyranny of the Soviet
Union on full display. But my tears were laced with joy, because
the fall of the wall represented such hope to so many people. Really,
it was an unbelievable event that led to an almost immediate im-
provement in the lives of millions—probably one of the most
consequential political events we'll see in our lifetimes.

Another trip that made an impression on me was the one we

made to Saudi Arabia in the run-up to the first war in the Persian Gulf. For me, the most important part of the trip was the trek we made into the desert to talk to our fighters stationed there. I didn't seek out the commanders or the generals. I sat with the fighters— the men on the ground, on the line—and they told me we couldn't just keep them sitting out there, with no clear directive. They'd been left hanging for so long while the United States considered its next move that they didn't know if they were coming or going. I was pretty young at the time, so maybe these guys felt they could relate to me, or that I could relate to them, because they really opened up to me on this. They told me how they couldn't always talk to their wives or girlfriends. They couldn't talk to their superiors. All they could do was sit in the desert and wait for their orders. But, of course, the longer you sit in those kinds of conditions, in full preparedness, the more you start to lose your edge, the more you begin to doubt your mission. Those guys wanted me to tell the folks in Washington that we needed to make up our minds about what we were doing there.

So, I did—and to this day, I don't limit my briefings to reports from the people who wear the stars and bars. I want to hear from the people in the field, because their perspective matters, and it's too often overlooked.

Back home in Washington, I partnered with Tim Penny, a Democrat from Minnesota, on a bipartisan deficit reduction plan that got a lot of attention—one of the first shots fired in the effort to balance the federal budget. Our idea was that we could take a penny out of every dollar of federal spending, and in this way, bring our expenses into line. We were able to attract a number of our colleagues to the effort, and ultimately, we put together a proposal that offered sensible reforms in every part of the federal budget. Still, the Penny-Kasich plan was rejected by a 219–213 vote. I was thrilled that it was such a close vote, but disappointed that we couldn't get it through. One of the people who fought us on this was First Lady Hillary Clinton, but it felt to us that we'd moved the needle a little bit on budget reform.

We continued to push the issue. I helped to introduce welfare reform legislation known as the Personal Responsibility and Work Opportunity Reconciliation Act, which President Clinton signed—a significant part of the Republican Party's "Contract for America." Still, my focus was on brokering a deal to balance the federal budget for the first time since 1969, and passing the Balanced Budget Act of 1997. More than anything else I accomplished while in Congress, that balanced budget stamped my time on the Hill, just as it has stamped my time going forward. It reinforced my long-held belief that the budget is all—it drives our economy, whether at the state and local level or the national level. We simply can't spend money we don't have, and it took battling over every single line item to make the point and set things right.

Just how did we get it done? Well, I'd been working on it for years. Starting in 1989, when I was just a low-ranking committee member, I began preparing and presenting my own budgets, as a kind of counterpoint to the budget debate—picking up on the habit I'd gotten into as a rookie state legislator. President Bush (the Elder) had presented a budget that year that I thought was just terrible. The Democrats had presented a budget that I thought was even worse. So, I went ahead and presented my own. This alone was a bit of an accomplishment, because the White House and the Democrats had virtually unlimited resources to help them prepare their budgets, while I had only six staffers. The joke I made at the time, to explain away the disparity, was "We might be slightly overstaffed, but I think we can work it out."

It was no joke, really. The way it worked out, the president's budget received 213 votes of a possible 435 on the House floor. The Democrat's rebuttal budget received 230 votes. And the Kasich budget received 30 votes. Not exactly a resounding victory by any stretch, but I tried to convince my staff that even though our budget hadn't passed, we should consider it a win just the same. Indeed, it would set us on the road to an outright win.

I called my staff together after the vote and said, "We just presented a budget on the House floor, and somehow managed to convince twenty-nine other members of Congress to adopt our budget to run the United States government. Are you *kidding* me? Pretty great, don't you think?"

From there, we were able to build a team that believed in fiscal responsibility—no easy assignment on either side of the aisle, I'm afraid. It was tough to get Democrats on board, but it was a difficult issue for my Republican colleagues as well.

Year after year, we'd go through these motions yet again, and each time out, we'd gain additional support, such that when I became chairman of the committee we had a stronger, more viable budget, and a broader base of support. In 1995, some readers will recall, the Republicans looked to shut down the government. People thought we were being reckless and irresponsible, but I thought it was a powerful, principled stand against a Clinton budget filled with phony, trumped-up numbers and built on false assumptions. It was, in many ways, a career high note for me, and out of that we were able to begin negotiations on a budget that made sense for the country.

Understand, the numbers supporting Clinton's budget didn't actually support his budget at all, and as soon as we were able to convince enough members of Congress to stand against it, we started battling long and hard over priorities. I was not willing to stand behind Clinton's counterfeit numbers and tell the American people that we were achieving something when I knew we were not. Out of that shutdown we were finally able to balance the budget in 1997—for the first time since man walked on the moon, according to the headlines that dominated the newspaper coverage that followed.

The great lesson for me, and for anyone paying attention, was that if you have a good idea that's not in favor at first, it pays to keep at it. Conversely, if you're opposed to a terrible idea, or one that's built on a false premise, it pays to push back on it. Over time, if you're able to present your arguments in a sound, compelling way, you'll begin to generate support. You'll win people over.

# 5.

# Faith Above All

The time of tumultuous change that found me in Washington was not limited to the politics of government or the government of politics. Some of these changes were profoundly personal, and just as there were all these high notes during my eighteen years in Congress, there were low notes as well. The lowest of these was rock bottom: when my parents were killed on an August night in 1987 as they were exiting a Burger King parking lot. They'd stopped in for coffee—they'd always loved Burger King coffee, especially the price. Going out for coffee there was part of their routine.

I got the call about the accident around midnight. The news was devastating. My parents had been hit by a drunk driver. They'd done nothing wrong—it's just that they were in *precisely* the wrong place at *exactly* the wrong time. A doctor told me my father had been killed and my mother was in critical condition, and in that moment, I don't think I heard too many details beyond those. All I heard was that my father was gone, and that my mother was fighting for her life. All I knew was that I had to be there with them, so I drove all night with my girlfriend at the time to a hospital in Pittsburgh. It felt as if I were inside a bad dream. About the only thing I remember from that long, dreadful drive was falling in behind a tar truck that sprayed a fine film of tar in its wake. It's strange the things you remember: the truck was in front of me for only a few miles, but my windshield was quickly covered, and I couldn't see a thing. We actually had to pull over and rub some shampoo on the glass to cut through the tar. (The shampoo was my girlfriend's idea, and it turned out to be a good one.) It struck me as an absurd metaphor for what I was feeling. It was as if my vision had been tarred over and all I could see was blackness, emptiness. My thinking seemed tarred over, too.

Nothing made sense.

Nothing seemed real.

My mother hung on until I got to the hospital, but I don't think she ever knew I made it. I never got a chance to tell her I loved her, or what her great example meant to me. I sat for the longest time trying to get my head around what had just happened—but of course there was no way to understand it. I was comforted that night by a man named Stu Boehmig, who'd become close to my parents as the assistant pastor at their Episcopal church. At that time in my life, though, I wasn't open to what he was telling me about God and faith, so I guess I should say Stu *attempted* to comfort me. Truth was, I was beyond comforting in that moment. As I've written, I had been deeply connected to the church as a child and as a young man, but I'd drifted from my spiritual life in recent years. So, as I sat there trying to process the enormity of what had just happened to my parents, I wasn't interested in talking about God's plan. I was angry, confused. I'm not proud of it, but I actually yelled at Stu, who was only trying to help. I told him there was no place in my heart or in my thinking for a relationship with God. Stu kept at me, though. Over the next few days, he kept reaching out to me, telling me that a window had been opened for me with this tragedy, and that it was up to me to climb through it or step away from it.

"Where do you stand with God?" he kept asking me.

At first I had no answer, but I guess I was open to the thought that I needed healing, guidance. I saw that this terrible, terrible accident had opened that window Stu kept talking about, and that I had better climb on through it if I wanted to make myself whole.

Out of the darkness of that day came the light of tomorrow, and now that I look back on it, I don't understand how people get through such a sudden, tragic loss without faith. It just doesn't seem possible.

Out of that day, too, came a point of connection that would attach to the rest of my days. During the course of my 2016 campaign, I'd meet countless folks at our town halls who would take the time to share some of the tragedies of their own lives, maybe because they knew my story and felt encouraged to share their own. And do you want to know something? People can sense when they're in the company of someone who understands them, and when you feel understood, you're inclined to share. There is safety in numbers, yes? There is succor in community. And when we are able to recognize others who have walked their own hard road, our tough times might seem just a little easier to navigate.

Throughout the campaign, I'd hear from voters about the loss of a loved one, about a life-threatening illness, about a devastating accident, about any sort of difficulty—and together we would see our way through the pain to a place of possibility. I know that the sustaining relationship I've built with God out of the darkness of that day has been my strength, my salvation. Without it, I fear I would have crumbled. To be sure, the pain would have eased over time, the holes in my life would have been filled with work and friends and a family of my own. But those things on their own would not have led to a fundamental transformation. Those things would have bandaged the wound, but the wound would never have healed completely. That's not to suggest you ever really get over the loss of your parents, especially when they're pulled from this earth so suddenly, so senselessly. But with a deep and abiding sense of faith—of the kind my mother had come to know herself, toward the end of her life—there is a measure of peace.

For me, it was as if a switch had been flipped, and I set about on a lifelong journey to rediscover my relationship with God—helped initially by the great kindness showed to me by Stu, who must have seen me as a blank canvas. Stu had some help in this, because I was joined on this faith journey by my great Washington, D.C., friend John Palafoutas, who was working at the time as a congressional aide, and by Tom Barrett, who remains a dear friend and who ran a Bible study group on Capitol Hill. These were the Three Amigos who helped to change my life in so many positive ways.

Here's the thing: I wasn't *just* out to reconnect with God. I was out to do a deep dive, to really understand what it meant to live a life in His image. I'd always been a voracious reader, but now I started in on the biblical texts, the theological scholars. I joined Tom's congressional Bible study group, which might sound by its designation like a doomed enterprise, but to surround myself with like-minded souls, each of us bound by a search for meaning in our lives, even as we circled one another in Congress, sometimes at cross-purposes, offered me a kind of ballast.

My abiding faith informed the rest of my time on Capitol Hill. It was foundational, fundamental—transformative, even. It's the underpinning of my family, my friendships, and it was a bedrock of my two campaigns for president. I offer it here as the core element of my backstory, for it is my relationship with God that stands at the heart of everything I believe, and everything I do in service of those beliefs. I don't mean to suggest that I get it right all the time. Not at all. In fact, I get it wrong more often than not. I fail time and time again. I live most days at that base level I wrote about earlier. But that's the great thing about faith—you can always try harder. I can always find those moments of grace or inspiration or purpose—and rise to meet them. I'm working on it, and I am not alone in this. Still, I worry for those who go about their days without the moral and spiritual guidepost a life of faith can offer. I do.

Be assured, there are good and noble humanists all around. I count a great many of them among my closest friends. Yet, for me personally, and for millions of Americans, it's also unthinkable to live a life without God. We are, after all, a nation built on a Judeo-Christian ideal, and there is now room in that ideal for faiths of all kinds.

One of the books I have in my library is *Christianity: The Witness of History,* by Norman Anderson. As I write this, I'm reminded of a passage: "No one in their senses would deny for a moment that the other world religions include much that is true and helpful, or that Christians can learn a great deal from the earnestness and devotion of their followers."

The key, really, is to believe in *something*—something bigger than you, bigger than we can know. How are we to be accountable for our actions if we are not accountable to a higher purpose?

In all societies, there's a tendency to drift from transcendence to individuality, to put Man on the throne instead of God. But that's when we get into trouble. That's when we start thinking it's okay to be jealous of what other people have, to covet the riches or the ease or the success of our neighbors. That's when we turn from a pursuit of the greater good to the vanity of our modern world. So, we need to have rules and laws and moral codes in place to help guide our behavior. We do—we're humans, after all.

Faith, at bottom, is our moral code. If we are to flourish as a society, we must live by the laws of a higher purpose. If it works out, in your heart of hearts, that the higher purpose in your life is service to others, to the community we share and the freedoms we enjoy in order that we might live peaceably and purposefully in these communities—well, then that's great. And if it works out that you find this purpose in service of the Lord and anticipation of a joyful eternity—well, then that's great, too. But I believe there needs to be a shared feeling of transcendence. It just so happens that, for me, I live in the light of the Word. I know that I am here on this earth to build a life and legacy in service of my Lord, and in anticipation of the great hereafter.

Faith for me is a freeing thing, an affirming thing, and it gives me perspective.

Faith for you might be something else entirely.

But faith, for *us,* must lift us all to where we can be, in the words of the great Welsh theologian Matthew Henry, the "lights of the world."

"A city that is set on a hill cannot be hid," he wrote in his *Complete Commentary.* "The disciples of Christ, especially those who are forward and zealous in His service, become remarkable, and are taken notice of as beacons."

## MOVING ON

Where do you go when the water rises?

That's a question I put to readers in a book I wrote about the Bible study I helped to organize in Columbus in the late 1980s with a good group of like-minded souls—a Bible study that's still going strong. My book was meant to be an exploration of faith, and a touchstone for readers looking to build their own relationship with God through a deepening sense of community and connectedness, and in the writing, I ended up sharing a lot about myself and my family. I believe it's my most personal book, because I gave myself permission to be myself. Yet, a lot of people close to me told me I shouldn't write it. I'd been out of office for going on ten years when I started working on it, but my closest friends and advisers knew I wasn't quite done with politics. At that moment, I wasn't so sure about this myself. I enjoyed being in the private sector, doing my own thing—writing books, hosting a television show, working at Lehman Brothers, giving speeches.

Life was pretty, pretty good.

But these close friends and advisers knew me well. I took their point when they told me that politicians weren't supposed to talk so openly about faith and God and eternity—meaning I listened to them on this, and then I went ahead and talked about it anyway. That's the great tug-of-war in America today. We expect our political candidates to make room in their lives for organized religion—it's a litmus test of their character. But more than that we don't seem to want to hear. More than that and it starts to feel like we're encroaching on someone's privacy.

Still, I went ahead and wrote that book anyway, against all that advice. I called the book *Every Other Monday* because that's when we Bible study guys got together—it had been a sacrosanct "date" on our calendars for more than twenty years (and it still is). I mention it here as a reminder that we need to seek our own touchstones, and listen to our own hearts, as we go about our lives.

Where do *I* go when the water rises? Where do I turn in moments of crisis and fear? Well, I turn to God. I reach for the Bible. I study the teachings of our great scholars and philosophers and theologians. I discuss these matters, at length, with my Bible study guys and my other friends in faith. And I've come to the conclusion that, at its best, faith gives perspective. It helps us to recognize that our time on this earth is short, and it is only to prepare us for a time yet to come. Underneath and alongside all this, though, I also turn to my wife, Karen, and to my daughters, Emma and Reese, who also stand as my moral compasses, my strength and solace, my voices of reason.

Of all the good things to come out of my time in Congress, I'd have to put meeting my wife Karen at the very top of that list. She is my light here on this earth, and the wonderful life we've built in Columbus with our twin daughters is my proudest accomplishment and my dearest treasure. It's my grace, really. I've got to tell you, one of the main reasons I didn't endorse Donald Trump as the Republican presidential candidate after I suspended my campaign was because I couldn't stand in front of Karen and the girls and look them in the eye and tell them I supported this man. I could not accept how he carried himself during the campaign, nor could I accept how he had carried himself prior to it, based on what came to light during the election cycle. I could not condone how he seemed to treat women and immigrants and minorities, or the way he looked at the world. And I said these things during the campaign, before he was elected.

You might wonder why I'm including a discussion of Donald Trump in a chapter on faith, but I believe it ties in. I believe that in order to understand some of the ways I responded to some of the things President Trump did and said during the campaign, it helps to know my heart. It's also helpful, I think, to revisit some of the concerns many people of faith had about President Trump's language and demeanor. They just didn't jibe with how I was raised or with how I believed people ought to treat one another—whether they were running for president or stopping in for a piece of pie at the local diner.

Realize that Karen and I had participated in the campaign with our daughters. And now we were looking on together in shock at some of the things Donald Trump was saying—indeed, at *a lot* of the things he was saying. And it wasn't just Donald Trump, mind you. There was enough bad behavior and unseemly rhetoric going around on those debate stages and at rallies across the country to suggest the death of civilized discourse and respectful discussion at the societal level.

Realize, too, that over on the Democratic side of the campaign, Hillary Clinton didn't distinguish herself in this regard. She wasn't exactly taking the high road. She referred to half of Trump's supporters as "a basket of deplorables" and started putting people down in order to make her point. I couldn't look Karen and the girls in the eye and tell them I was for Clinton any more than I could have told them I was for Trump. Forget that Clinton's political philosophy was stuck somewhere in the nineteenth century—I just didn't think her behavior was all that presidential, either.

Here, again, I don't mean to set myself out as a paragon of virtue. Sometimes I'm not so nice. I can get tired, frustrated, disappointed in myself for not doing better. I can get my back up, same as most folks. I've even heard people say I have a short temper (which I suppose is only slightly better than having a *long* temper). I can hold my own firm opinions, same as most folks. But I try to treat people decently, and I expect them to treat me decently in return. If it's pointed out to me that I didn't show someone the respect he or she deserved, I'll usually go out of my way to apologize for it and look to make it right.

So, during the 2016 campaign, as I sometimes sat and discussed the news of the day with my family, I was embarrassed by what they were seeing on television. There was no decency. There was hatefulness and disrespect. There was no humility. There was only solipsism and self-aggrandizement. It was a blight on this great country, the way some of these candidates were behaving, and it left me feeling that we should all have been ashamed of ourselves. As I exited the presidential stage, it was unthinkable to me that I could ever endorse Donald Trump, who I believed had set the ugly tone for the campaign. Moreover, it was unfathomable to me that party leaders could even approach me seeking support, or that reporters would even think to ask.

All I could think was, Did any of these people in my party even listen to anything I said during this campaign? And do they not realize how meaningful my words were to me?

I thought back to my coming of age as a politician, to stepping into my role as leader, and to finding my way to God and faith after my parents were killed in that terrible accident. I worried about how to reconcile the man I had become with the crass, crude behavior we were seeing on the national stage. To be sure, Donald Trump wasn't the only offender on this front, but in an election cycle filled with conduct unbecoming a presidential candidate, I'm afraid *his* conduct was the most unbecoming of all.

Alas, Donald Trump is our duly elected president, and we must now stand with him and look forward with optimism to a bright American future. That doesn't mean he gets a free pass. That doesn't mean we brush aside the first and second and lasting impressions that attached to his campaign.

As long as we're weighing matters of the soul and spirit in this chapter, let me share with you the moment my concerns over Trump's behavior took a marked turn. It was the night after the Miami debate, which turned out to be the twelfth and final debate on the calendar, a pivotal point in the campaign and, in my assessment, for our perception of the man who would go on to become the Republican Party nominee and our next president.

(Note: there was a thirteenth debate scheduled for two weeks later, in Salt Lake City, but Donald Trump refused to attend, stating that he was tired of answering the same questions from essentially the same group of reporters alongside the same political opponents. Personally, I thought it was pointless to debate without the front-runner in attendance, so my team let it be known that I would not participate without him, and then the whole thing fizzled after that.)

The Republican field was down to four candidates for the Miami debate: Trump, Ted Cruz, Marco Rubio, and me. The debate fell on March 10, five days ahead of the second Super Tuesday slate of primaries, with more than 350 delegates at stake. It was an important moment in the campaign because two of those primary states were Florida and Ohio, where Marco Rubio and I expected to do well. There was widespread speculation that without a win in our respective home states, each of us would be forced to consider exiting the race.

Up until that time, I'd been saying I would support the eventual nominee, no matter who it was. At the debate in Detroit the week before, I even tried to make a joke out of it, saying of Trump that "sometimes he makes it really hard." It was no joke to me, though, the way Trump was behaving, the tone he was setting, some of the things he was saying. Still, coming out of that Miami debate, I was inclined to support him if it worked out that he won the nomination, just as I would have been inclined to support Ted Cruz or Marco Rubio. I wouldn't have been happy about any of those outcomes, because I believed I was the right person for the job, but I would have supported the eventual nominee for the good of the party, for the good of the country.

Then, the very next day, March 11, Trump had to cancel an event in Chicago when there was rioting in the streets and protestors were threatening to disrupt his rally. It was an ugly scene, and my people were telling me that Trump was out there inciting this type of violence. I'd heard about all that, of course, but I wasn't really paying good and close attention to everything the other candidates were doing and saying. My focus was on my own message, my own events, my own campaign. But this incident in Chicago was troubling—not just to me, but to right-minded, thoughtful, compassionate leaders all across the country. So, I asked my communications director, Chris Schrimpf, to put together a list of some of Trump's comments and maybe some footage showing examples of his inciting rhetoric.

I didn't know what I expected to find, but I wanted to see what I could see—and what I saw was appalling.

Now, I don't pretend to know what was in Donald Trump's heart or his soul when he spoke to the crowds at his rallies. I'd met him on only a few occasions, and engaged in only brief, surface-type conversations. And voters didn't *know* Donald Trump any more than they *knew* John Kasich or Ted Cruz or Marco Rubio. All we can do is judge a candidate by his words, and the manner in which those words are delivered matter a great deal.

What did I see and hear? Well, there was damning video evidence of hateful, rabble-rousing conduct from more than a dozen Trump rallies, going all the way back to an event in Birmingham, Alabama, in November 2015. Taken together, I found these incendiary incidents so profoundly disturbing that I felt I had to say something about them—so I did, the very next day. I issued a statement reading, "Tonight, the seeds of division that Donald Trump has been sowing this whole campaign finally bore fruit, and it was ugly."

I share these concerns here, in the context of a broader discussion about faith, because I saw Trump's reckless entreaties as a weakening of our shared American values—even more so, a *coarsening* of our shared American values. To be fair, Donald Trump himself was not the *cause* of this weakening; his behavior was merely *emblematic* of it. And it wasn't just Trump behaving in this way, but it troubled me that a strong plurality of Republican voters didn't seem to care that the candidate they supported was operating at the basement level I wrote about earlier in these pages. Instead of rising to these meaningful moments, and demonstrating a clear set of values that could stand as a positive flash point for a country in search of leadership and inspiration, Donald Trump gave the impression of a man who would do or say anything to get attention, even incite a crowd to violence.

Have you ever been out in the woods, relying on a compass, when, all of a sudden, the magnetic component stopped working and the needle started fluctuating like crazy? That's kind of how it felt to me as I looked at all these incidents—that we were all somehow broken . . . and *lost*. You see, it's not that Donald Trump was merely hanging on in this campaign due to the weight of his "self-funding" or the size of his celebrity; it's not that his bad behavior was being quietly tolerated or generally ignored until his candidacy drifted into irrelevance; and it's not that he was any sort of fringe candidate or novelty. No, he was dominating the discussion, the coverage, and the voting—all in a way that could only signal that this type of behavior was being ratified by the American people.

Most alarmingly, to me, it signaled a spiritual disconnect at play in this election cycle.

All along, I'd disagreed with Donald Trump on policy issues and questioned his experience for the job of president. All along, his surging popularity, in the polls and in the primaries, had been worrisome. Yet now those worries took on a whole new dimension. Now I was reminded of how essential it was for Americans to move about the planet with a kind of shared moral compass, and for the first time, I pushed myself to imagine a future with Donald Trump as president, and what it might mean for the soul of this country.

## WHERE I STAND

I didn't shy from my faith on the campaign trail. As the field of hopefuls began to thin and the positive values I'd been sounding in my town hall events began to resonate with voters, I spoke my mind, and my heart, more and more. Those values are rooted in my McKees Rocks upbringing, as I have written, but they are also found in the lessons of the Bible and the teachings of Christ. They are written on my soul, and I want to share them with you here.

Yes, I was raised in a churchgoing household. Yes, I was taught to believe in God and in the goodness of man and the fullness of a life well and purposefully lived in His glory. Yes, I was an altar boy, and for a long while there, I thought I'd be a priest. But it wasn't until those dark days immediately following the deaths of my parents, at the urging of my good friend and spirit guide Stu Boehmig, that I began to truly explore what it meant to believe in God, to consider if there even *was* a God—and if there was, what kind of place I would make for Him in my life.

That was in 1987, just about thirty years ago, and I'm pleased and humbled to report that I'm still at it—and where I'm at these days is that there is indeed a God, and He is indeed active in our world and present in our lives. Surely, He is present in mine. I've come to this conclusion after years of study and meaningful reflection, recognizing full well that others might see the same evidence and come to an entirely different conclusion. All I know is what I know—and what I *don't* know, because I've also come to realize that you can't figure out how God works; it's an unknowable puzzle. Still, I've spent a lot of time developing my thoughts and trying to place my relationship with God in a kind of cultural context.

What does God expect of me? I believe He expects me to live on a higher plane, all the while knowing that I will surely fail. I believe the higher plane he sets before me is a call to resist the gravitational pull of life on earth, which is just a lot of the base stuff that can fill our days in negative ways: envy, hatred, jealousy, intolerance, self-aggrandizement, looking merely to accumulate wealth or fame. If you think about it, when it's time for us to leave this earth, these negatives can all seem kind of mundane. Yet, in the ills of society we see these negatives on full and forceful display. It's the way we sidestep those negatives and walk in the light that will come to define us after all.

I believe God expects us to be caring and kind and forgiving to our neighbors—here, again, knowing that we will invariably fall short. But I also believe that religion is a little bit like going to the gym. You have to exercise all the time, get in the habit of doing it, work tirelessly and endlessly to keep fit. Go ahead and set your faith aside for a stretch and see what happens. You'll see that it gets tougher and tougher to get back to the longer you've been away from it, so why not keep it going? It takes time and care—but what could be more deserving of our time and care than our relationship with the Lord? Our workaday world has a gravitational pull of its own that directs too many of us, too much of the time, to negative impulses, to base behaviors. That's just human nature, right? Some things we know better than to chase, and yet we can't keep ourselves from chasing them.

Religion is a little like golf. You'll have to forgive me on this, and perhaps indulge me a little, but I find that the game of golf holds a great many lessons for life itself. In golf, if you spend all your time thinking about the bad shots, the missed putts, the time spent in the rough, you'll set aside your clubs in frustration. But if you focus on the joys the game can offer and the successes you can find on the course, the game takes on a different hue. The same holds for religion. If you dwell on the negatives—on, say, the *don't*s in the Bible—you might be driven away. But if you underline the positives, the *do*s, you'll keep at it. The way we live our lives these days, it sometimes feels that, as a society, we focus on the bad shots, our time in the rough, as opposed to the potential in all of us to live more purposefully, to *do* better.

Just to finish up with this golf metaphor before readers get tired of it—because, let's face it, there's nothing more tiring than a middle-aged man going on and on about his golf game—let's acknowledge the bad shots, but let's also accept that we can make an adjustment and turn those bad shots into good ones.

We can improve our game.

So, when it comes to religion, I keep my focus on the positives, on what I *can* do. In one of my previous books, *Stand for Something,* I write that "when the central message of religion is fear and punishment, the true meaning of faith, hope and grace is lost." I still worry about this. Try as I might, I can't live constantly on that higher plane God has set before me, and I used to struggle over this. These days, it feels like the struggle has eased—not because it has become any *easier* to live on that higher plane, but because I've learned to forgive myself my failings. Don't misunderstand, I'm *always* working on it—it's not like I let my gym membership lapse, like I toss my golf clubs into the lake after a tough front nine. Sometimes, though, I just can't seem to carry the weight set out in front of me, so I keep at it, build myself up to it.

I press on.

## LOVE THY NEIGHBOR

Now, when I talk about religion, I don't want to shove my beliefs down anybody's throat. But I do want to give them voice—hoping, perhaps, that they might be of some help to people who are searching for meaning in their lives. If you don't want to hear from me on this, you can skip ahead to the next chapter. It's like I used to joke with people in my town halls, whenever someone seemed to want to challenge me on religion. I'd say, "Look, I'm the one running for president. When you're running for president, I'll come to *your* town halls and listen to what *you* have to say."

Michael Novak, the great philosopher whose best-known book is probably *The Spirit of Democratic Capitalism,* warns us that life can be nothing but a vale of tears. This is true: life is tough. We're all made to walk our own hard road from time to time. Just because you have faith, it doesn't shield you from devastating hurt. However, it does offer you perspective. In fact, if you do have faith, it really gets down to connecting the wisdom of God, who controls this whole world, with the question of why bad things happen to good people. Nobody can answer this question for Him, but we all have an idea. Job, from the Old Testament, asks God to help him understand why He has visited so much suffering upon him. God replies, "Who are you to try to figure out the way that I am?"

Over the past decade or so, I've discovered some new truths

about the afterlife. I've come to the conclusion that we're not going to leave this earth and be sitting up in the sky playing harps. We're going to be in a position to re-inherit the earth, and that means we're going to have some work to do.

This world can only prepare us for the world yet to come—and in those preparations, we find the seeds of a life well and purposefully lived.

What does God mean when he commands us to love our neighbor? He's telling us to enable our neighbor, to help him achieve what he is meant to achieve. If somebody's experiencing hard times and is in need of a job, help him out. If someone is in pain, comfort her. If someone has a great victory, don't let him celebrate alone. If someone is angry at you, find a way to make amends.

Celebrating together, crying together, sticking your neck out for people who can't help themselves—these are the things that pull us together and give us a sense of community. They bind us as a nation: to one another, to the common good, and to a shared set of ideals. We're not in this world alone. Though sometimes it feels we have to go out of our way in order to connect with our neighbors, we've got to make the effort.

Go out of your way.

Reach out.

Give of yourself.

Love your neighbor and be loved by your neighbor in return.

You don't have to do it *my* way. You just have to do it *some* way.

I know a bunch of people who don't share my beliefs, and yet they do a lot of great things. They're tremendous people—some of my closest friends. But here's where I set a lot of these people off with my views: I happen to believe that you can't guide an entire society without a shared religious foundation. On an individual basis, sure. Among small networks and tight communities, sure.

But in a country as big as ours, I think you need a compass on a societal level, and it can't be a compass with the magnetic component all out of whack.

I think we've lost that compass over the years. There are explanations for this all around. The secularization of our American society has its roots in the heat and haste of our lives. It is not surprising that as nations mature, they also drift, and I don't believe the religious enterprise has responded well to that drift. Many of the people who describe themselves as religious leaders have failed us. To some, they no longer seem relevant, because their message is frequently about judgment and punishment (the *don't*s of religion), rather than grace, love, and connection (the *do*s). And for some people, when those leaders look to involve themselves directly in politics, it's a turnoff.

As my friend Stu Boehmig often reminds me, "Preachers should guide their congregations in values and let the people conclude who their political leaders ought to be."

Let us recognize that the seeping of religion into our politics can only divide us and create cynicism. Martin Luther reminded us that religion is the conscience of the state, not the governance of the state—and we would do well to keep this distinction in mind as we are called to worship. Our religious leaders ought to be spending more time feeding the poor and helping the downtrodden than getting involved in politics and seeking the limelight.

Let us recognize, too, that, at bottom, we're all hypocrites. We say one thing and do another; we say we lean one way and then act another. We must accept that there are consequences when we set aside our values, and that the secularization of our society comes at a cost. When you think about it, a lot of the religious wars that have developed over some of the pressing issues of our times are really about telling people how to think without letting them figure it out for themselves. To me it's these negatives that drive people from organized religion, and I like to tell people to turn the car back around and keep heading to the light they started out for in the first place.

We see this hypocrisy in all walks of life, not just religion and politics.

We see it in sports, as team owners look past the unforgivable transgressions of players in order to keep them on the field or on the court and winning games.

We see it in business, as CEOs put profits ahead of principles.

We see it in music, as rappers and pop stars offer lyrics and videos that marginalize some listeners and leave parents reaching for the Mute button.

We see it in movies, in video games, and on television, as we struggle to make sense of so many senseless images of violence and gore.

We must expect *all* our leaders to celebrate the grace and positivity all around them, and to walk a good and noble path. Those who are believers must make an effort to shine meaningful light on their world, and to transmit the feelings of hope and connectedness that can come with a life of faith. As a politician, as a leader, I focus on issues that help us to engage positively in other people's lives. We need to get these resolved before we battle over the social issues that have come to dominate our national debate, issues that have come to divide us. Still, I know people of great faith who see these issues in completely different ways.

We have to be tolerant of other people's points of view; we have to be able to disagree without being disagreeable, without claiming that we have a monopoly on the truth.

Personally, I have my own views, but I'm ever mindful that others might see things another way. I don't condemn or judge, and I expect not to be condemned or judged in return. I can have an opinion of somebody else's behavior, but the ultimate authority on these matters is the higher power. And when I say that, I don't want people to feel I'm trying to convert them to my way of thinking. I'm just offering my thoughts, sharing what I've learned from my own life, my guiding principles.

Because, just saying, life is not easy.

My feeling is that we all need to be on the same page with this one. We have to be pointed in the same direction. Otherwise, we're working at cross-purposes; we're *living* at cross-purposes. In a world where everything is changing, the Judeo-Christian values that reside at this nation's core should not be changed. Everything is *not* up for review or discussion or reinterpretation. Our principles are our principles, and we must hold fast to them as a society— because without them we're lost. It's only when we set down our shared moral compass—the one that points us to honesty, integrity, personal responsibility, faith, humility, compassion, forgiveness—that we start to lose our way. We become less tolerant of one another.

We become weaker as a nation.

So, I'll put it to you again: Where do *you* go when the water rises? How do you celebrate your successes? The path before us is not always certain, in good times and bad, so my thing is to walk in the light of God and trust that He will help me to find the way. And do you know what? I've found that the more I study Scripture, the more I read the great biblical scholars, the more I think and pray, the better I am as a person. I'm not perfect—far from it—but each day, I try to walk in His glory and carry myself as He would have me carry myself, and I get a little closer to where I need to be.

# 6.

# A Crisis of Leadership

There I was, with my feet up on the couch, my buddy Rondo joining me for a glass of wine after dinner, Karen and the girls off doing their own things around the house, and I realized I needed to start making some calls. There were people waiting to hear from me on this. A lot of people, because when you decide to run for president of the United States, it's not like you can snap your fingers and will it so. There are all those moving parts I mentioned earlier. You need to put a team in place. You need to get your financing in order. You need to have a vision for the country and a way to articulate that vision. And you need a good group of dedicated folks who share that vision and who have the insight and experience to push you in the right direction.

You also need a bit of wind at your back, a substantial Twitter following, and the apparently undivided attention of television news executives who have determined that stories about you and your campaign are good (very good!) for ratings—all factors that were just a little beyond our control.

Happily, a lot of those moving parts had already fallen into place, at least on the personnel front, so that when I finally came to my decision to run, it was a little like starting the launch sequence on a much-discussed mission. What had been discussed most of all was probably the money. Like it or not, it costs money to seek the presidency. How much? Well, we didn't really know. We had an idea, though. We kicked around some numbers. Early on, when the prospect of a presidential run was still just a prospect, we thought we'd need to raise about $10 million to jump-start a viable campaign. How did we come up with that number? We were scoreboard watching, basically. We read the reports on what all the other candidates were raising, looked at the money that was likely available to us and came up with the money we already had in hand, and came up with $10 million as a viable goal.

Later, we amended that number to $12 million, and then $15 million. It was a moving target, but it was a moving target we all felt we could hit, and a number that would give us a bare-bones chance at a running start. Would we have liked to be able to raise $50 million? You bet, but as we were ramping up and considering our options, that number didn't seem reasonable—not just yet.

My one hard rule whenever we discussed money, early on *and* once we were up and running, was that my campaign would never go into debt. I would run an *affordable* campaign or I wouldn't run at all, and if it ever got to the point where we were overextended, we'd suspend our efforts. (Indeed, at the very end, we had about $100,000 left in the bank, so I'm proud to report that we stuck to that rule.)

Here's a story to illustrate how focused I was on money.

I never got involved in the day-to-day running of our finances, but I paid attention in a big-picture way. I'd notice if we were staying in a hotel that was a little too high-end for our budget, for example. My team was well aware of my concerns about overhead, so from time to time they'd put off telling me about a major expense, or a new hire, or whatever. Well, as our campaign got going, we needed to grow our staff accordingly, and at one point we hired an advance man no one seemed to want to introduce to me. An advance man helps set up town halls and coordinate various events for us in all the different towns a candidate visits—a good and necessary addition to any team. One day, I saw this guy on the plane and I had no idea who he was. Everybody was so afraid to tell me we'd made another hire, because they knew I was a little nuts about the money. I kept saying, "We're not going into the hole. We're not going into the hole." It was a mantra.

Finally, someone found the courage to tell me what was going on, after which I immediately sought out Doug Preisse, a longtime supporter of all of my political endeavors. Doug was my ear to the ground *and* my eyes on the prize—his friendship and loyalty and dedication were essential to the effort. He ended up traveling with me throughout the campaign, and I came to value his insights, his focus, and his good company—only, in this case, I just wanted to know how we'd come to have an advance man on the team.

I said, "Are you kidding me? We have an advance man? What's *that* costing us?"

Doug just looked at me and said, "Governor, we're running a national campaign for president. Of course we have an advance man. Deal with it."

So, I dealt with it.

Why was I so worried about the money? Because I was the one who had to raise it. There's a tendency in a campaign to spend money a little too casually, but for the most part, it falls to the candidate to raise it. Of course, there are people on the fund-raising side of the campaign who do a great job lining up potential donors and coordinating the events; I don't want to diminish their essential role. But I was the one out there making the ask and closing the deal. To give credit where credit is due, Brooke Bodney helped lead the effort on fund-raising, and she did an outstanding job. She worked countless hours, to the point of exhaustion, and of course I wouldn't have been able to do my thing without her extra effort. Despite the support from Brooke and the others, though, it still felt like the pressure was on me.

Now, there are some on my team who remember our front-end fund-raising concerns a little differently. They remember that the magic number started a little higher—say, at $17–$18 million— and that we kept adjusting downward as reality caught up to our expectations, and as all the other candidates started declaring and we could see how much money they had in hand in their filings. This might have been the case, but these details were a little beyond my pay grade at that early juncture. What do I mean by that? Well, I'd been at it long enough to know that politics is an art, not a science. You run by feel. You start out with one strategy and then perhaps you pivot, based on the response of the electorate, or the media, or your opponents. You figure it out as you move along, and my job early on was simply to decide if I was in this thing and, while I was deciding, to speak from my heart and from my experience.

We couldn't know exactly how much money the other candidates were going to have until they filed. All along, we'd been hearing that Scott Walker had raised $40–$50 million, but then he filed with less than $20 million, so we adjusted our thinking accordingly. Jeb Bush was said to have raised over $100 million. And then there were the other candidates, like former Arkansas governor Mike Huckabee and Kentucky senator Rand Paul, each checking in with about $10 million, according to reports. It wasn't so much about what that money could buy you in terms of salaries and resources and advertising as it was about what it bought you in terms of credibility. A respectable, credible number was what we were after, and it would grow from there—or not, if our message failed to resonate with voters and donors.

You know, when you're watching the scoreboard in this way, as we most certainly were, you're not doing it in a vacuum. Everybody's out there doing what amounts to the same thing, but it helps to keep in mind that the money means different things to different candidates at different stages in their campaigns. It's fluid—and subjective. As a popular incumbent governor of Ohio, who had just been reelected by a wide margin, who had served eighteen con-sequential years in Congress, I had a certain kind of story to tell. And Bobby Jindal—just to throw out another example from the Republican field—as a two-term governor of Louisiana, had *his* story to tell. So it followed that each of our campaigns would re-quire different sets of resources in order to tell our separate stories. We each had different objectives, and different needs, so compar-ing the others' campaign war chests in a dollar-for-dollar way wasn't the best way to keep score. Still, in the early going, it was just about the only way to keep score. You couldn't always trust the polling, but the money was a reliable tell.

You have to realize, too, that our ability to raise money going in was hurt by the fact that I didn't know if I was going to run. I guess you could say that as strategies go, mine was not a particu-larly good one. But the clock was working against us—meaning, the first debate was approaching. Obviously, I couldn't start raising money until I made the decision to run, and my ability to raise meaningful money would take a serious hit if I missed out on the first debate entirely. So, now it fell to me and my team to start making up for lost time.

Clearly, we had to make some sort of a formal announcement, so that became our public priority, but at the same time, we had to start ramping up for the first Republican presidential debate, which was just a couple weeks away. That debate had been one of the hard-and-fast dates on our calendar as I considered whether to run. With my announcement, I became the sixteenth candidate in the field, but the ground rules for that first debate were that only the top ten candidates, based on an average of five national polls, would make it to the main debate stage, to be conducted in prime time and aired on Fox News. The rest would be invited to debate on a kind of undercard, which a lot of pundits were suggesting was akin to being assigned to the kiddie table. (My daughter Reese, who has a terrific ability to see things as they are and a great way with words, said it was like having to play on the junior varsity team; I loved that!)

As it happened, that first debate was to be held in my own backyard—in Cleveland, which of course would be the site of the Republican National Convention the following summer. As the governor of Ohio, I considered it doubly important that I make it onto that main stage. Really, it would have been a giant hiccup, perhaps even an embarrassment, for that debate to take place on my home turf without me, and for me to be consigned to the junior varsity. We all worried we were a little late to the game on this.

Two weeks just wasn't a whole lot of time to move the needle.

One of the ways I could have helped myself in this regard was with a formal announcement of my candidacy. Typically, there's a bump in the polls attached to the launch of a national campaign, if you time it right and hit all the right notes, which was just what we were trying to do. A well-timed, well-executed event to announce my candidacy could help us get the bump we needed, and for a while, my advisers thought an announcement at the Rock and Roll Hall of Fame, in Cleveland, would do a lot of business for us in the hitting-all-the-right-notes department. There'd be a photogenic backdrop, which would help us capture that all-important media attention. I was told it'd make me look young and hip, standing there in front of the famous institution. And I suppose there was a certain integrity and synergy and excitement to it, given the Cleveland setting. Strategically, the venue was also better located for national media—meaning, it was easier for reporters to get in and out of Cleveland than any other city in Ohio. Location alone wasn't a guarantee you'd get a ton of coverage, but holding an event in the middle of nowhere, as the sixteenth candidate jockeying for position at the starting gate, could pretty much guarantee that you'd be ignored.

Yet the idea of holding the announcement in Cleveland felt forced, contrived. (Besides, I thought I already looked young and hip.) An announcement in my hometown of Columbus was more appropriate, I thought, more in keeping with the homespun values I'd be putting out in my campaign. So, we turned our attention to local venues that could accommodate a good crowd and offer a media-friendly location.

There weren't a whole lot of options. We talked about Everal Barn and Homestead, a beautiful, pastoral setting in my hometown of Westerville, where I'd announced for governor. But that was outdoors, and we didn't want to take a chance on the weather. We all remembered those tense moments back in June 2009, when storm clouds rolled in just a couple of hours before I was due to make another such big announcement—luckily, those clouds blew through and it turned out to be a great event. Still, we all thought it made sense to look for an indoor venue. We talked about the Franklin Park Conservatory and the student union at Otterbein University, but we finally set our sights on Ohio State, my alma mater, a choice that later felt inevitable.

The Ohio State campus made all kinds of sense. I had a long relationship with the school, going back to that weekend visit with my father, as a prospective student. I'd also taught there for a time, after leaving Congress. But my connection to the school goes beyond rooting for the Buckeyes to all the ways the school has lifted me to a place of purpose and possibility—as it seeks to do for *all* its students. Ohio State will always hold a special place in my heart. I felt that way the moment I set foot on campus as a brash, fresh-faced eighteen-year-old from McKees Rocks. I can still remember walking onto the football field late one night during my freshman orientation. I don't think I was supposed to be there, but there was no one around to stop me. I just walked right out onto the field, stood on the fifty-yard line, and thought to myself, Either this place is going to own me, or I'm going to own it. It was one of those formative, rallying moments, and it left me feeling grounded and inspired, both. Every time I've stepped into that stadium since then, I've been taken back to that late-night visit to that fifty-yard line, and in my head, I'm still that eighteen-year-old kid with all those big dreams, out to change the world, held up by the sweep and grandeur of that storied stadium, smack in the middle of that storied campus.

We'd gone back to that stadium just the summer before my announcement to run for president, during my run for reelection as governor. It was a beautiful, sunny day, and my whole team was with me for the shooting of our final campaign ad. As the production crew finished prepping, I called everyone together for a huddle on the fifty-yard line. We had a little talk, said a little prayer, shared a little hug. It was a very emotional moment because, at the time, I truly believed this would be the last ad of the last campaign of my political career—and a lot of those emotions were captured in the resulting campaign ad.

I had this in mind as we were looking at places to hold the announcement for 2016. I wanted it to be personal, and at the same time to offer an iconic setting. In the end, we settled on the student union at Ohio State, and everything worked out pretty perfectly.

We had some terrific speakers lined up to offer their support: Archie Griffin, the two-time Heisman Trophy winner and an Ohio State legend; Tom Moe, the director of the Ohio Department of Veterans Services, who spent five years as a prisoner of war in Vietnam. I had Karen and the girls at my side. Even the audio and visual elements were spot-on; we had a state-of-the-art sound system, with beautiful lights, decorations, the works—right down to a custom carpet at our feet. It was all very . . . presidential.

As I spoke, I took the time to look around the packed room, at the students and supporters and hundreds of volunteers looking down from the rafters above—my entire Ohio team!—and I allowed myself a small, sweet moment of reflection.

"The Lord wants our hearts to reach out to those who don't have what we have," I said at one point. "That shouldn't be hard for America. That's who we are."

I also said this: "The sun is rising, and the sun is going to rise to the zenith in America again. . . . The light of a city on a hill cannot be hidden. America is that city, and you are that light."

I'd written down my thoughts in an outline beforehand, which meant I ended up speaking mostly from the heart—an approach that would become a signature of my campaign, once I found my footing. Yet, in this moment, I was inclined to follow a certain kind of script. There's a way campaigns are meant to run, that's all I knew. I'd been down this road before, with that short-lived run for president in 2000, but I told myself that this time would be different—but only in terms of the outcome. I'd go at it in much the same way, the same way I'd run all my campaigns. I'd run on my record; I'd run on the issues; I'd run as if I were 20 points behind. But this time, the results would be different.

As I spoke, I looked out across that great hall and considered this election and what it might mean—for my country, for my family—and as I did, I had another one of those fifty-yard-line epiphanies. I was that eighteen-year-old kid from McKees Rocks all over again, only now I also felt this tremendous sense of purpose, this pride of place and moment. When I allowed myself a breath, to step back and reflect on what this campaign might mean, it was humbling, exciting, inspiring—all of that.

*Either this place is going to own me, or I am going to own it. . . .*

But there was no time to dwell on how far I'd come, because there was still a long way to go.

## BUILDING A TEAM

That dedicated team I needed to put together? A lot of those folks were already in place by the time I decided to run. They were people such as Don Thibaut and Rondo Hartman, my longtime sounding boards; and Jai Chabria, who'd started with me nearly twenty years earlier, as a political assistant on Capitol Hill, and who always had my back. There was Beth Hansen, my chief of staff as governor, who would now pivot and become my campaign manager; and Bob Klaffky and Doug Preisse, both forces in Ohio politics, who'd long been part of my inner circle and who would now serve as key policy advisers. Greg Wendt, a trusted friend who'd been helping me for years with his insight and savvy, was a natural addition to the team; as was Jeff Polesovsky, who had worked so diligently to help me get elected governor, together with my dear friends and advisers Wilber and Janet James.

Most of my key staff during this exploratory period had come from within, with the exception of John Weaver, a political consultant best known for his work on John McCain's presidential campaign. John signed on a couple weeks before our Ohio State announcement, so our core group had just enough time to put their heads together and come up with a strategy.

Before I lay out that strategy, though, I want to take a moment to honor the happy band of dedicated campaign staff and volunteers who signed on to our effort. Truth is, a national campaign is only as strong as its team, and here we were gifted with a tremendous group of enthusiastic professionals. It amazes me when I look back on how many good people we were able to attract to our effort. Think of it: dozens of folks actually quit their jobs in order to come work for us full-time in our headquarters office. It was just incredible. They worked, for the most part, in cramped conditions in an old house in Columbus—seated on folding chairs, at folding desks, many of them working on computers they had to supply themselves.

By the end of the campaign, I'd say we had about forty people working for us in this way. And it's not as if they were doing menial drudge work; many of them were working in essential roles: people we couldn't afford to pay what they were worth, but people we couldn't afford to be without. And yet they signed on, willingly, joyfully, purposefully. Many of them had worked for me before, or volunteered for one of my gubernatorial campaigns, and I was only too happy to welcome them back into the fold.

Without them, we would never have gotten the campaign off the ground. (And let's not forget that in our state and regional offices around the country, there would soon be dozens more signing on to the campaign.)

With our team in place and our headquarters office now bursting at the seams, our first strategic decision was to determine whether we could win the nomination without really going to Iowa in a full-on way. Nothing against the good people of Iowa, who, like the good people of New Hampshire, relish in their first-in-the-nation role in the presidential primary and caucus process. But we simply didn't have the resources to campaign aggressively or effectively in both states. Plus, most of the other announced candidates had already spent a good chunk of time in Iowa, so there was a feeling among our group that any effort we made in the state would be of the "too little, too late" variety.

You have to realize, there's a lot of ground to cover in Iowa—it's a big state, with so many counties, and towns and populations spread out all over the place. New Hampshire, by contrast, is like a postage stamp. That's what makes it such a great proving ground for a grassroots campaign. There's an incredibly diverse population there—one that's also incredibly interested in presidential politics. You can travel to all eighty-eight counties in New Hampshire fairly easily. Also, you can do a lot of what we call "retail politics," meaning, finding ways to connect with people where they lived, such as at a town hall event.

We looked at the scenario from every conceivable angle and concluded that an all-out push in New Hampshire made sense and that it could be enough to see us through to the next phase of our campaign. So that became the plan. We would go to Iowa and show the appropriate respect for its history and people, but we knew we hadn't left ourselves enough time to make a good showing there, so we would keep those visits to a minimum. Whatever resources we'd devote to Iowa (time, money, media), we'd keep those to a minimum, too. We just didn't have it in us to make Iowa a focus, not if we also wanted to focus on New Hampshire, where we believed we had a good shot.

The timing of our announcement was critical, we all agreed. The first debate was scheduled for August 6, and we'd looked on with great interest as all the other candidates declared their candidacy and watched their poll numbers spike then very soon fall into place. There was a predictable pattern to it. To be honest, I didn't pay as much attention to all this stuff as my advisers did, but their interests were mine, so I took their point. The idea was to slot my announcement between the launch events of other candidates, hopefully on a day that was relatively free of any significant news stories coming out of other campaigns, and then to make sure that we weren't too far away from the final debate polling to land a spot on that main debate stage before the inevitable soft fall of my polling numbers. Here, again, it was more art than science. We were going by gut, by feel—but I want to be clear that it wasn't necessarily *my* gut, *my* feel. My instinct was to have at it, to hit the ground running, but I was willing to be guided on this one, and now that I'd decided to run for president I wanted to do a thorough job of it.

We'd quickly assembled a formidable team to lead our New Hampshire effort, including former senator John E. Sununu, who was one of my key advisers; former senator Gordon Humphrey, who not only endorsed me but also campaigned tirelessly on my behalf; and former New Hampshire attorney general Tom Rath, a Yankee sage who really knew the electoral workings of the state.

Almost immediately, national polling put me in sixth or seventh place among the announced candidates (depending on the national polling), but because it was such a crowded field, my support was registering only in the single digits. Still, I counted this a promising start, since the other folks had been at it for months and months. The front-runners back then were Dr. Ben Carson, Marco Rubio, Jeb Bush, and Donald Trump, with the last beginning to edge out in front, but not yet by any measure beyond his ability to command media attention. The general feeling in our camp was that Trump would take his turn as the lead dog, and then fall back to the middle of the pack soon enough—a general feeling that never quite took into account his appeal to a growing plurality of disenchanted, disenfranchised Republican voters.

In the minds of most analysts, the field was wide open. The announced candidates tended to be grouped in bunches; there were the outsider candidates, looking to change things up in Washington; there were the upstarts, looking to grow their base to launch a national campaign; and there were the established Republican conservatives, many of them sitting governors like me, looking to build on their records of leadership and party loyalty. For the moment, it appeared that each of us would be driving in our own lane for a while, so Jeb Bush remained the candidate to beat as far as my own candidacy was concerned. The whole time I was weighing a run, we kept hearing that despite all the money he'd been able to raise, despite the long run-up to 2016, when he moved about the country as a kind of presumptive nominee, voters weren't too terribly excited about Jeb Bush. So there was an opportunity here. The idea was to keep viable and relevant and to appeal to his hoped-for supporters in what ways I could.

That bump we were all counting on to propel our campaign to that first debate stage? It didn't exactly happen for us in a big-time way. There was a good amount of media coverage coming out of my announcement, but it was becoming clear to us that this presidential election cycle was unlike any other. It was also becoming clear that the name recognition I'd been counting on, as a nine-term congressman and current two-term governor, wasn't nearly as strong as I thought it was. On some of the cable news shows, there were panelists and commentators who couldn't even pronounce my name—that's the kind of uphill battle I was fighting on the name-recognition front. (If I had a dollar for every time I had to tell someone my name was pronounced "KAY-sick, as in *basic*," we could have raised enough money to plant a lawn sign at every home in the state of New Hampshire, or so it seemed.)

For a couple days, we got only a little more than our fair share of media attention, but by the time the week was out, the "bump" had appeared to flatten. In golf terms, we were polling at just about the cut line—meaning, if we missed an easy putt for par, we wouldn't get to keep playing in the main draw. We'd left ourselves very little margin for error.

I'd never been involved in such a crowded election, one where, right out of the gate, your first and only job was to make yourself heard. Forget connecting with voters in a personal way. Forget trying to communicate on a substantive level. Forget holding an event and expecting the press to cover it. Forget raising money in any kind of predictable, meaningful, sustainable fashion. This was nothing like the two-, or three-, or four-person races I was used to running. And it wasn't even remotely like the 2000 presidential race, where there may have been a dozen other candidates, but we were all scrambling for attention with a measure of decorum and decency— and without the surface-level distractions of social media.

Still, we'd all known this going in. What I didn't fully appreciate, though, was how little known I was outside of my home state of Ohio. I mean, I'd been a congressman, involved in a lot of big moments on Capitol Hill, and not just in a sideline way. I'd been on Fox News, not just on my own show on Saturday nights, but also as a guest host, filling in for Bill O'Reilly on the network's top-rated program. I'd just been elected to my second term in one of the biggest, most influential states in the country, by a big, influential margin. But in the heartland, folks don't really care about any of that. And it's not that I wasn't *well* known, we were learning. I wasn't known *at all*, and that would turn out to be a major strike against us in the early going.

How's that for the understatement of our campaign?

Still, in the media centers of New York and Washington, the folks who were covering the campaign didn't really care about any of that. That's one of the frustrating realities of national politics: if you're not located in one of the media centers, you'll have a hard time getting anyone to cover you. If you're in their backyard, they'll know who you are and send a crew if you're up to something; if you're out in middle America—in, say, Columbus, Ohio—they'll leave it to local media to handle the coverage.

Another major strike: I wasn't nearly as *loud* as some of the other candidates—meaning, I wasn't about to raise my voice or pander for votes the way some of my cohorts seemed to have no problem doing. I'd never been the sort of person who would talk someone down just to lift himself up, or to run his mouth and start making wild promises he couldn't possibly keep—and I wasn't about to start becoming that person now, just to keep pace with the others.

My campaign strategy, leading into that first debate, was to talk about the issues, and at that time, I thought the driving issue that would galvanize voters was the economy. If I was known at all beyond Ohio, it was for the push I'd been making in recent months for that balanced budget amendment, and for the fact that I had a history of practicing what I preached, having been one of the chief architects of the balanced budget under President Clinton. Basically, I planned to present a clearheaded, bipartisan argument for conservative fiscal responsibility that would stand at the heart of my campaign.

At least, that's what I thought. As it turned out, the 2016 presidential race was unlike any other campaign we'd ever seen, unlike any other campaign we're ever likely to see again. The old models simply did not apply. One of the big strikes against me in this group was that I was the governor of a big state like Ohio, in charge of looking out for more than 11.5 million people. In any other year, this would have gone right in the plus column, but everything was upside down during this election. All around me, candidates were making wild promises and outlandish statements, while I was out there trying to offer up sound strategies and proven approaches—in other words, trying to be *responsible*. But you know what? That was seen as boring. Nobody seemed to care—at least, not in any kind of measurable way in this early going.

Being governor changes you. It makes you a different kind of leader. When you work in Washington, it's easy to stand on the floor of Congress and wail about an injustice. You can always blame somebody else for why things aren't going the way you'd told the folks back home they would be going. When you see something wrong, you don't have to fix it; you just have to rail about it. But when you're governor, it's on you. You've got to make sure the snow is removed from the roads, and the bridges are rebuilt, and there's money in the budget to keep the schools open.

I'd spent my entire political career working to bring about change. And the thing of it is, when you're the governor, you can actually achieve more from a reform point of view. But while you might be able to *achieve* more, your newfound responsibility leaves you in a position where you are able to *promise* less. This doesn't mean you can't be a revolutionary, a visionary, but you have to be a *responsible* revolutionary, a *responsible* visionary. This can strengthen you and make you a better leader, but at the same time, it can weaken you—especially when you're fighting to make yourself heard in a crowded field of presidential hopefuls who'll say just about anything to get elected.

So, there I was, feeling a little bit like I was walking up a down escalator in this post-truth environment, wondering how the heck I was supposed to get my ideas across in this crazy election year.

It's pretty interesting, don't you think? To be the governor of Ohio, in this field, at this point in time, it was more a weakness than a strength, and it would take me awhile to find a way to flip the script and turn my position to some kind of advantage.

## HAT IN THE RING, FOOT ON THE GAS

July 21, 2015—that was the date I announced my candidacy at Ohio State. Everything that happened before then was just preamble. That's just getting your team together and thinking things through. That's just keeping your options open and assessing the field, and giving yourself the best chance to win, because you don't go through these motions just to go through these motions. You don't run just to run. And even on this late date, just a couple weeks out from the first debate, we were still thinking of Jeb Bush as the elephant in the room. Or the pace car in our mainstream Republican lane. Or the presumptive nominee. Or whatever tired metaphor or cliché you want to use to say that Jeb Bush was the guy to beat.

Yet, a lot of the preamble stuff was essential business, so I don't mean to dismiss it. There were all kinds of deliberations, machinations, and preparations going on behind the scenes. Understand, I wasn't too involved in a lot of it, but it was kind of interesting, all these little details you had to take care of if you hoped to give yourself a shot at winning. So, while I was mulling over whether to even run in the first place, there was groundwork being laid on the assumption that I would. For example, before we could consider ourselves up and running, we had to have a Super PAC in place, and someone to run it. Matt Carle moved over from my administration, where he'd been head of legislative affairs, and took on that responsibility.

Matt had just run my reelection campaign for governor and had become a valued part of my team—a member of my Bible study group, too. Yet, once he took over our New Day for America Super PAC, I had no contact with him. Nobody on the campaign side had any contact with him. This was both a good thing and a frustrating thing. It was good because I knew we were in capable hands, but at the same time it was frustrating because I had come to rely on Matt's instincts and missed having him to call on whenever I wanted his take on something.

During this campaign, Brooke Bodney would continue to head our traditional fund-raising efforts, seeking "hard money" from political donations that were regulated by the Federal Election Commission—monies that would be used to fund the day-to-day operations of the campaign. Meanwhile, Matt Carle would spearhead efforts on the "soft money" front—raising monies to be used outside the campaign's purview.

The way it works under Federal Election Commission rules is there can be no communication between a candidate and his or her campaign committees and the Super PACs that exist in support of that candidate and those campaign committees. They're two entirely different organizations, bound by two entirely different sets of guidelines. The best way to understand the split is through the getting and spending of money. On the campaign side, we could raise a maximum of $2,800 from individuals and $5,000 from political action committees, and that money was used to fund the campaign, including candidate travel and advertising. On the Super PAC side, there was no limit to the amount of money an individual could donate, and corporate donations were allowable as well. That money went mostly to advertising and to advance certain policy initiatives. In terms of advertising, the campaign could buy television time at the lowest available unit rate—meaning, at a predetermined rate that was the same for all candidates across the board and was often substantially below market. The Super PAC, for its part, could buy time only at prevailing market rates—meaning, those ads would typically cost a whole lot more to run.

What this meant in practical terms was that one hand couldn't know what the other was doing. Matt could bring on a media guy like Fred Davis, for example, and together they could create a television spot they thought might set the right tone and send the right message. But over on the campaign side, we wouldn't see the spot until it started airing, and even then, we could weigh in on what we thought about it only through the media or comments I might make publicly along the campaign trail.

That kind of thing happened a couple of times during the campaign. Once, early on, the Super PAC put together an unconventional campaign ad that featured an unidentified candidate getting into an unidentified helicopter, beneath the voice of an unidentified narrator talking about public policy issues. The voice-over was all about how there was only one candidate who had created jobs, cut taxes, balanced budgets, and so forth—as the camera pulled back to reveal a scene that gave the viewer the impression the "one candidate" being discussed was Donald Trump. After all, the "one candidate" was being shown stepping onto a helicopter pad at a private airport, so the suggestion was clear. Then came the surprise reveal: as the camera panned out, you could see a "John Kasich" sign affixed to the tail of the helicopter.

The day after the spot first aired, a reporter asked me about it, and I said I didn't think we should be comparing ourselves to other candidates—so Matt felt he had no choice but to pull the ad. He and his team had spent a lot of time on it, a lot of money on it, and now, looking back, I can appreciate what they were trying to do in distinguishing my record from Donald Trump's in that way. But at the time, it just didn't feel right to me—a message I would much have preferred to deliver to Matt privately, if I could have done so within FEC rules.

A good example of the logistics we needed to consider ahead of my announcement were the efforts made just to ensure my name was on the primary ballot in all the states. You'd think, in this day and age, in the greatest country in the world, we'd have a much more streamlined, much more efficient process in what's essentially a national election, but that's not how it works. We take our democracy seriously, and one of the great strengths of our democracy is the power and autonomy we leave to our states. This is nowhere more in evidence than in the way we nominate our candidates for president. Really, the ballot-access rules in some of these states are wild, and varied, and hard to figure out. And they keep changing from one election cycle to the next, so it's not as if you can compile a handbook for future candidates. What's valid one year might be invalid the next; what makes sense and seems to follow a logical pattern in one state makes no sense and seems entirely illogical in the next, so that what you're left with is a kind of patchwork quilt.

Turns out there are attorneys who specialize in federal and state election laws, and we put together a volunteer army of them, mostly in Ohio, but some in Washington as well. Turns out, too, that no single attorney has all the answers on this, so we had to cobble together a group of folks who knew where to look for all the answers.

Every once in a while, I'd check in and see how things were going, but Ben Kaiser stayed on top of this effort for me. And it really was an effort, to hear him tell it. In every state, there was a whole new set of hoops we had to jump through. In some states, you had to complete the process sixty days before the primary; in others, it was ninety days. In some states, there are steep filing fees (maybe $25,000 or $40,000); in others, you need only a certain number of voter signatures to file a petition. Very often it wasn't just the *number* of signatures, but the *distribution* of those signatures. In Indiana, you had to collect a fixed number of signatures in each congressional district. In other words, you couldn't just go to Indiana and collect one thousand signatures; you needed a certain number in each district, so we needed guidance on this.

Quite a lot of fine print to be gotten through, don't you think?

Vermont had some of the toughest ballot-access rules—the toughest as in the most difficult to meet, because the state's population was sparse and so spread out. The way it was set up, voters could sign a petition for only one candidate. We were looking high and low for registered Republicans in the state, traveling the back roads through these rural areas, because at that point, there were sixteen candidates in the field and not a whole lot of signatures (and in a state like Vermont, not a whole lot of Republicans) to go around, so we were all scrambling.

Our thinking was that we were in this to the end, and we weren't about to be tripped up by poor planning. I might not have had the name recognition of some of my Republican rivals for the nomination, and I certainly couldn't raise the kind of money they were raising, but we were determined to outwork, out-plan and out-hustle the field. I would run a sound, viable campaign or I wouldn't run at all. In my thinking, there's just no way you let all these good, hardworking people put in all this good, hard work on your behalf only to find out that you haven't even gotten on the ballot in some of the states. If you remember, that's what happened to Rick Santorum in 2012, when he had some momentum in the early primary states but looked up one day and realized he wasn't on the ballot in an upcoming contest. I don't set this out as a knock on the Santorum campaign—it was just to indicate the pitfalls we kept in mind. That kind of thing could derail your entire effort, so we wanted to control what we could.

We had our team pouring over election laws, talking to the secretary of state or the chairperson of the state party, and even then, some of these local folks didn't have the latest information on what was going on in their own state. We didn't do this in all fifty states at once, mind you; we followed the primary and caucus calendar, and started ticking them off one state at a time, one deadline at a time. The Republican National Committee had its own effort in place to help candidates trouble-shoot the various ballot-access laws. We didn't want to rely on them, however, so we went ahead and did our own thing, but many of my rival candidates were playing catch-up. We might have been playing catch-up, too, in terms of name recognition and fund-raising and making up for lost time, but in this one regard at least we were out in front, doing the groundwork we needed to do to move our campaign forward.

One of the great side benefits to this kind of preparedness, other than making sure we dotted all our *i*'s and crossed all our *t*'s, was that we'd get a little media attention out of it as our campaign unfolded. In Kansas, for example, it worked out that I was the first candidate to make it onto the ballot, so a couple of reporters turned this into a little story. When this happened, our team would then hear from their counterparts on some of the other campaigns, who were wondering how it was we'd been able to figure all this out when the RNC had yet to issue its guidelines.

How? We had our act together. We took the painstaking approach to understand what was required of us, what was expected of us—and to consider what *we* could reasonably expect from our efforts.

## SETTING THE FIRST DEBATE STAGE

As predicted, my standing in those national polls began to drop a little bit as the cutoff for that first debate lineup drew near, but I did manage to hold on and earn the tenth and final spot for that first prime-time debate at the Quicken Loans Arena in Cleveland, to be moderated by Bret Baier, Megyn Kelly, and Chris Wallace. And in the process, I'm afraid my candidacy pushed Rick Perry to the undercard along with Bobby Jindal, Rick Santorum, Lindsey Graham, Carly Fiorina, Jim Gilmore, and George Pataki.

I tended to take these things in stride, thinking it would have been no big deal if I had had to play with the junior varsity for a debate or two, so I don't recall breathing any kind of sigh of relief when I got the news. All along, my advisers had been telling me we would be okay if I didn't make it to the main debate, and I took them at their word. It was only later that they let slip how important they all thought it was for me to be debating in prime time. No, we weren't about to fold up our tents and call it quits if we didn't make it. And yes, there would have been another debate in just a couple of weeks, and with it, another chance to make a main-stage impression, but appearances count for a lot in politics, and this was our first chance to make a lasting first impression on a national audience, so they gave this first main-stage invitation a lot of weight—a lot more than they were letting on.

Eventually, we would reach out to a guy named Tim Downs to help me with my debate strategies. He flew in for a couple sessions and worked with me on my body language, my tone, my closing statement, things of that nature. But for this first debate, it fell to me and my core advisers to make sure I hit all the right notes. Indeed, as the Cleveland debate approached, we took the time to stage two mock debates with our team. (These sessions are not to be confused with our ongoing debate prep sessions.) We still didn't know whether I'd make it onto the main debate stage, but while we were waiting on the final polling numbers that would determine the candidate lineup, Bob Klaffky went ahead and organized a couple of full-scale mock debates. The idea was to run through an entire debate in real time, just to help me find my footing and my rhythm. We set up a room with seven lecterns, because that was as many as we could find. And we had a table down in front for the moderators. We even had a replica of the timing lights I'd have to face, to recreate the sense of urgency I'd be made to feel in the actual debate.

About five minutes into our first mock debate, I threw up my hands and said, "Okay, guys, I get it. It's gonna be impossible to stand out with this many people onstage."

I might have known, but it took going through these motions for me to get a sense of what it would actually be like to get a word in among such a big group. It was a useful exercise, and out of those mock debates I learned that it didn't make sense to try and *out-zinger* my opponents or pit myself against one of the other candidates. No, the best strategy, we all agreed, was simply to survive the first debate and do what we could to get invited back to the second one, and the one after that, and the one after that. Our thinking was that, eventually, the stage would get smaller, and there would be an opportunity in those later debates to take a more tactical, more substantive approach. So our goal going forward, rather than to score points, was not to make any mistakes.

As it happened, the debate was set up in such a way that the candidates were fanned out across the stage by their position in the polls. Basically, they had us seeded like swimmers in the final heat at the Olympics. You know how that works, right? The swimmers with the best qualifying times are assigned to the middle lanes, with a distinct advantage because they're in the thick of things, able to see the action all around, while the last to qualify are placed in the outside lanes, off in Siberia. So, there I was, at the very edge of the stage, trying to get into some kind of rhythm and make myself heard above the din coming from the lecterns in the middle.

And oh, that din! That Cleveland debate wasn't so bad compared to some of the debates that would follow, but it was the first time the country had seen the down-and-dirty and divisive tone that would come to characterize this presidential election cycle. There'd been indications that this was how the race was leaning, but only in an isolated way, in the sniping that goes on between two candidates from their separate lecterns at their separate events. But here we were all in one room, on prime-time television, and folks were starting to take the gloves off. Donald Trump seemed to set the tone in a now-infamous back-and-forth with Fox News anchor Megyn Kelly, so *that* was the exchange that dominated the headlines and analysis the next morning. Remember, that was the debate where Trump angrily dismissed Kelly for challenging him on his characterization of women as "fat pigs, dogs, slobs and disgusting animals."

I could only stand there at my end of the stage and try not to cringe—and to answer with civility the few questions that came my way. As I did, I realized that this "debate" wasn't really a debate at all. I think I did a decent job of it, given my spot at the edge of the stage, but it was more like a scrum for attention than a serious exchange of ideas or a discussion of the issues—more like a high-stakes rap battle, where each candidate took his or her best shot and kept at it until time was called. The format just didn't work when you had so many people up on that stage, and what you got instead of a debate was a bunch of candidates desperately searching for one-liners or easy sound bites that might make it onto the news shows the next morning. There was no way for any of us to highlight our leadership skills or articulate our positions.

I came away thinking that the debate format was more about surviving than thriving. It was quite a lot of noise and nonsense, really, but I kept telling myself it was elemental noise and nonsense. At this still-early stage in the campaign, it was another one of the few ways we had to keep score, so we went through the motions as if they mattered. And they did, even though there wasn't much to them. What you had, mostly, was a bunch of candidates—including me, at the outset—looking to tap into snippets of their rehearsed stump speeches in ways that might have been only loosely connected to the question put to them by one of the moderators.

We were all just scrambling, I'm afraid—and that's no way to begin to nominate a major-party presidential candidate. And yet, there we were.

Some of my opponents suggested I might have had a home field advantage going into this first debate, being in my home state, and I suppose there's some truth in that. Outwardly, it was meant to be a level playing field: each campaign was given the same number of tickets, but then the RNC distributed a bunch of tickets to registered Republicans from the local community, and these folks appeared to have my back on this. That's just how it worked out. There were times that night when one of the other candidates would say something I thought would connect with the audience, and there'd be boos. Or I'd hear something I thought would outrage the audience, and there'd be cheers. Then, when it was my turn to speak, I'd get a pretty favorable response, so I was happy to be on home turf. Still, it was all out of whack—and like nothing I'd experienced in all my runs for elected office.

As much as possible I tried to highlight my experience in Washington, my experience running the great state of Ohio. This was the underlying message of the campaign when we were just starting out, and it spun from my core belief that the economy is all. At the time, in that moment, this was how I thought campaigns were run, how we went about fixing our problems. You go back to basics, and you tell people the truth, even if it's a truth they don't particularly want to hear. Remember, when I ran for governor in 2010, it was also all about the economy. Ohio was dying. Governor Ted Strickland had fumbled the ball, and a lot of people were hurting. So, I ran on my record in Washington, and on my vision for our great state. I told voters I had a plan to create jobs and shore up our economy, and the people responded, not by a great big number, by the way—I won by just a 2 percent margin— but it takes a lot to unseat an incumbent who's been elected with over 60 percent of the vote, so we all counted it a great victory.

Remember, too, that I'd had some rocky times in my first year on the job, and in a lot of ways this frame of reference would inform how I set off on this presidential campaign. In my first year or so as governor, I'd go into meetings and talk about fixing the economy, and I could only see the big picture. Looking back on my first year or two in office, I see I was acting more like a congressman than a governor. I was more of a doer at first. In politics, in government, you can *do* or you can *lead*. There's a profound difference, and it took me awhile to recognize it. Part of the reason for this was that the demands of *this* elected office, governor, were substantially different from the demands of that *other* elected office I'd held in Washington for nine terms. As a congressman, I was operating at some remove from my constituents, from the community of interests I was meant to serve. As governor, however, I was right there in the middle of things. In Congress, I governed more with my head than with my heart. But back home in Columbus, I was realizing, the heart would have to play a bigger role.

At one point early on in my first term as governor, Karen took me aside and gave me a talking-to when she thought I could have shown a little more compassion on the job. She said, "You're the father of Ohio. Act like it."

You'd better believe I took her advice.

For me, this wasn't a change in style or approach so much as it was an opportunity to be myself, a chance to abandon style in favor of substance, I guess you could say. Mostly, it was a chance to be a better leader. This turned out to be a seamless shift for me, because I'd always been a champion of the underdog. I got that from my parents, who lived by this example. We were taught to be a light for others who might be a little less fortunate, to ease our neighbors' struggles if we were in a position to do so, to share if we were in a place of plenty. So, as I became a leader of our great state, I became more of a servant of the people, rather than just being a strong force for change. I went into the office one way, and I grew into my role in another way, particularly around issues that had to do with people who lived in the shadows. The mentally ill, the drug-addicted, the working poor, the developmentally disabled—these are the folks society tends to discount and dismiss, yet I felt a tremendous sense of responsibility toward them.

Let me just finish up this thought about my first term as governor, before turning back to that first presidential debate in Cleveland, and you'll see how it all ties in. Economic growth was the bedrock principle of my administration, which we were achieving in Ohio. It was job one, our moral purpose—because it sets up an environment for job creation, because it allows leaders to do other things. For example, once we balanced the budget in our state, once we started experiencing economic growth and began to pull Ohio out of the recession, we were able to expand Medicaid—angering a lot of people in our party, by the way—and in the fallout, I said something to the Speaker of the House that got a lot of attention. I said, "Mr. Speaker, when you get to Heaven, St. Peter is not going to ask you if you balanced the budget. He's probably not going to ask you much about what you did to keep government small. He's going to ask you what you did for the poor. And you had better have a good answer."

Perhaps you remember that moment. It got a lot of play at home in Ohio—in fact, it was picked up all over the country once I decided to run for president. As you can imagine, I caught a lot of flak for that remark. There was one woman in particular, at a Koch brothers donors' forum in Palm Springs, who accused me of hiding behind my faith for this Medicaid expansion. I had all these people attacking me, and there were all these Republican governors out there, like Bobby Jindal, Nikki Haley, and Sam Brownback, not exactly coming to my defense. I thought it was an unfair charge. Yes, I was a little outside party lines on health care, but it didn't have anything to do with my faith. It had to do with what I thought was right. We determined that the people in my state needed help. My faith may have been a factor in my thinking, but it was a faith ratified by the facts, and emboldened by a long history of going my own way and voting my conscience on matters that might have strayed from my party's platform.

Yet, despite the ways I'd leaned as governor to create opportunities for folks in the shadows, to try to give them a voice, I relied on familiar ways as I began this run for president. It worked out that I was able to pivot as our campaign got under way, and I started to realize that people were looking for something more. They were looking for a candidate to help them believe in something bigger than themselves. Getting our economy moving—that was a part of it, because if you don't have economic growth, everything else falls apart. But alongside that, I was hearing from people whose lives had become increasingly difficult, people who were looking for hope, for a reason to believe they mattered.

All this helped set the stage for me at that very first debate, where I had to fight just to be heard. When I was asked how I'd explain my opposition to same-sex marriage to a daughter who might be gay, it was my one opportunity that night to speak personally on an issue, and I grabbed at it. I answered with my heart, and the full force of my faith. I said, "Look, I'm an old-fashioned person, and I happen to believe in traditional marriage. But the Court has ruled, and we have to accept it. Just because somebody doesn't think the way I do, it doesn't mean I can't care about them or I can't love them. If one of my daughters happened to be gay, of course I would accept her, of course I would love her. That's what we're taught when we have strong faith. And I've got to tell you, issues like that are planted to divide us, but let's treat everybody with respect, and let them share in the great American dream we have here in this country. I'll love my daughters no matter what they do, because God gives me unconditional love, and I'm gonna give it to my family and my friends and the people around me." (For what it's worth, Emma was watching the debate, and it occurred to her that her friends might think we were talking about *her*, so she took the time to set the record straight and tweeted, "I am not gay.")

People all across the country responded to my comments, and in a vacuum, that might have been the all-important headline we needed to propel my candidacy forward from that first debate. Yet that was not the way of things this election year, when the noise and nonsense seemed to get all the attention.

Speaking of that noise and nonsense, when I started telling people I was working on this book, one of my friends joked that I should call it *Fear and Goading on the Campaign Trail*, in a nod to the gonzo journalist Hunter S. Thompson and his classic book about the 1972 presidential campaign, *Fear and Loathing on the Campaign*

*Trail.* I took his point, because at times it felt like *most* of my fellow candidates were spending *most* of their time stoking the fears of voters and goading one another, instead of exchanging ideas and focusing on the issues.

## FINDING AN EDGE

When I talk to people around the country about the campaign, there's a lot of emphasis on the debates, and they're often surprised when I tell them the debates weren't that important to us. Oh, they were essential—*elemental,* even—but not in the ways most people think.

Here I believe it helps to realize that the candidates had a very different perspective on the debates than the general public. The debates were mostly media events, and didn't really reflect what was going on while we were out there on the trail. In this way, they were more akin to sporting events than to political gatherings. The settings for some of the debates only reinforced this comparison. Typically, they were held in downtown arenas or on college campuses. Just getting to the venue was a lot like going to a stadium before a game, and there was always a row of news and satellite trucks outside. A lot of times, there'd also be temporary sets and mobile studios built in the middle the road, or on plazas in the shadow of the venue, and you could usually find vendors selling campaign merchandise and souvenirs, and protestors and supporters lined up in protest or support of this or that candidate.

We'd make our way in through a back door, and be assigned to a dressing room or green room. In New Hampshire, we were sent to a locker room. For the CNN debate in Las Vegas, we were in a theater at the Venetian that had been built to house a production of *The Phantom of the Opera*, where we were given a dressing room that had been customized for a country music star, complete with a marble bathroom and shower. In Houston, we were put in the office of a music professor, so there was a grand piano.

The locker room was especially appropriate, we all thought, because you weren't allowed to talk to your team during the run of the debates, just like tennis players aren't allowed to receive coaching during a match. However, not all the candidates followed this rule—at least, not all the time. Perhaps the most notorious violator was the eventual Republican nominee, and I mention it here not to grouse or throw shade, but to give readers an inside perspective. It turned out there was a bit of a loophole in this restriction, because Donald Trump was in a different position than most of the other candidates. Why? Because he had Secret Service protection. The way it works is that any candidate can request Secret Service protection, which is then assessed and assigned based on a perceived threat level. President Obama, for example, was given Secret Service protection during the 2008 campaign, before the Democratic convention. Once you've received the official nomination of your party, of course, you're automatically assigned a Secret Service detail, which doesn't go away until after the election. (If you're elected president, you receive Secret Service protection for life.) Before each party's convention, it's offered on a case-by-case basis, by request—and here, too, it doesn't go away until you're out of the race.

In this election cycle, on the Republican side of the campaign, both Donald Trump and Ben Carson had Secret Service protection. We didn't want it, or feel we needed it—in part because it's a hassle, but mostly because I was already being protected by the Ohio Highway Patrol. A lot of my fellow candidates felt the same way, especially those who were sitting governors. But the protection allowed a candidate's campaign team unfettered access to their candidate, even during a debate, so on at least one occasion during one of the Fox News debates, you could see a Trump adviser sidle up to Trump's lectern during a commercial break, where they were presumably going over notes and discussing strategy. The other campaigns took note of this, and a number of candidates complained about it. So, during the next commercial break, the Fox News producer lifted the "no coaching" restriction on the rest of us, to level the playing field.

Eventually, the RNC intervened and arranged with United States Secret Service officials to issue five special lapel pins for each candidate to distribute to campaign staffers. The pins effectively acted as passes, allowing wearers to be in the proximity of the "protectee" candidate at all times. The idea was that we still weren't supposed to be in communication with members of our team, but at least now there was equity in terms of access, and we were all able to move about a little more freely as we made our way with our campaign teams into and out of these debate venues.

As readers will probably remember, that first debate in Cleveland offered a bad taste of what was to come. As I stood there on my end of the stage, I couldn't believe what I was hearing. Still, I stuck to our game plan and tried to stay out of the fray and keep my campaign on message. There was some sniping among the other candidates, together with some name-calling and chest-thumping and finger-pointing. It all set a negative tone, and the decorum of the debates would go downhill from here. Yet, as I left the stage, I thought it had gone well enough—for me, at least. It wasn't exactly a rousing night for our party, or for our country, and I hadn't gotten a lot of questions thrown to me over there in Siberia, but I had to think my answer on gay marriage, together with another response to a question on Medicaid, would help to position me as the voice of reason, especially when it was set against all those voices of unreason coming from that debate stage.

Almost immediately, we started to see a shift in how I was being perceived, just on the back of a few answers to a few questions. From that point forward, it was more and more about people and doing the right thing and taking good care of each other, and less and less about economics and experience. Don't misunderstand me, the economy and my time in Washington and as governor were still at the core of everything I talked about, but after that first debate in Cleveland, I tried to connect with people in a more personal way. By the response of the media, social *and* traditional, I was encouraged to start being myself and to stop trying to sound like the politicians I'd grown up admiring.

This shift in focus didn't happen right away, of course. I think it took me awhile to respond to it, but that first debate marked a kind of turning point for me. It was on that stage in Cleveland that I started to realize that the issues that had brought me to the campaign (balanced budgets, tax cuts, paying down the debt) were not the issues that were going to drive this election. No, for me at least, this campaign would be one of connectedness—and the shift came about, I think, as a kind of reaction to the negativity all around me. I've always tried to be a positive person, and as a leader, I've looked for ways to fill the spaces between our differences. Yet, there, in the toxic, antagonistic environment that had already begun to permeate the campaign season, people were responding to something in my demeanor, in my message.

And my demeanor, my message, could only respond in kind.

# 7.

# A Crisis of *Followship*

We live in a strange time, and we're still getting used to the strangeness of it.

That's another all-time understatement, I know, but this feels like a good spot in the narrative to consider how these strange times might have come about, how they might have impacted the 2016 presidential campaign, what they might mean for us as a country going forward, and what we might do to set things right, if we're so inclined.

Let's start with the media: It used to be that we got our news and analysis from the three major networks and from our major newspapers and local radio stations. There was a standard of objectivity in the news media that wasn't always adhered to, but it was nevertheless a standard, something to shoot for. Journalists aspired to a level of fair-mindedness, and on the back of these aspirations, the American public became conditioned to expect at least the semblance of balanced reporting from members of the "fourth estate." Granted, objectivity was sometimes hard to find; newspapers leaned liberal or conservative, Democratic or Republican, this way or that. Still, you could usually count on a somewhat accurate interpretation of events, with notes and comments and inside analysis from both sides of an issue. That's not the case anymore. With the advent of social media (the "fifth estate") and the fracturing of our mainstream news organizations, there has been a sea change in the ways we keep one another informed, and I am not alone in believing that this shift is at the heart of all this strangeness.

There's a chicken-and-egg phenomenon at work here: it's tough to say which came first, the decline in the breadth and scope of our traditional news coverage or the growing disinterest in that traditional coverage. You could make the argument either way. What's clear is that network news budgets are down because viewership is down. What's clear is that newspapers are folding or are cutting back on publication because advertising revenues are down. (In some cities, the one or two surviving "daily" newspapers no longer publish a print edition seven days a week, giving new meaning to the term *daily*, I guess.)

As a result, viewers and readers are looking at fewer, more efficient ways of staying informed. What that can mean for a lot of viewers and readers, though, is they wind up getting misinformed. They know less because they seek to know less; they believe they know all there is to know because the news outlets they choose to follow keep telling them their deeply held opinions are right and good and true.

As I look at today's news media environment, I see it as the Wild, Wild West, where anything goes and nothing is sacred. These days, many Americans also seem to want to get their news and information from a reinforcing media—meaning, from news organizations inclined to tell them what they want to hear or what they already think they know. When did this happen? How did this happen? And why is it suddenly okay for liberals, say, to read only certain newspapers or follow certain websites? Or for conservatives to watch a certain type of newscast, or listen to talk radio hosts who share their perspective? When did we become so entrenched in our thinking that there's no longer any room in that worldview for a differing opinion?

Now, let's set our changing media landscape aside and take a look at how a great many Americans have started to move about that landscape with a post-truth worldview. These days, many of us tend to live in our own little media silos, and what results for dominance of widespread narrowcasting is a society of widespread narrow thinking. It becomes harder and harder for people to open their minds or broaden their views, because they want to be reinforced in their beliefs instead of challenged in them. They'll listen only to those analysts and talking heads who share their point of view, or reaffirm that view in some way, instead of talking heads who challenged that view and maybe open them up to new ideas. They're not open to a difference of opinion or even to the idea of questioning an opinion, because they've set their own opinion in stone. This is a dangerous thing, and it's especially dangerous when there are deep-pocketed, media-savvy candidates on the campaign trail peddling those same set-in-stone tablets. They're out there yelling at us, telling us that they're right and we're wrong, and that the only way forward is to fall in line behind them.

When we silo ourselves in this way, when we surround ourselves only with affirming views and selective reporting and analysis, we become more and more convinced that our way is the only way. We become intolerant of other people's opinions or alternative approaches. In a post-truth environment, where utter falsehoods have become the order of the day, we give no quarter to any politician who doesn't line up with us on each and every issue, at each and every moment; whose "facts" don't confirm the "facts" we've created for ourselves; and who stands in conflict with the ways we've chosen to feel. With this kind of narrow outlook, there is no room for compromise or negotiation. Indeed, elected officials who reach across the aisle and look for common ground are viewed as sellouts, as are candidates who might pivot to embrace an opponent's idea. What we're left with is a system where very few politicians are willing to risk the anger of the electorate and be defeated for bending to achieve a compromise. As a result, nothing gets done. There's gridlock all around.

When politicians carve out safe seats for themselves, they find no room to maneuver in those seats because their base won't tolerate it. It's a real toxic mix, and we need to shine a light on it and hope people start paying attention.

Relatedly, let's look at how the constant gerrymandering of our voting system only reinforces this problem of a fractured media and a stubborn electorate. Politicians delineate what they think are safe districts for their party, but then there are all these watchdogs out there, making sure those very same politicians don't step from the narrow party lines they themselves have drawn. It used to be, if you got elected in what was traditionally a conservative or liberal district, you could go to work each day and fight to bring about change for the common good without worrying you'd be voted out of office if you took a position a little outside party lines. But as the political map keeps getting redrawn, those "safe" seats have swiveled, and now we have a situation where politicians are looking over their shoulders constantly, concerned about their jobs. If you're a Republican, you have to look to your right; if you're a Democrat, you have to look to your left. If anybody tries to reach a compromise, he's called out and hammered for it by the folks who sit at home in their news silos and monitor their partisan news sources as if it's some sort of hobby. And whatever deeply held points of view these politicians *deeply held* going into it are now etched even deeper in their thinking.

Let's not forget that this type of redistricting has been going on in this country since the nineteenth century. Gerrymandering itself is nothing new. The term itself dates to 1812, when it was coined by a Boston newspaper in reaction to a partisan redistricting bill signed by Massachusetts governor Elbridge Gerry. (When considered on a map, one of the districts whose redrawing Gerry was responsible for looked like a salamander.) What's new is that the reach of social media has ratcheted up the stakes, while the immediacy of our information age pushes party leaders to reexamine district lines at every opportunity. In the old days, politicians could take a risky position on an issue and there'd be time for that position to succeed or fail on its own merits. The court of public opinion had a long rope. But today, everybody watches every move every elected official makes, at all times, to the point where if you dare take a risky position, you'll be challenged on it immediately. You'll have to worry about a primary. In all my time in Congress, I never really worried too much about the primaries. It was always the general election that had me concerned, but if I was doing a good job, I knew I could count on the support of voters in my own party. That's not the case anymore, is it? Now we seem to have made it harder for the elected official who's out there trying to bring about meaningful change to keep his or her seat, and easier for an outsider insurgent candidate who's merely pushing all the right buttons to take that seat away from him.

Yet, even today, there are strong leaders in government who stand against these challenges. They'll say, "Bring it on!" And good for them—many of them manage to hold on to their seats and withstand the attacks against them. Still, it's no fun being attacked. It's not easy for your spouse and children to have to hear that you're a sellout or a fraud, or that you can't do the right thing because you're concerned about your job. There's no dishonor in trying to do what you can to keep your job. Who do you know in your life who doesn't try to keep his job? How many people march into their boss's office and tell him he's wrong and that they're going to start working against him? But politics is unusual, and if you seek a life of public service, you must continually ask yourself, "What is my purpose? And am I being true to myself and my principles?"

What seemed to have tilted in the post-truth presidential election cycle of 2016 was the emergence of news stories that had no merit to them—the persistent drumbeat of the nonstory. Just look at the proliferation of "fake news" circulating on the Internet—the websites and blog posts and nontraditional media reports that tease us with wild headlines from unreliable sources, stories that are nevertheless shared and cited as if they were objectively reported and second-sourced and vetted according to traditional news standards. I'm not suggesting here that people shouldn't make an effort to keep informed, or to share what they know or believe they know with friends and contacts in their social networks. It is a good and welcome thing when you can access a world of information on the Internet. Still, what a lot of voters failed to recognize this time around was that this news-gathering business is a two-way transaction. We can't just disseminate fabricated bits and pieces of propped-up "news" and believe we have somehow contributed to the national conversation. We can't read a comment or a headline on Facebook and Twitter and share it or retweet it without considering the source. We need to understand that we now live in a world where we are not only consumers of news media but participants in the dissemination of news and information as well. A sense of responsibility ought to come along with that participation, don't you think? We ought to take the time to understand where the news we choose to share is coming from. Is it a firsthand account? From a reliable source? Is it even a recognizable source? Are there other people or organizations out there corroborating it?

Another troubling trend that seemed to surface during this election cycle was the way the media was fixated on profits and ratings. Our twenty-four-hour news engine must be fueled constantly, yet our news organizations can't keep from filling that cycle up with stories that are popular to readers and viewers. How do they know what's popular? By the number of times we repost or recirculate the stories on social media. I got so frustrated at the imbalance in some of the reporting I saw during the campaign that I called a network news executive I knew to vent about it. I urged him to follow his values and his conscience, to tune out the voices trying to tell him he should be chasing profits and ratings. And you know what? Instead of telling me to buzz off and mind my own business, he thanked me for the call. He said he appreciated it very much, and admitted that it was a challenge to keep viewers watching his broadcast when so many of them believed they could get their news and information from the Internet.

During the 2016 presidential race, throughout the debates and primaries and on through the general election, you could see candidates in both parties playing to these narrow points of view and to these silo-reinforcing news organizations. They were relying on them, in fact, because they knew that, in the harsh light of objective media scrutiny, the public just might have realized that there was no *there* there, that people might start to look elsewhere for someone to lead them out of the muddle.

What happens when you have all these candidates telling voters only what they want them to hear? It closes people's minds instead of opening them. It contributes to the polarization of our culture, because the checks and balances that used to buttress our news organizations are no longer in place.

What happens over time when people tune in to a news channel already knowing what they're about to hear? When people have closed themselves off from a different outcome or possibility? Well, for one thing, it puts an end to an all-important national discussion on the issues before such a discussion has a chance to happen. For another thing, it encourages media outlets to look to drive their ratings or subscription renewals with incendiary reporting that merely reinforces what their viewers or readers already believe— and then it's just a race toward the bottom line.

This drives us down when what we need is to be lifted up, pushed forward, moved along the path to what's possible.

## THE GAME HAS CHANGED

Like a lot of folks who care about such things, I was aware of this seismic shift in the way we communicate and share ideas with one another, but only in a sidelong way. In my sheepish defense, I wasn't paying good and close attention to how the information silos can impact political campaigns—probably because they'd had yet to impact one of my political campaigns. When you're trying to run a great state like Ohio, or represent the voters in your district in Congress, you're not paying attention to who's yelling the loudest or who in the media is giving you favorable coverage. Your focus is on leading the good people who voted you into office, not on trying to convince them to return you to office when your time is up.

I should mention here that in my two runs for governor, which both took place in our social media age, the ground hadn't fully shifted beneath my feet. The Ohio media tended to do a good and fair-minded job of covering those races—which, though conten-tious, never quite lapsed into the narrow-mindedness (or the *single*-mindedness) we sometimes saw during the 2016 presiden-tial campaign. So, a lot of my observations here on the fracturing of our media didn't really apply. However, years from now, gen-erations from now, I believe we'll look back on this election as a kind of tipping point, a dividing line. There will be everything we once knew on one side, and all this stuff we've yet to process on the other. Historians will scratch their heads and wonder what the heck was going on with us in this election year.

Still, I'm not out to sound the call of doom and gloom, or to sug-gest that the 2016 race might have signaled the last gasp of our American way of life. I'll leave it to others to put that kind of nega-tive spin on things. Sure, I'm distressed at the ways our supposed or would-be leaders have taken to treating one another. Absolutely, I worry for my kids' future, for my country's future. Like many of you, I find the tone and tenor of our political discourse deeply troubling—and hardly presidential. And I'm distressed at the bias and lack of preparedness on the part of many journalists and media organ-izations, who, with their election coverage, should have placed the public interest ahead of their ratings and readership concerns.

I choose to see the good in people and in our institutions, and to look for light and hope where others see only darkness and de-spair. I look at the gerrymandering of our political system, and what we can also regard as the resulting gerrymandering of our news media, and know that we can find a way to set things right. We must. And the way to do so is for leaders of both parties to come together and take a look at redistricting in a bipartisan way, to reimagine the map of our shifting electorate so that it might speak for the good of our states and our country, instead of for the good of whichever party happens to be in the majority at the time.

The game has changed, that's all. There's a new playbook yet to be written, although I have to think that by the 2020 presidential election, that playbook will no longer apply. The game will have changed yet again. But the good of America stands at our nation's core, and it will continue to stand at its core. To paraphrase Alexis de Tocqueville, America is great because America is good. That's a line I echoed in my remarks when I suspended my campaign on May 4, 2016, just a day after Texas senator Ted Cruz dropped out of the race and left me as the last traditional Republican standing against the populist candidacy of Donald Trump, a man who would go on to win the general election despite trailing in almost every major poll and despite the predictions of almost every pundit and prognosticator in our traditional news silos. For less than twenty-four hours, I was the only mainstream, experienced politician in this man's path to the Republican Party nomination for president of the United States—a position most of my opponents could never have imagined when I became the sixteenth candidate to enter the race the previous summer. Back then, I was all but counted out before I was fully counted in.

How did *that* happen? Well, for now, let me tell you how it *didn't* happen. It didn't happen that I'd raised a bunch more money than all the other variously qualified, variously experienced candidates; and it didn't happen that I'd won a bunch more delegates than they did, either. It didn't happen that my voice was just a little louder, or that my ideas connected with a greater percentage of Republican voters. And it certainly didn't happen that I was running second in a kind of war of attrition, and had succeeded merely in outlasting the rest of the field.

Here's my take: it happened that there was a crisis of *followship* in this country, and we were all caught in its swirl. It's a crisis we'll probably face for the next while. I'm betting you've never heard the term *followship* before, because I think I just came up with it. I was setting these thoughts to paper, trying to address what a lot of folks commonly refer to as a crisis of leadership in this country, and wondering if there was some way to understand the strangeness of this past election in this context, when it occurred to me that what we were facing was just the opposite of a leadership crisis. To be sure, there were good and qualified candidates in the presidential field, and I like to think I was one of them. There were good and qualified leaders in Congress, in our statehouses, in our local communities. So, it's not that there weren't good and qualified people out there, willing and able to lead us in government. And it might just turn out that President Trump is able to lead this country in a positive way. As I write this, at the front end of his presidency, I'm hoping he's going to do a great job. He is, after all, our president, and it's in our shared national interest to try to lift him up and see him succeed, instead of dragging him down and waiting for him to fail.

No, there was a crisis of *followship* because candidates like Donald Trump tapped a wellspring of anger and pain and frustration among voters who were already entrenched in their own little silos, taking in only the news and information they needed to feed that anger and pain and frustration. Prominent Republicans who at another time in our history might have stood in opposition to Trump, or even questioned him or pushed him to discuss his policies, were reluctant to do so because they worried Trump's followers might turn against them. This was reinforcement of a kind, but there were other reinforcements all around. Voters found reinforcement in their self-selected media, and in their social networks—the ones on the Internet and the ones they'd knitted together in their day-to-day lives. They found it in the like-minded people they worked with, socialized with, compared notes with. It came from friends and family who probably shared a lot of the same anger, a lot of the same pain, a lot of the same frustrations. And then it all kind of folded in on itself and grew to where we as a nation didn't quite know whom to follow or what to believe or how to move the nation forward.

## DON'T JUST FOLLOW THE LEADER

I've spent a lot of time thinking about what it means to lead and what it means to follow, and how the two roles are connected, both in the context of the campaign and in the world around us. I've seen how government works, and how organizations work (including the U.S. Congress)—and now how presidential elections work— so, I want to offer up my observations on what it takes to move *any* enterprise forward.

1) You need to be a leader with a vision—a vision that excites people, challenges people, and offers the promise of a bright future.
2) That vision needs to be something that can take people to a better place and make them feel as though that place is not only right and good but that it can give the entire organization a lift.
3) The leader needs to develop a team. I found this out in Congress, where you need to bring people together if you hope to get anything done. I've even seen this as governor, where I've learned that a carefully assembled team of dedicated individuals can accomplish great

things. This one might seem obvious, but we've all
encountered a leader or a would-be leader who be-
lieves he or she can go it alone.

4) You must acknowledge that a leader needs followers,
but not just *any* followers. You need followers to assent
to the direction the leader lays out, with a willingness to
follow in that direction. If all you've got are a bunch
of subordinates who shrug their shoulders and say
they can't accomplish the task in front of them—well,
then you're doomed to fail. Conversely, if all you've
got are people willing to follow a leader blindly and
fall into lockstep behind him or her—well, then you're
also doomed. It isn't always easy to achieve a leader's
vision, but there must be agreement among the followers that the goal is within reach.

5) From among the followers, there must emerge a group
of leaders. These are the ballplayers in the locker room
who support the coach's direction. These are the soldiers who help to rally the troops in the general's absence. These are the department heads looking to
bring their units in line. Sometimes it works out that
the followers become tired or disillusioned or even
disgruntled, but, to reiterate, the system breaks down
when all you have are mindless followers who merely
go through the motions laid out for them by a leader.

6) Within each group, you must have a few disruptors.
The purpose here is to have people in place who might
question authority, not challenge it. You're not looking
for a contrary view, or someone out to advance his or
her own agenda. What you seek is constructive criticism, not destructive criticism. What you require are

other sets of eyes and insights to complement your own.

7) An effective leader must keep reinforcing the message, keep laying out the vision, keep inspiring the followers. You cannot simply flip a switch and trust the effort to move forward without a gentle (and sometimes not-so-gentle) push every now and then.

8) Finally, an effective leader must constantly drive the team. It's not enough to set out a vision and recruit good followers and expect others to implement that vision on your behalf. It's not enough to accommodate a disruptive point of view, and to remind your team of the importance of your shared mission. You must keep ever vigilant, make course corrections when necessary, and redeploy your team members as needed.

In sum, if you expect to be a good, strong leader, you need good, strong followers. Here, I believe that we're coming out of an election cycle where we came up a little short on both ends of the equation. Yes, there were responsible news outlets doing a responsible job of fact-checking the trumped-up claims coming out of the campaigns, but there was no one to fact-check the fake news stories circulating like brush fires across the Internet. And there was no one to check the runaway egos of some of the candidates, or maybe to steer them toward a more hopeful, more helpful, more presidential strategy. This, of course, only reinforced the destructive tone of the campaign.

Meanwhile, on the media side of the equation, with news outlets disinclined to challenge the candidates most in favor with their particular subset of viewers or readers, it seemed to many that there was no place to turn for thorough, objective election coverage.

Lead, follow, or get out of the way—that's an oft-quoted line you're likely to find in quite a lot of bestselling leadership and management books, and on inspirational posters tacked to dorm room and locker room walls. It comes from a comment first attributed to General George S. Patton: "We herd sheep, we drive cattle, we lead people. Lead me, follow me, or get out of my way."

But in a divided society, followers cannot merely follow. They must lead as well. They must, from time to time, stand as disruptors, who of course have their place in any organization. To succeed, a leadership team needs buy-in across the board, but organizations fail when leaders are conditioned to expect blind loyalty from their followers. Therefore, I believe it's healthy for an organization to have whistle-blowers in its ranks, folks who call attention to something that just doesn't make sense or doesn't seem right. That said, you can't have disruptors running an organization, but they need to be acknowledged and accommodated.

When I put together my administration as governor, I made sure to surround myself with people who shared the spirit of my vision for the state of Ohio, but who would also have the strength of character to argue with me if they thought I was straying from that vision. A smart leader is willing to listen to a voice of dissent, to really consider it. If you build your organization with a bunch of yes-men, people who go along to get along, the enterprise will collapse. That's kind of what happened over at Wells Fargo, where they had all these people creating all these phony accounts to generate fees—although, in fairness, there were later reports that certain employees were trying to put a stop to the practice. Still, at the highest levels, nobody had the guts to stand up and say what they were doing was unethical for the longest time, until someone finally did and the company was taken to task.

The more I think about it, the more I look at ways to attach the term *followship* to our current state of affairs in politics, the more I realize that a crisis in *followship* is exactly what we're facing. We as followers need to demand that our leaders actually do something when we elect them to office. We don't vote them in just to continue the stalemate that's taken shape in Washington and in some of our state and local governments. No, we need them to put forward new ideas, and to start working to advance those ideas.

Congress is a very dysfunctional organization these days. It didn't used to be. When I was there, we could figure out ways to get things done. We could vote on the budget, say, or on trade agreements, and we'd come at the given issue from opposing positions and find a way to meet in the middle—or not, but we would at least have at it.

Nobody seems to want to have at it anymore, and this is a worrisome thing.

Look, I'm no social historian or political analyst, but I believe in my bones that a crisis of *followship* played a role in the 2016 presidential campaign, and it seemed to flow from the disintegration of our news media and the shared unwillingness of many American voters to consider viewpoints outside their own. It all ties in. I believe that we looked up one day and found ourselves in this mess, saw that a wellspring of frustration had bubbled up and boiled over. Now we can only look inward and to one another to set things right. We can't look to Washington to fix this for us. Our state and local governments can't help us, either.

We can only help ourselves by falling in behind the good and qualified folks who continue to want to work for the public good.

I'm not suggesting that our news organizations aren't a little bit broken; they are, and more than a little, in some cases. And I'm not suggesting that we need to check America's pulse and make sure we're still breathing—although we might want to rethink the ways we take America's temperature during a close, contentious election, with an overreliance on polling measures that fail to calculate human error alongside traditional margins of error. And I'm not suggesting that we need giant news monoliths to keep us informed. Not at all. But we do need to climb out of our silos and take a good look at the world around us. We do need to consider points of view other than our own. We do need to consider the source of an inflammatory story or statement before reflexively sending it along to our fellow followers, ones who already share our fixed point of view. We do need to insist that our leaders speak the truth, and we need to hold them accountable when they don't. We do need to take particular care before we buy into the slickly packaged (and, frankly, not so slickly packaged) rhetoric of those who would lead us down a dangerous path.

Most important, we do need to talk to one another, compare notes, find points of connection in the issues of the campaign, and do our own due diligence to determine which of the candidates has our back.

A crisis of *followship*? It's as good an explanation as any, and I have to believe this crisis will pass. It must. Because good leaders need good followers, people to step up and become leaders themselves, working in support of a shared, hopeful future. Because when we fall in lockstep behind purported leaders who feed us lies and distortions that we no longer recognize as lies and distortions— well, then we can only walk in darkness.

And why walk in darkness when there is light all around?

With my parents and siblings in 1961, dressed in our Sunday best. *(Photo courtesy of author)*

With my girls, Reese and Emma, on the campaign trail. *(Photo courtesy of Doug Preisse)*

Meeting President Nixon in the White House while I was a student at the Ohio State University. *(Photo courtesy of author)*

I returned to Ohio State, where in many ways it all started, to announce my candidacy for president. *(Photo courtesy of Kasich for America)*

On the elevator with some of my senior staff: John Weaver, Beth Hansen, and Chris Schrimpf. *(Photo courtesy of Kasich for America)*

Arriving to a warm welcome on a cold New Hampshire night, with Karen and the girls. *(Photo courtesy of Kasich for America)*

Watching the results of the Ohio primary with lifelong friend Don Thibaut. *(Photo courtesy of Doug Preisse)*

John Sununu *(left)* convinced me that I should take our message to New Hampshire, where former senator Gordon Humphrey *(right)* became an ardent supporter. *(Photo courtesy of Kasich for America)*

San Diego town hall. We took the campaign around the country. *(Photo courtesy of Kasich for America)*

Colonel Thomas Moe was a "roommate" of John McCain's in the "Hanoi Hilton" and has been an example of perseverance and faith to me and many others. *(Photo courtesy of Kasich for America)*

One of my favorite shots from the campaign: this young man, who was fighting cancer, was attracted to our message and stopped by for a visit on the bus in New Hampshire. *(Photo courtesy of Doug Preisse)*

Newport, Rhode Island, town hall. *(Photo courtesy of Kasich for America)*

Bedford was the site of our one hundredth town hall, a New Hampshire primary record. *(Photo courtesy of Kasich for America)*

Seeking solace on the trail: a reflective moment at St. Paul's Church, Concord, New Hampshire. *(Photo courtesy of Doug Preisse)*

I love this "backstage" photo from the American Israel Public Affairs Committee Conference in Washington, DC. The response to our hopeful message of consanguinity with Israel was amazing. *(Photo courtesy of Kasich for America)*

The spin room after the first Republican presidential debate, in Cleveland. As you can see, the eyes of the national media were upon us. *(Photo courtesy of Kasich for America)*

On a snowy primary eve in New Hampshire, several hundred people turned out for a stirring rally at Robie's Country Store. Spirits were high. The temperature? Not so much. *(Photo courtesy of Kasich for America)*

Delivering the "Two Paths" speech, April 12, 2016, at the Women's National Republican Club in New York City. *(Photo courtesy of Kasich for America)*

# 8.

# On the Trail

When you run for president, you're bound by the map and the calendar. I'm stating the obvious, I know, but I can't stress this enough. Most of your decisions (where to campaign, how much to spend on advertising, when to shift your focus to another part of the country) are driven by the upcoming primaries and caucuses, which are, for the most part, scheduled years in advance and which tend to follow the same pattern each election cycle.

When you run for Congress, or campaign for governor, your schedule is more fluid, more manageable, more predictable. You move about your district in ways that make sense, or travel the state to events and appearances that will help to get your message to voters in a meaningful way. You can limit travel, if you're on a tight budget, target your advertising in such a way that it doesn't break your campaign, keep your staffing costs to a minimum, and still reach out to voters in viable ways.

A national campaign is a whole other ball game, though—and it fell to my team to focus on all these big-picture logistics. My focus had to be elsewhere. For one thing, I had a day job. The people of Ohio had just reelected me governor, so my first order of business was to keep our state thrumming. Every day, throughout the day, wherever I was, I thought in some way about what was going on in Ohio. For me, that was job one. Running for president was a different sort of priority; it was job two. Oh, I was deeply committed to it, but I had an obligation to my home state that I meant to honor, so I set out on the campaign trail with one eye on the home front and one eye on the road.

As far as the campaign itself was concerned, it was up to me to bring my message to voters, to *campaign,* while it was up to my team to keep the lights on in our effort, to schedule my events, and to make sure I got to them on time and then got back to Ohio often enough to make sure things were moving forward at home.

It's kind of interesting the way the whole operation came together, and I was blessed to have some enormously talented, abundantly experienced and endlessly devoted people working with me. I trusted them implicitly, which was why I was able to concentrate on the message while they worried over the best ways to communicate that message. Most of the heavy lifting on a day-to-day basis fell to my campaign manager, Beth Hansen, and she was all over it. She'd wake up each morning and start in on making sure all the members of our team were pointed in the right direction, our comings and goings all arranged. Then she'd sort through the headlines from the night before and plug into what was going on with all the other candidates—basically, assess what was going on politically as it may have impacted our efforts. She was the one who stretched every dollar as far as it would go, made sure we had the cash on hand to pay our bills, and kept thinking two and six and twelve steps ahead.

Beth and I were talking one night and she described her job as like being in the ocean, getting pummeled by giant waves. You'd get knocked down and fumble around underwater for a while, and then you'd finally scramble to your feet and catch your breath. But then there'd be another wave, and you'd have to fight your way to the surface all over again. The waves just kept on coming.

We'd set our sights on the New Hampshire primary, on February 9, 2016, but then, right after that, we had South Carolina on February 20, and Michigan on March 8, and right on to Super Tuesday after that. As soon as you got through one, you'd have to concentrate on the next one, and it just so happened that this election, the primaries were running on a tighter schedule, with more multistate primary days than ever before. Why? Well, in 2012, and in previous presidential election years, the Republican National Convention was held later in the summer. Remember, Mitt Romney didn't formally receive the party's nomination until the last week in August 2012, even though he'd essentially clinched it in late May. Even before that, he'd had a commanding lead in the delegate count, with the nomination looking all but certain. Still, it was extremely difficult for him to fund his campaign during this intervening period, before the convention and the financial support of the party that came with it kicked in, so one of the things that came out of that frustration was a more compressed schedule for 2016.

This put the 2016 Republican National Convention in the middle of July, so a lot of things were pushed ahead. Essentially, we solved one problem and created a whole bunch of others. Most of those had to do with the fact that there was now less time for us candidates to catch our breaths between primaries, to sprinkle in events in states where the voting wouldn't happen until late in the cycle. So, all those moving parts I talked about earlier seemed to move a whole lot faster than anyone on our team could remember—and all those waves Beth was talking about, they kept rolling toward us.

You can't imagine the size and scope of the effort. It was

impossible for any one person to get a handle on it. We had to set up a headquarters office, and local offices around the country, and each of these had to be staffed. We put together a whole social media team, which was now considered an essential component of an effective campaign, and social media *wasn't even a thing* when I first ran for Congress in 1982. Come to think of it, it wasn't even a thing when I *last* ran for Congress, in 1998. But the world had changed, and now I had to listen in on conversations about buying Google ads and getting a Snapchat filter and making sure our official Twitter account was verified. Half the time, I had no idea what we were talking about.

Most of our money went to candidate travel, which of course didn't cover just *my* travel, but that of my entire team. Early on, we leased a fitted-out tour bus that had been used most recently by Lady Antebellum, the well-known country music group out of Nashville. It cost a bunch of money, about $25,000 a month, and that was before we had to pay a full-time driver and cover gas and tolls. But we figured out it would be more cost-effective to travel to all the various events by bus, where there'd be room to accommodate different members of my campaign team on a last-minute basis. Forget that we got to travel the country in a bus that had been fitted out for a bunch of musicians; you could get a lot of work done as you motored from event to event. And once we pulled into town, the bus did a lot of business for us. People would stop by, pose for pictures alongside it—it became a real iconic image of our campaign. On most days, we'd ride six or seven hundred miles in it, so it became a tremendous traveling billboard for us. After a while, we started calling it the "4 Us Bus," named for our "Kasich 4 Us" campaign slogan.

When we'd leave the Northeast for the Midwest or the South, our core traveling group would fly and the bus would meet us there. So, at the front end of the campaign, we were never away from the bus for long.

I wasn't the only candidate with a tricked-out tour bus, but none of the others seemed to get the same mileage out of their setup. Donald Trump had a bus, of course, and it was probably the *best* bus, but as far as I could tell, he never set foot in it. His people would drive it around to events, and in some spots, they used it as a mobile voter registration site. That was smart; we did a little bit of that, too. Still, we really got our money's worth out of that thing. We'd take meetings in it. We'd invite folks on board. Sometimes, we'd even work out in it. That was always a big concern of mine when we were on the road: finding time each day to do some meaningful exercise. If we had some time between events, I'd get some of our staff together on the bus and we'd do some planking, which was about all you could really do in that aisle. Turns out you can really work on your core when you're planking, so my core was in great shape by the time we were through. We kept a basketball on board, and whenever we found ourselves with some free time and a hoop nearby, we'd be playing. And even if we had only a few minutes, I'd make sure I never missed an opportunity to hit some golf balls.

Very quickly, the bus became a kind of clubhouse for our team, a place to unwind at the end of each long day. And let me tell you, some of those days were *long*! We'd get going at about eight o'clock each morning and be running until ten or eleven o'clock at night. Typically, we'd do three or four town halls each day, with a lunch event and media appearances slotted in throughout the day. Most evenings, there'd be a fund-raising dinner, too. At night, we'd unwind on the bus with a bottle or two of wine, which for some reason we took to calling Wayne, as in "Where's the Wayne?" For the life of me, I can't tell you how *that* started, but that became shorthand whenever it was time to kick back and unwind and set aside the events of the day.

We ate a lot of Cape Cod potato chips, as I recall, and listened to a lot of Justin Bieber, Pink Floyd, and Twenty One Pilots, the duo out of Columbus that's fronted by Tyler Joseph, a young man who'd gone to my daughters' high school, Worthington Christian. (Oh, man, we just loved those guys, and not *just* because it felt to us like we had a rooting interest in their success.) And we talked deep into the night about popular culture and the Cleveland Cavaliers. I remember one particularly heated discussion about whether the music or the lyric was more important to a song, and in case you're interested, we were pretty evenly split on this one. We would snack on the bus, but we wouldn't take our meals there—that was one of our rules of the road—which meant we ate at a lot of local joints. We'd try to get recommendations from the local campaign volunteers, but every once in a while, we'd have to pull in to a fast-food place, or take our chances on a random restaurant that happened to be open late enough to accommodate us. Once, after an impromptu meal at one such restaurant in Iowa, our entire team got sick from something everybody had eaten—everybody, that is, except me. I didn't eat anything—try as I might, I *couldn't* eat anything. The place we'd wandered into was one of those generic-looking restaurants, with every different type of food, and my meal tasted terrible. I thought I was better off going hungry, but when I pushed my plate aside, Doug Preisse had the presence of mind to suggest that someone at our table ought to eat it, because we didn't want the waiters and kitchen staff thinking we didn't like their food. After all, people knew who we were; there were reporters following us around. We didn't want to put it out there that the food at the place was lousy, so Doug ate his meal and most of mine, too. Alex helped out a little as well, and by the time we got to the airport to fly out that night, everybody in our group was doubled over.

(I'll usually eat anything, but this was one time I was saved by my discerning palate.)

Oh, and as long as we're on the subject of food, my wife, Karen, was in the habit during the campaign of watching what I ate—*literally*. Let me explain: She was always good about making sure I put my best foot forward while I was out campaigning. I'd been crisscrossing the country, doing all these events, posing for all these pictures, and Karen would be back home in Ohio paying close attention. If she saw something in the press coverage that struck her as *off*, something I could maybe do a little better or avoid doing altogether, she was all over it.

It was in this context that she called me up one evening and said, "John, I really think you should stop eating all these different foods in front of people."

She was right, of course. (She's right about most things, I'll have you know.) What she was responding to were all these photos turning up in the news of me stopping at the locals' favorite haunts, sampling the fare. It's a wonder I didn't pack on the pounds, with all the campaign stops we made at all these different restaurants and state and county fairs. No matter where we went, people wanted me to try the food—and here I'd just been to New York City, where we went to a famous local pizza place and I'd made the mistake of using a knife and fork. In my defense, the pizza had just come out of the oven. It was ridiculously hot. There was no way I could have taken a bite out of the thing without burning the roof of my mouth. Yet, to use a knife and fork on an authentic slice of New York pizza—well, that's a cardinal sin, it seems. And I was teased mercilessly for it—so much so that even Donald Trump weighed in and mocked me for the way I'd eaten the pizza.

He was right to mock me, I'll admit. That's no way to eat a slice of pizza. However, I ended up getting more publicity out of that than I did at any of the other stops we made on that trip to New York. You never know how folks will respond to even the smallest misstep or miscalculation.

With all that food, and all that time sitting on those long bus rides, we had to make an extra effort to get up and move around. We made sure that the hotels we stayed in had halfway decent gyms, so I worked out every morning. If we had a breakfast event, I'd hit the gym extra early and, in the quiet of a (mostly) empty fitness room, do my cardio, lift weights if they had them, and meditate. Those moments alone in a quiet hotel gym were some of the most calming and reflective of the entire campaign—a chance to assess where we were, where we were going, and how we might get there. Then, whenever we'd arrive somewhere ahead of schedule, I'd go out for a long walk. It was a great way to stay in shape and clear my head, and if there was something to discuss with a member of my campaign team, I'd drag him or her along with me for a good old-fashioned "walk 'n' talk." In this way, we kept moving and kept connected. Some of our guys even started running. Chris Schrimpf led the way on this, and before long, he had Doug Preisse out there logging miles right alongside him—a commendable feat, we all thought, and a curious sight, given Doug's disinclination to break a sweat over anything other than unfavorable polling numbers.

And since we were tooling around the country in our rock star tour bus, I figured I was entitled to a couple of perks when we checked into a hotel for the night—only my particular tastes were basic. My team knew to put me in a room far away from the elevator and the ice machine. They knew to call ahead and ask for extra pillows and to make sure I had plenty of water—because, hey, that was just how I rolled.

## UP IN THE AIR

That bus wasn't our only means of transportation of course. We spent a lot of time on planes, and most of that time we'd fly the same plane, with the same crew. Our go-to was a Cessna Citation CJ3. Jetting around the country in a private jet was hardly as glamorous as it sounds. It wasn't nearly as comfortable as the bus. Really, it was like a sardine can in that thing: a seven-seater with just about no headroom if you happened to be over five feet tall. There'd usually be six or seven of us crammed on board: me, Doug, and Chris; my assistant, Alex Thomas; and our digital media guy, Zach Prouty, with room for one or two more if someone from the campaign wanted to travel with us for a stretch, like John Weaver or Beth Hansen.

With a plane that size, we couldn't fly coast to coast, but it was perfect for our typical short hauls. Frequently, we were on and off that plane three or four times a day. Bob Klaffky would travel with us every once in a while, and he remembered one time, when he joined us for the debate in Houston. He arrived the day before the event in Atlanta, and from there we all flew to Gulfport, Mississippi, for a town hall and a fund-raising lunch. Then it was on to New Orleans for an early evening fund-raiser and a Fox News town hall. After that, we hopped back on board the Cessna for the short trip to Houston, where the debate was scheduled for the next day. Four cities, four states, one day.

Poor Bob was exhausted, but then he realized the rest of us

were moving around like that every day, so he really couldn't complain.

We watched a lot of movies on the plane; it was an excellent way to pass the time. On the bus, it was mostly sports; on the plane, mostly movies. It took awhile for us to figure out how to connect one of our laptops to a set of speakers someone had bought so we could all hear the soundtrack, but once we got it going, we'd all look forward to that day's feature. It fell to each of us to take a turn choosing the movie, and we each took the assignment seriously—our downtime was such a precious commodity during the campaign that nobody wanted to squander it. And since we couldn't always agree on such matters, the movie would frequently lead to a discussion on the merits of this or that actor or actress, this or that director. One of our greatest debates came after we'd screened all three *Godfather* movies, and we were split on which one was the best. (Personally, I couldn't decide between *The Godfather* and *The Godfather Part II*; it was a toss-up, really. I tended to regard both movies as of a piece, two parts of one long, epic film. They were both great. Also, I was in the minority among our group because I also liked *The Godfather Part III*, which a lot of people tend to overlook. It wasn't in the same league as the first two, but it was still pretty good.)

For some reason, the plane was also conducive to deep, contemplative conversations on the meaning of life—quite often, with an assist from a bottle of Wayne, although we tended not to eat or drink until we were within forty-five minutes of landing. The bathroom on board wasn't exactly luxurious, and nobody wanted to have to use it. On the bus, our hot debate topics tended to be about popular culture, but while we were soaring through the clouds, we turned to more ethereal matters. We talked about God and faith and religion, and the values we shared. We had some great discussions—and many of them wound up informing the conversations I'd have the next day with voters at my town halls.

One of the great things about the plane was that it let us move around the country at a moment's notice. The flip side of that was that we were sometimes fooled into thinking you could be in two places at the same time—like when I told Karen and the girls I could make it to Dixville Notch (all the way in the northernmost corner of New Hampshire, by the Canadian border) and then back to Columbus in time for my daughters' birthday dinner. We all thought it was important that I make an appearance in Dixville Notch, and this was the one date on the calendar that seemed to work—only, it didn't work all that great for us Kasichs. Still, I decided to go for it. We flew to the nearest airport in New Hampshire and then rode the bus to Dixville Notch. The one thing I didn't count on was the snow. You'd think, in the middle of January, that I might have factored bad weather into our plans. Sure enough, it was snowing like crazy when it came time to leave after our event, and I remember getting agitated that the roads were in such terrible shape. Still, we managed to make it back to the airport to get me home in time to have dinner with my girls.

For those of you keeping score at home, I won the Dixville Notch primary vote, beating Donald Trump 3 votes to 2, while Bernie Sanders made a clean sweep on the Democratic side of the ledger, collecting all 4 votes cast—so I put that trip in the middle of a snowstorm in the plus column.

We had some harrowing moments in the air, too—like the flight I wrote about in the opening pages of this book, when we flew from Chicago to Mackinac Island in Michigan in the middle of one of the worst storms anyone on board had ever seen. Let me restate for the record, that was the worst flight I ever took. You don't know what turbulence is until you fly around in the middle of a great storm in one of those tiny planes—and that twin-engine turbo prop was even smaller than the CJ3 we were used to flying.

Yet, for every white-knuckle moment, there was another of pure majesty. Oh my, we were treated to some spectacular sites as we crisscrossed the country. The country never looked so grand and magnificent as it did from ten thousand feet, and it was always a thrilling, faith-affirming thing to look out the window and see the sun splashing across Bryce Canyon in Utah, or see the lights of the New York City skyline at night as we flew past the Statue of Liberty, or glimpse an open field in the heartland running as far as the eye could see. Doug and Zach would usually track our flights on their computers and give the rest of us a heads-up whenever we were passing some glorious landmark or another. Of course, we couldn't all rush to the same side of the plane at once, or the plane would list in that direction. (The plane was so small that Doug used to ask the pilot if we'd get where we were going any faster if we all leaned forward.)

All kidding aside, however, it was during these "pinch me" moments of thrilling splendor that I could step outside myself for a beat or two and think of what was at stake in this election. I'd look out and think what an honor it would be to lead this great nation, what a blessing.

I'd look out and see the glory of God.

## THE MOOD OF THE ROOM

Meanwhile, we put together an army of volunteers in New Hampshire. They were the difference makers for us as our campaign got under way. The passion and enthusiasm of our volunteer corps was just incredible—led by people like Bruce Berke, who'd supported me in my previous presidential run and was now back in a key role; and Chris Shays, a great friend of the campaign who traveled with us all over the state.

The volunteers were outstanding—too much to be believed, really. You could make the case, and you'd get no argument from me, that these (mostly) young people sowed the seeds of our grass-roots campaign. They knocked on doors, made phone calls, canvassed voters at shopping centers. Some of them had driven up from Ohio to be a part of our New Hampshire effort, sleeping on air mattresses in houses all over the state. Others had come from clear across the country. And then we had our share of New Hampshire locals, who opened their homes to our volunteers and dug into their linen closets for extra blankets and pillows. Because of them, *all* of them, we were able to connect to almost every voter in the state in a decidedly personal way.

With just a couple of months to go before the New Hampshire primary, this became our focus: connecting with voters. Really, it was the heart of our campaign, and I want to spend some time on it here. You see, running for president is a team effort, as I hope I have already indicated, but let me double-back and make the point again. I was blessed to have a group of dedicated, like-minded political professionals working with me on this campaign, and that blessing spilled over into our nonprofessional campaign workers. This was never more essential than in our efforts in New Hampshire, where by some wild alchemy, we were able to put together an assemblage of volunteers and staff to help us cover the state like no candidate in anyone's memory.

How we did this, I'm not quite sure, because this effort, like so many others, was one of those moving parts I always talk about when I talk about the campaign. This was what went on when I was acting as governor, or traveling the country, or preparing for one of the debates. I couldn't always know firsthand what was taking place at the ground level, where a national campaign is really run, and *won*. New Hampshire offered a tremendous case in point. We all knew the state was key to my chances in the race, but we were outsiders looking in, which meant we had to bring in members of our Ohio-based team to work with local volunteers. On the campaign side, we tapped our national political director Jeff Polesovsky to lead the effort, together with Dave Luketic, our national political director of New Day for America, on the Super PAC side. Understand, in New Hampshire as elsewhere, there had to be a wall between the campaign and the Super PAC. This meant we had to double up. We used to joke that we were like Noah's ark, with two of everything. We had Jeff and Dave running these parallel efforts, unable to talk to each other or coordinate with each other in any way. In a small state like New Hampshire, each was always hearing what his opposite number was up to, but the two never crossed paths—and if either one of them ever heard that the other one was in town, he'd head in the opposite direction.

I'd worked closely with Jeff and Dave for years—they'd helped run my campaigns for governor and had worked in and around my administration. Jeff, for one, was such a fixture in our world that he still carried a nickname given to him by my daughters when they were about ten years old. They called him "the Dude"—and the name stuck.

As I sat down to gather my thoughts about New Hampshire for this book, I realized that *most* of what went on in the state happened on the Dude's watch, so I started to pick his brain. Then, as he shared all these great stories about what it was like to mobilize more than 800 volunteers from all across the country, and to put them to good and meaningful use in a state of 1.3 million people, filled with counties and townships with names some of our guys couldn't even pronounce, I realized that he was in a better position to tell some of these stories than I was.

Here, let him tell you about it and see if you don't agree:

Sometimes you can't figure out what you really need until you get there and see it for yourself. So, soon after the governor announced, we took our whole team from Ohio to New Hampshire for a day-long strategy session. We already had a tremendous amount of data on the voters of New Hampshire, through polling and modeling universes and making nearly a million phone calls into the state out of volunteer phone banks back in Ohio. But what we needed was an army of volunteers who could spark a movement on the ground, create momentum, and help our campaign break through the noise of too many candidates who were all about to be spending more time in the state.

After that daylong meeting, we decided to send our regional political director, Scott Blake, to New Hampshire for a few days each week. At the time, Scott was overseeing state campaign operations in half the country, but his presence and leadership in the state was a turning point. He was able to work directly with the New Hampshire team to take advantage of the data we had and to plan for the influx of volunteers.

Then, in the middle of November, two talented operatives from Ohio took leaves from their jobs and moved to New Hampshire full time. They got to Manchester in early December and lived in a cold room upstairs from our campaign headquarters, above the kitchen. These two spent literally every hour of the day in that office—sleeping on mattresses on the floor, cooking food on a hot plate, and showering in the bathroom that was connected to the kitchen. It wasn't uncommon to have one of them come out of the shower in a towel and walk directly into a group of volunteers getting fueled up on donuts and coffee before going out to knock on doors.

In December, Ben Kaiser and I were still spending most of our time in Ohio, focusing on the rest of the country, but Ben would soon prove essential to our effort in New Hampshire as well. We now had people on the ground in the state who were preparing for the volunteer arrival. National headquarters staff started recruiting people in Ohio and managing all aspects of their upcoming trips to New Hampshire. That team lined up rental houses and apartments and bed-and-breakfasts to accommodate our volunteers. Money was tight, so we negotiated cheap flights and talked prices down on rental cars, vans, and RVs. We also asked people to pay their own way, or drive their own vehicle if at all possible—from Ohio. This sometimes meant fourteen hours in the snow!

Many nights, New Hampshire staff would be up until after 4:00 a.m. preparing the manifest for the next day. We had to have a handle on who was coming in, how and when they would be arriving, where they were staying, where they would be going door-to-door. It was a massive operation, and Ben finally moved to New Hampshire after the first of the year to oversee the whole process full time.

It's impossible to overstate the good work of these good people who were making regular trips to New Hampshire to organize events while others were planning for life after the primary.

A real key to our effort was bringing Governor Kasich to New Hampshire for a few events between Christmas and

New Year's Eve. There was bad weather, which was to be expected that time of year, and of course there were the usual holiday conflicts, but he was there when other candidates were not. And something clicked that week. The momentum we so desperately needed was kicked up a notch—crowds were bigger and there was a buzz around our effort as we moved into January. In fact, the buzz was so great that volunteers would come back to Ohio and start telling their friends about their experience, and they'd want in, too.

Our transplanted team brought a relentless drive and a midwestern confidence with them. People started growing "rally beards" and wearing "Ohio Against the World" T-shirts. Volunteers were flooding the tiny Manchester campaign headquarters to get their marching orders and to deck themselves out in the "Buckeye Brigade" gear I'd created to spur the troops on. There was a real sense that we were all in this thing together. Reinforcements were coming every day—and at first, we thought they were coming mostly from Ohio. Then I had a staffer go through our tracking documents a day before the primary and we discovered that we were actually hosting volunteers from more than thirty-five states!

Every night, we would join the volunteers for an hour of making phone calls before Scott hosted a 9:00 p.m. call with our staff from around the state to see if we'd hit our goals and to prepare for the next day. I spent many mornings working with Scott to adjust our targeting, write new phone scripts, and change our message if our conversion rates were low. We didn't just have to turn people out on Election Day. We had a small window of time to identify, motivate, inspire, and maintain a universe of voters who had a lot of choices.

Housing assignments, daily schedules, lunches and dinners, transportation, event staffing, and other utility work was being handled by several dedicated interns. Over the final two weeks, there were fifteen interns and volunteers living in the campaign headquarters, sleeping on air mattresses on any floor space they could find.

There was so much volunteer activity going on at the headquarters that we often used a large sign to hide the door to a room on the second floor, where our team leaders all worked around one table. Right outside the window to that room was a massive Jeb Bush billboard, which we loved to pelt with snowballs. I spent much of the final week working on a staircase at the back of the house, making calls and refining our strategies in South Carolina and Michigan. There was nowhere else to work in the whole house!

The communications team worked diligently to get the word out—and to let the rest of the country know about the energy and excitement we were tapping into in the Granite State. And then we had people working tirelessly (and selflessly) in support of the governor and his message; one relocated from Chicago, where he'd been living with his fiancée, and moved in with our state director's family. (Our director's mom kept us all in line, and made sure we had what we needed, morning, noon, and night!)

Meanwhile, back in Ohio, we had supporters send handwritten letters to people in New Hampshire, sharing heartfelt stories about John Kasich and what he had done (and was still doing) for the people in Ohio. We never really knew how impactful those letters were until one of our volunteers was canvassing door-to-door one day outside Manchester. He stopped to have a conversation with a woman on her doorstep, and she went and retrieved a letter she had received from someone in Ohio. As it turned out, the letter had been written and sent by the volunteer's wife!

Small world, huh?

It was at that moment that I knew we were connecting with voters in a fundamental way—connections that found us more and more as we got closer to the primary. Volunteers marched through the campus of Saint Anselm College for a rally before gathering together to cheer for Governor Kasich at a debate party. Dozens of volunteers gathered at the airport to welcome the governor and his family back to New Hampshire. And, with the snow falling, hundreds of people from all over the country gathered at Robie's Country Store, in Hooksett, for a late-night Election Eve rally. We even had a volunteer from Chicago who showed up in an Airstream trailer and cut a deal with the gas station owner next to the campaign headquarters to park it there and sleep in it. We crashed two rental vans, lost a minivan for a week, and broke a furnace, fixed it, then broke it again. Dozens of volunteers from Washington, D.C., flew in for the final push and campaigned around the state in RVs. Then a snowstorm kept them in the state for two extra days when all flights were canceled. My brother came in from D.C. to volunteer and ended up walking more than twenty-six miles in two days, going door-to-door in the snow. When I went to meet him to watch a few minutes of the Super Bowl with him, he was having dinner with two guys from Toledo, Ohio; a college student from Georgia; a retired businessman from Tennessee; and four state legislators from Illinois who'd brought along their own camera crew.

There were no VIPs. Everyone just marched together.

We had CEOs of large companies in Ohio canvassing with college students and state legislators, interns making phone calls side by side with lifelong friends of Governor Kasich, volunteers who got lost in their van on a sixteen-hour journey and ended up in Manhattan instead of Manchester, eating pizza in a campaign office kitchen with a group of business leaders who'd flown in on a private plane.

It was all so remarkable, so wonderfully astonishing, the way these people came together in pursuit of a common goal. I will be forever grateful for their extra efforts—the very definition of "above and beyond the call of duty." Someday, maybe Jeff Polesovsky will write a whole book about it, instead of just a few paragraphs. For now, let me reiterate that we had a lot riding on New Hampshire. Check that: We had *everything* riding on New Hampshire, because as I've written, we could make only a bare-bones effort in Iowa, and we didn't think we'd do too well in South Carolina, even with an all-out push there. It was extremely important for us to do well in at least one of these three early contests, and since voters in the Deep South tended to be more socially conservative than voters in New England, we turned our attention northward. A strong showing in the Granite State wasn't our only path to the nomination, we believed, but it was a clear path (perhaps our best path). The plan was to ride a hoped-for bump in New Hampshire all the way to Super Tuesday, and then on to Michigan and Ohio. A win in my home state on March 15, a little more than one month out from New Hampshire, would set us on a sure and viable course—this time, with enough momentum, it was hoped, to carry us to the northeastern states.

All we had to do was capture enough momentum in New Hampshire to help us drive our message home (literally as well as figuratively)—no small task, but a task within reach. Our stated mission, therefore, was to develop the best "ground game" in New Hampshire among all the Republican candidates, and I believe we succeeded on this front, as you can begin to see from the Dude's account. Most political analysts, and even my opponents, would probably agree on this, because we covered the state like a blanket of fresh snow. In the months leading up to the New Hampshire primary, we visited hundreds of town and cities in the state, and held 106 town hall events.

One of the great things about campaigning in New Hampshire is the snow. Of course, there were a lot of people on my campaign team who felt a little differently about this, because the snow could make things difficult. It messed with our schedule, it messed with our travel, and sometimes, well, it was just a mess. But I didn't have to worry about any of that. I just had to show up and take in the beautiful scenery all around.

There was one night in there, at the tail end of a fresh storm, when the snow was just perfect for making snowballs. So, naturally, that's just what we did, and before we knew it, a good old-fashioned snowball fight had broken out. We got the press involved; even some of our supporters were in the middle of it. At one point, I ran over to Doug Preisse and tackled him—knocked him right down into the snow. We were laughing like kids, and as I look back on that moment, it stands out as a highlight for the way it reminds me of how much fun we looked to have, wherever we could find it. And it worked out that we were doing a little more than just blowing off steam. It wasn't *just* fun. Out of that one impromptu snowball fight, mixing it up with some of the reporters who'd been traveling with the campaign, we got some of the best media coverage we received up in New Hampshire—perhaps on the learned truth that when you let your guard down like that in front of a group of journalists, away from the microphones and the town halls and the staged photo opportunities, they get a chance to see you as you really are.

And when you give them an opportunity to let *their* guards down and cut loose—well, so much the better.

It wasn't just the number of events we held, or the fact that we held them in each and every county, that made the difference for us in New Hampshire. It was what happened at those events that mattered most of all—and what happened was by turns heartening, surprising, uplifting, and, well, remarkable. You see, we ran the events a little differently from our Republican opponents, because our town halls were open to Republicans, Democrats, Independents—whoever wanted to come by and see what we were about. In the beginning, this was one way to make sure we had a decent-size crowd, but even then, we'd sometimes turn up to a local school or an American Legion hall or an Elks Club and find only a couple dozen folks in attendance. By January, though, word must have gotten out that we were putting on a good show, because our crowds were getting bigger and bigger. People were responding to our message.

In order to understand that message and the positive energy that came along with it, it helps to understand the people of New Hampshire. One of the things voters across the country don't seem to fully appreciate is how seriously the folks in the Granite State take the primary process. The eyes of the nation are upon them, and most New Hampshire voters are determined to make a thorough-going assessment of each and every candidate. To the folks in New Hampshire, it's an honor and a privilege to vote in the nation's first primary every four years, and they mean to honor that privilege.

Just to give you an illustration, one of my guys stopped into a bar in Concord one afternoon, hoping to grab a late lunch, and he told me the place was filled with locals who'd been running around to all these different campaign events. They were all comparing notes, and you could tell by the hats and T-shirts and campaign buttons they were wearing which candidate they supported—or, at least, which events they'd attended. The bartenders at this place both seemed to be about college age, and they were having a good-natured but nevertheless heated discussion on the merits of Donald Trump vs. Bernie Sanders, arguing that each candidate was really appealing to the same base of disenfranchised voters. Over in the corner was a group of women just back from a Hillary Clinton event, opining that it had conflicted with one of my events and making plans to drive to the next town the following afternoon to catch my town hall there. And then, at the other end of the bar, were two young women in Marco Rubio gear, arguing amiably with a Ted Cruz supporter over an immigration issue.

It's an encouraging picture, don't you think? Yet sights such as these were the order of the day all across the great Granite State. For months leading up to that first primary, New Hampshire residents plan their comings and goings around all the different town halls and rallies and events. They do their due diligence. They make sure to see every candidate, and in a lot of cases, they go back two or three times, just to make sure their first impression still holds. Like I said, they take this stuff seriously up there—and I took the job of trying to present my ideas to them seriously as well. Trouble was, it took me a few weeks to realize that what people seemed to be responding to in my message was not my ideas or my experience. That was a part of it, to be sure, but what voters were connecting to was the *connectedness* of my message.

What voters were connecting to was—well, *me*. Only it wasn't *me* exactly; it was the ways I tried to connect everyone gathered in these town halls to one another.

It was those letters, those phone calls, those knocks on the door from one of our volunteers.

## POINTS OF CONNECTION

I'd always loved these town hall events, although few candidates seemed to embrace them in quite the same way. I've done them my whole career—only, in the very beginning, when I ran for the state senate, they were often held in people's living rooms, over coffee, and there'd be maybe a dozen of the host's friends from the neighborhood in attendance. I tried to bring that same flavor to the town halls in my presidential campaign, and it just worked out that my events were a little different from everyone else's. The other presidential candidates billed their events as town halls—probably because the term had a folksy ring to it, a whiff of Americana, but they went ahead and read from a prepared speech, or ran it like a rally. Everybody has his or her own style, I guess. Everybody has his own strengths, and the idea is to play to those strengths. Some candidates just didn't feel confident working without a net, which is how a town hall format can feel. More to the point, some of the other campaign staffers didn't have confidence in their own candidate to let him or her go off script or take impromptu questions from the crowd. But I cherished those events, and my team knew they could trust me to work the room in a meaningful way. They knew that a *true* town hall, conducted as it's meant to be, is the only effective way to reach the diligent voters of New Hampshire. It's the difference between sending a mass e-mail to get your message out there and sending the handwritten notes our volunteers were circulating. It's a conversation, really, a chance for candidates and voters to connect in person, in a free-flowing way. It's not a sales pitch or a stump speech. It's more intimate than that, more personal. It's an opportunity for a candidate to show up in shirtsleeves and roll up those shirtsleeves and start talking, plain talk—about himself, about his experiences, about his hopes and dreams for the country, and, most pointedly, about his hopes and dreams for the people in attendance.

Very often, at a town hall, I'd borrow a line of conversation from one of our late-night bull sessions on the bus or plane to get things started. But I never had a script, and even if the organizers had me set up on a stage or at a lectern of some kind, I'd very quickly work my way into the crowd and start interacting directly with the folks who'd come out to hear what I had to say.

Anyway, that was the idea. And be assured, I wasn't just there to talk. I was there to listen as well.

Do you want to know something? I never had a cynical exchange with a single voter in New Hampshire. Not one. We might have had a couple of hecklers in there, but I almost always tried to engage with the person who stood to challenge me on an issue. The challenge was usually offered in a respectful way, and often led to a meaningful exchange. I wasn't always able to bring each critic around to my way of thinking, or to win his or her support, but each time out, there were moments of deep connection, sometimes in a way that had nothing at all to do with politics as usual.

It's difficult to bring across to readers the energy and informality of a town hall. If you want to get the full flavor of these events, I suggest you do a search on YouTube; a great many of our town halls are archived there, at least in part. Take a look. But one way to explain a town hall is to compare it to one of those single-topic episodes of *The Oprah Winfrey Show*. Certainly, most readers will remember the way Oprah found so many wonderful points of connection when she moved about the studio audience, sharing emotions and experiences. I certainly don't mean to compare myself to Oprah, but it's the visual I'm after here. It's the sense of movement and excitement and unpredictability—because, really, our town halls felt a whole lot more like a television talk show than a traditional political rally.

It took me a couple of weeks to find my footing as a candidate. At the outset, I was focused on economic growth, a balanced budget, the debt clock, jobs—what John Weaver always called Cut and Rope Politics 101. But as I traveled the state of New Hampshire and really *listened* to the folks at my town halls, I started to realize that our campaign was about touching people where they lived—in their kitchens, in their living rooms, in their hearts. Absolutely, the economy is all important. You can't have these deeper, more emotional conversations until you fix the economy, but the people of New Hampshire took this as a given. They wanted to talk about people in their families who were living in the shadows. They wanted to talk about making sure their adult children could afford health care. They wanted to know how to deal with the drug problem, or racial tensions, or the apparent erosion of family values in their communities.

When it started out, I went at this thing intellectually. I campaigned on these foundational issues because, let's face it, when people don't have a job, they don't have hope. But I very quickly turned and started addressing the emotional issues more and more, and as I did, I was reminded of Karen's admonition that I start acting like the father of Ohio. We'd gone through so many challenges as a state (a school shooting, human trafficking, parents wondering how to care for their adult children with autism), and here

in New Hampshire and all across the country there were challenges as well. Once we were able to get Ohio on stable financial
ground, we started reaching out to the people of the state in ways
that were unusual for a Republican administration. We created
programs to lift people in need. We gave a voice to folks who were
struggling. Inevitably then, once I was at a town hall, as a presidential candidate, I started speaking to those struggles, ever mindful
of the fact that the conversation was always built on the supposition of a strong economy.

I once read a study that said people would rather live in poverty
than live in a community where there was no work, and I gave that
a lot of thought. Work is a good and noble thing. It helps people
realize a purpose in their lives. It gives them satisfaction. But once
that's addressed, I started realizing, a leader needs to start looking
out for the people of his state or the people of his country the way
a father would his children. Once your kids are educated and land
a good job, you then help them face myriad issues related not to
how much money they have in their pockets, but to the challenges
they are made to face along the way. Too often these challenges
can lead to fear, to a feeling that things are spinning out of control.

That fear turned out to be the driving emotion of the 2016 presidential campaign, and the front-runner tailored his message to
stoke that fear. In response, the American people elected a strongman who they believed could help them address that fear and
get control of their lives once again. Hopefully, that's how it will
work out.

I took a different approach. I could not offer simple solutions to
complicated problems. I could not present myself as a strongman
to voters, because, to my thinking, the answers to many of the problems people were facing don't rest with our top leaders in government but in our communities. And there are just some problems

that can't be fixed from the top down, even though they must be addressed and considered. When I went to visit a drug and alcohol rehab center in New Hampshire, for example, it was clear to me that the real heroes in the lives of these patients were the people who worked in the facility, the men and women who woke up each morning before dawn to try to heal these broken individuals. It didn't matter who the governor was. It didn't matter who the president was. It mattered who was coming in for the morning shift.

One of the great things about these town halls was that no two were alike. By the time we had to fold up our tent in early May 2016, we'd done about 250 of them—some big, some small, most somewhere in between. The way it worked was our team would identify a venue, such as a fire station, a high school cafeteria, or a community center, and we'd set it up and get the word out. It didn't cost a whole lot of money to put on one of those events—about six thousand dollars, on average, to cover the lighting, the sound, the staging, and the rental fee for the space. From time to time, a local organization would sponsor the event, such as the time we rolled out our economic plan at Nashua Community College or when I presented my "Two Paths" speech at the Women's National Republican Club in New York. That was a great way for us to keep our costs in check and fill the room with an engaged group.

The format of these town halls didn't change all that much over the course of our campaign, but the content surely did. In the beginning, the notes I made sure to hit were the same notes I had been sounding on the first few debate stages, and in my prepared speeches and press interviews, with a focus on a stable economy. The only difference here, at first, was that the message was delivered in this informal way, and that there was room in the format for dialogue with the audience on related issues such as jobs and the rising cost of health care. But what I began to realize, almost as soon as we started lining up town halls in a back-to-back way, was that this election was about so much more than politics. It was about people. It was the politics of the personal. That's one of the reasons so many people responded to Donald Trump's populist message, I think: he hit them where they lived; he spoke to their feelings of disenfranchisement, disengagement, disempowerment. The difference between his message and mine, though, had to do with the way people responded to those feelings—indeed, with the way they were *encouraged* to respond to those feelings. At a Trump rally, many people were driven to anger and blame; there was name-calling and finger-pointing; there was a certain "my way or the highway" tone. At a Kasich event, people were given hope and all kinds of reasons to lift each other up instead of holding each other down; there was a "we're all in this soup together" tone.

Looking back, I find it tough to pinpoint exactly when I started leaning away from the central themes of my campaign and toward the more personal themes that found me as we got going. As I was gathering my thoughts for this book, I asked some key members of my team what they remembered about the way I pivoted. A number of them pointed to a very specific town hall, in the small town of Colebrook, in Coos County, New Hampshire. We were at an American Legion hall, and it was probably the twentieth or thirtieth such event we'd held in the state, so we'd been at it awhile by this point, with a long way still to go. There was snow on the ground, and folks seemed to be settling in to the idea of another long, cold New England winter. And I guess I was feeling a little nostalgic for a time in our lives when neighbors came together at that time of year and made sure everybody had what they needed. This was my mind-set as I addressed this collection of friends and neighbors in New Hampshire's Great North Woods. While I had their attention, I just happened to ask if anyone in the hall that day who'd been married a long time had recently lost a spouse. I knew there were probably a few people in attendance who lived alone, and that it's always tough being alone over the holidays.

The question just came to me—it was just something to ask, given the way our "conversation" had been going up to that point.

An elderly man raised his hand in response, and I walked over to him. He looked to be about eighty years old, and he told me he'd just lost his wife of fifty-five years. I consoled him in what ways I could, in that kind of setting, and then I turned to the hundred or so who had gathered for the event and said, "Who here is going to take this man to dinner and spend some time with him tonight?"

Here again, it all just seemed to flow from the warm and welcoming mood of the room. I suppose it also came from the thought of what I would have done if I happened to live down the street from this man and had just learned of his loss. And wouldn't you know it, people started crying and going over to this man and hugging him and exchanging phone numbers. It was a beautiful, heart-lifting thing to see. And at first I thought it had nothing at all to do with my campaign, really, but then I realized that it had everything to do with my campaign.

Out of that moment, and dozens more just like it, folks started responding to this type of personal message. Soon, the town halls were *mostly* about the people who were coming out to them. They became safe havens for voters to voice their concerns for the country, their worries over how their families were struggling, their disappointment at the rage that seemed to flow from the other campaigns. At our events, people could express their deep concerns, and maybe talk about a challenge, an anxiety, a hurt, loneliness. Word spread, and in our own homespun way, our campaign took on dimensions we hadn't really anticipated—especially as it stood in

comparison to the politics-as-usual campaigns of some of my opponents. All across the state, at bars and restaurants like the one
my guys had visited in Concord, people started comparing notes
and talking about this governor from Ohio with the hard-to-
pronounce name who seemed to really *get* them, to really care
about them.

This all came to a head, famously, at a town hall at Clemson
University in South Carolina, just a week or so after our strong
second-place showing in New Hampshire. A young man named
Brett Smith took the microphone and started telling me he'd been
in a dark place. He told reporters afterward that he hadn't come out
that day expecting to tell his story, but he'd found himself in that
"safe harbor" we'd somehow created and he'd felt moved to speak.
He said his parents had recently divorced, his father was out of a
job, and a close friend had just committed suicide. But rather than
shutting himself in and grieving and worrying, this young man
said he'd found strength and solace in the Lord and in his friendships. "And now," he said, "I've found it in the presidential candidate
I support." That got a big response, which I certainly appreciated,
but of course the moment was not about *that*. The moment was
about the fact that all of us gathered there had been in similar dark
places, and this young man seemed to recognize that—and he asked
for one of the hugs I'd been known to give out at such events.

Somehow those hugs had gotten to be a big deal—my version
of shaking hands and kissing babies, I suppose. So, I worked my
way through the crowd and gave this young man a hug. There was
a lot of *ooohing* and *aaahing* and all that, and when the moment
had passed, I turned to those assembled and tried to put it all in
some kind of context.

I said, "I've heard about the pain of people all across the country, and what I've learned is we're going too fast in our lives. Let's

care about one another and not be disconnected, and together we will rise this country."

There was a sweet footnote to that moment at Clemson University. "The Hug," as it came to be known in the media, went viral. Go ahead and google the phrase alongside my name, and you'll see hundreds of articles, pictures, references. As a lifelong sports fan, I love how my gesture has been memorialized with this neat little handle, like "the Catch," which as football fans know, refers to the winning touchdown pass from Joe Montana to Dwight Clark that sent the San Francisco 49ers to the Super Bowl; or Bobby Thomson's "Shot Heard 'Round the World," the home run that sent the New York Giants to the World Series.

Alas, this moment didn't exactly propel me on to the general election, but it lives on just the same. In fact, as I write this, there's a news story making the rounds that Brett Smith has just been honored as the most inspirational person of the year in his hometown. How cool is *that*? Best of all, Brett is doing okay. He went on from that moment to graduate from the University of Georgia and complete an internship with Georgia governor Nathan Deal. After graduation, he landed a job as a field representative for his congressman. Since that town hall, he's been interviewed by CNN, MSNBC, *The New York Times, The Washington Post*, and a number of other national media outlets. He's even been stopped by people on the street who recognize him and ask how he's doing. Some folks even lean in for a hug of their own.

About the dark time in his life that drove him to our event in South Carolina, he now says this: "I learned [that] the more I talked about it, the better I felt, so the exposure I received really kind of forced me to keep talking about it. The more I talked, the easier it got. I still have bad days, everyone does, but personally I am in such a better place than I was at any time during the past two to three years."

How about *that*?

## PLAIN TALK

That moment in South Carolina got a lot of play in the media, even though it was nothing unusual to reporters who'd been following our campaign. I believe it struck a chord for the way it stood out against the sea of negativity that had washed over the presidential election cycle. It wasn't so much that the moment was unlike anything we'd seen before in previous campaigns; it's that it was so unlike anything we were seeing in *this* campaign. It was genuine. It was real. And it stood as a kind of light against the darkness we were seeing evoked across the country. Looking back, I came to realize that all that darkness and negativity flowed in some way from the debate stages, which moved from Cleveland to the Ronald Reagan Presidential Library in Simi Valley, California; from the University of Colorado, in Boulder, to the Milwaukee Theatre. That's where it started, in a *macro* way, but I really believe it became more insidious in the *micro* environment of all those individual rallies. And then it grew from there, as each candidate went back out into the field and tried to raise his or her voice to be heard above the shouting coming from all the other candidates. What you were left with, regrettably, was a group of determined candidates trying to fire up their bases with a certain brashness and bluster meant to convey a sense of leadership and vision.

Since the general election in November, there's been a popular line of commentary that suggests that this brashness and bluster were coming mostly from the Trump campaign, but if you look closely at the rhetoric that characterized those early debates, you'll see that there was bullying all around. And as a lot of the individual rallies in our early primary states became more hateful and inflammatory, my town halls seemed to stand as one of the last bastions of civil discourse on the campaign trail. This wasn't a calculation, mind you; it wasn't a niche in the marketplace we were looking to fill. It just felt to me like the right way to treat people in such a setting, at that moment in time. With me, there was no yelling or trash talking. With me, there was no rabble-rousing. There was only a call for reasonable people to come together and seek reasonable solutions to the problems facing the country.

Let's be clear: To the candidates—at least, to *this* candidate— the debates took up a very small part of our day-to-day focus, even though they loomed large on the national stage. It helps to remember that there was usually about a month between each debate, and that during those intervening weeks, there was a whole lot of jockeying for position as my fellow Republican candidates traveled the country and did what they could to make sure they earned an invitation onto the main debate stage, as we each kept driving in those "lanes" I talked about earlier. The way the whole thing was set up, it was as if we were caught in a political catch-22. In and of themselves, the debates were relatively meaningless; they revealed little about each candidate's policies or qualifications or preparedness because they weren't *really* debates at all. Yet, they were also essential to the health and well-being of each campaign, because they served as a kind of self-fulfilling barometer of how each candidate was doing in the polls, while revealing certain aspects of his or her character. A lot of the time, I felt that the key to "winning" one of those debates was merely to survive it—meaning, to get through it without a blunder or a dustup or an uncharacteristic flash of bad behavior; without getting caught in the crosshairs of one of your fiery opponents; without being tripped up by a question or a topic you hadn't considered.

I could only think that Donald Trump saw the debates as an opportunity to get under the skin of his opponents. To him, perhaps, the key to "winning" one of those things was to dominate the discussion, ruffle a whole lot of feathers, and put it out there that he was a kind of runaway train, unable to be stopped by the conventions and customs of our political systems or by the standards and practices of our mainstream media.

I didn't pay too much attention to what my opponents were doing. A lot of people, when I talk to them about what things were like for us on the campaign trail, have it in their heads that the candidates were running into one another all the time. They saw us all together on those debate stages. They saw reports from our events presented on the nightly news in such a way that it appeared that we were out on the same circuit. The truth was we never really saw one another—or, at least, *I* never really saw my opponents. For all I knew, they were all staying in the same hotels and eating at the same local hot spots, comparing notes, while we were off doing our thing.

There was one time, however, when a large group of us were all in the same place at the same time. It was in a freight elevator, of all places, in the Quicken Loans Arena in Cleveland, as we were making our way to the first debate stage. There's a great picture of us, all jammed in. Anyway, as we were riding that elevator, someone remarked that if we got stuck there'd be no debate. After that, the debate organizers appeared to have made other arrangements, because that was the last time we were thrown together like that.

I didn't pay too much attention to the polling, either—other than to worry for a day or two before each debate that my support was enough for me to make the cut for the next main stage. That's how it goes, when you're polling in the single digits and trying to get your message out there in a noteworthy way. There were people on our team who tracked the numbers closely, but I didn't want to hear about it. I wasn't interested in what the other candidates were saying at their events or in the media, because I wasn't about to change what I was saying as a result, so I tried to tune out the news of the day when we were on the road. On the bus, in the hotel, the only thing I'd watch on television was the Golf Channel or one of the other sports channels. Come to think of it, we watched a lot of sporting events, but the Golf Channel was my default option. Still, I've got to admit, there were times when I'd look up from the little screen we had for watching TV and I'd take a look at all my guys staring intently at their smartphones, or tapping away furiously at their devices, keeping in touch with whatever was going on in the rest of the world and in all the other campaigns.

I understood that, of course. I even counted on it. After all, it was their job to stay plugged in; it was mine to keep connected to the folks coming out to our events. Truth was, I didn't need the media to tell me if we were connecting with voters. I could tell by our town halls. You could feel the energy in the room, and you could see that each event was just a little bit bigger, a little more exuberant than the last one. In New Hampshire, I could tell by how folks were responding to me as I moved through each town, stopping at local fairs and diners and community events. That's what's so great about campaigning up there. There's time enough to visit every county, every nook and cranny, and connect with people on an individual basis—time enough, even when you're a little late announcing your candidacy.

It's kind of interesting to assess how the field took on new and curious shape as each debate unfolded. Following that first debate in Cleveland, for example, Donald Trump emerged as a clear front-runner in a crowded field, with Dr. Ben Carson polling pretty consistently in second place. And as the rhetoric from Trump's rallies became more and more hateful, the ugliness surrounding his campaign intensified. It was perhaps inevitable that it would spill over into some of the other campaigns—and, soon enough, we started hearing a similar brand of malicious invective from some of the other candidates who'd apparently looked on at the Trump juggernaut and concluded that name-calling and trash talking and bullying would somehow vault them to the head of the field.

By the time we all got together in California for the second debate, it was starting to appear that each candidate was running against Trump, and that Trump himself had come prepared to deflect every attack against him with a crude, crass response that had no place in a presidential campaign. At the time, I found this only a little bit troubling. I was concerned about the coarseness of some of the language I was hearing, some of the behavior I was seeing, but at this early juncture, I didn't think Trump's popularity was sustainable. He had yet to lay out a consistent, coherent platform, and he had yet to be challenged substantively on the issues. So, like a lot of folks, I was hanging back, waiting for the other shoe to drop on his campaign, and for this presidential election cycle to start spinning in more familiar ways.

That never happened, as we now know, so we are left to reconsider the Republican field as the debates dragged on and to reflect on the Trump phenomenon as it chased all the other candidates from the race. Heading back into that second debate in California, former Hewlett-Packard CEO Carly Fiorina was the only addition to the main stage from the "junior varsity" debate in Cleveland, and for a while it seemed that she was the focus of a lot of the questioning. Donald Trump had made headlines in the weeks lead-ing up to the debate after criticizing her appearance, so the two of them went at each other for a while. Then Rand Paul went after Trump on his insulting demeanor. Then Jeb Bush went after Trump on immigration. I was positioned once again off in Siberia, at the far end of the debate stage, and it felt to me that everyone was just trading prepared barbs and sound bites, hoping to connect with the moderators (this time led by Jake Tapper of CNN, with an as-sist from colleagues Hugh Hewitt and Dana Bash) and, by exten-sion, the viewers at home.

If you remember, I got off one of my better lines at that debate, meant to indicate my shock and disapproval at the behavior of some of the other candidates onstage. I said, "You know, if I were at home, I'd turn off my television."

## HOW WE LINED UP

I suppose it's helpful here to offer up a quick assessment of the Republican field, for ready reference, because the landscape kept changing, even in the last weeks of the summer of 2015, more than a full year before the election.

Rick Perry suspended his campaign a week before the Califor-nia debate, after being left off the main debate stage for the second straight time.

Jim Gilmore failed to make the cutoff for either the "varsity" or the "junior varsity" debate in California, but he was still hanging in there, vowing to press on.

George Pataki, Bobby Jindal, Lindsey Graham, and Rick San-torum participated in the preliminary debate, leaving Carly Fiorina to join the ten participants from the main stage at that first debate in Cleveland.

The lineup remained the same for the third debate, in Boulder, this one to be moderated by John Harwood, Carl Quintanilla, and Becky Quick of CNBC—and to be marked by intensifying attacks, not only from one candidate to the next, but from many candidates to the moderators, who came under scrutiny for their handling of the debate. From here on in, the size of each debate lineup began to thin—meaning, theoretically, there'd be a greater opportunity for each of us onstage to articulate his or her position.

I believed I was faring better each time out, getting more time, making more of an impression, and by the time we got to the New Hampshire debate—the eighth on the schedule, held at the New Hampshire Institute of Politics at Saint Anselm College, in Manchester, New Hampshire, and organized by ABC News—there was no longer any undercard, or "junior varsity," debate, only the main event. By this point, several candidates had dropped from the field (Rand Paul, Rick Santorum, Mike Huckabee, Lindsey Graham, George Pataki, Bobby Jindal, and Scott Walker), and in order to qualify, you had to have finished in the top three in the popular vote count in the Iowa caucus, which had been held the previous week, or poll in the top six across a spectrum of New Hampshire and national polls, as determined by ABC News. Predictably, I failed to qualify on the basis of my showing in Iowa, where I captured only 2 percent of the vote—a disappointing result, even though I'd expected to be disappointed. Still, I once again made the cut on the polling front and was invited to participate—an invitation my team thought was vital to my chances in the New Hampshire primary.

Carly Fiorina and Jim Gilmore were the only candidates still in the race who did not make it to the debate stage in New Hampshire. (They would both suspend their campaigns the week following the New Hampshire primary.)

The New Hampshire debate, you might recall, was the one where there seemed to be some confusion with the introduction of Dr. Ben Carson, which in turn led to some confusion with the introduction of yours truly. Basically, what happened was I wasn't introduced at all, so I just kind of sidled onto the stage and took my place. It was weird, but it wasn't that big a deal. People watching the debate at home told me it was one of the strangest things they'd ever seen at a national debate, but up there on that stage, or even out in the theater, I don't think people even noticed. You might also recall that Donald Trump had famously sat out the previous debate, held about a week earlier in Iowa and organized by Fox News, after clashing with the network and one of its anchors, Megyn Kelly, who was due to be one of that debate's moderators. This, too, was weird, but I didn't think it was either. It's only now, in retrospect, that I see Trump's grandstanding with regard to the debates as an early indication of how our future president seemed inclined to make the proceedings all about him.

That was my attitude throughout the campaign: to shrug off the weirdness and the glitches that were beyond my control, to ignore the histrionics of some of my opponents, and to focus on connecting with the voters and delivering a hopeful message. Some of that weirdness found me backstage, before the organizers even had a chance *not* to introduce me. They'd given every candidate his own "green" room—only, we were assigned to the locker room of the Saint Anselm baseball team. Some of the other candidates were given nicer digs, based on where they stood in the polls— kind of like the way they kept placing us single-digit guys at the end of the stage. I didn't really mind the locker room, but there were open pipes and uncomfortable chairs and a distinct aroma. It was cramped in there, too, so a couple of our guys moved to a nearby squash court—you know, the kind with the tiny doors you have duck down to pass through.

It was all a little surreal.

There I was, in a college locker room, and in my ear I had my team offering me last-minute advice. It felt like a scene from one of the *Rocky* movies, with the corner guy and the cut man and the trainer whispering strategy and support to the champ—only, I didn't feel like a champ at that moment. I didn't usually get nervous before any of the debates, but people told me afterward that I was a little on edge before the New Hampshire debate, so I guess maybe the significance of the moment was weighing on me.

Still, I took in all the words of wisdom from my people:

"You own this, Governor."

"These are your people."

"This is your moment."

It really was like a pregame pep talk, back there in that smelly locker room. I knew the stakes, for me and for my opponents—and what their likely strategies would be out there on that stage. I knew Ted Cruz hadn't really invested anything in New Hampshire and that he would be playing to a national audience instead of a local one. My team had told me that Chris Christie was probably going to look for ways to attack Marco Rubio, and we suspected that Rubio, in turn, had likely prepared a bunch of feisty comebacks with the hope of showing that he could be just as feisty as anyone on that stage. I knew that a strong showing in New Hampshire was essential for the Jeb Bush camp, and that he would be out there looking to connect with the locals a final time. And I knew that Donald Trump would be out to command center stage yet again, to get off a memorable one-liner or two, and to look for ways to let viewers know that this debate was so much more interesting than the Iowa debate he'd chosen to sit out, with much better ratings.

What I didn't know was that Ben Carson would be waiting in the wings, stage right, looking to all the world like he wanted to stay out of the line of the fire, out of the way of all the crosstalk that would surely find him once he stepped onstage and the debate got under way.

## "WE ARE ALL MADE SPECIAL"

As I wrote previously, the debates were a lot less important to me than the town halls, where I believed we were making a powerful impression on the folks in attendance. It was easy enough to see how we were connecting with young voters at our town halls, but our impact outside those gatherings was sometimes difficult to gauge. One notable exception to this came via a young producer at Fox News in Washington, D.C. Her name was Emily Judd and she was a year or so out of college. Her job was to pore over footage of all the candidates in the field, looking for clips to be used on the Fox News program *Special Report with Bret Baier.* She was never actually in attendance at any of these events, just monitoring them through her computer, but that's the nature of the television news business. In newsrooms across the country, young people like Emily were culling highlights from hours and hours of campaign footage to share with viewers.

Toward the end of the campaign, when the Republican field was down to Donald Trump, Ted Cruz, and me, Emily said she found herself drawn more and more to our positive message. Trouble was, none of the sound bites she was pulling from our events ever made it to air, because the network tended to focus on the negative messages. And if you looked at the coverage from other cable and network news outlets during that period, you saw much the same thing, across the board.

"It was so frustrating," Emily told me after the campaign. "Here I was responding to the hopeful message you were sharing with your audience, being really moved by all the positive things you were saying, but the fruits of my labor each day only reinforced the negative aspects of the campaign from the other candidates. I couldn't get your positivity on air, so the rest of the country never really heard it, not on Fox News."

One of the things I loved about Emily's perspective, which she shared with me when she got a chance to meet me and walk me to the stage at a presidential town hall in Philadelphia, was that she felt connected to my campaign even though she'd never actually been to one of my events. It all happened for her through the computer. This spoke to me, reinforced in me the genuine feelings of optimism and good cheer that seemed to fill the room at our events.

One of the other things I loved about Emily's story was that she'd just been accepted to Yale Divinity School, but had put off her decision to attend because she'd been thinking she might like to pursue a career in television news instead. What tilted her back in the other direction, she told me, was her growing frustration over the emphasis on negativity and sensationalism she witnessed among her colleagues in the news media—and a comment she heard me make, in this one-degree-of-separation way, through her computer, at a town hall on the campus of Villanova.

"I believe that we are all made special," I said to one of the young people in attendance. "The Lord made us special. You are unique and you've been given gifts, and nobody else has them. And they are critical and they are to be used for the healing of our world."

Well, Emily Judd heard those remarks and made up her mind

to go to divinity school. A couple of months later, she heard me mention her story in the speech I gave to announce that I was suspending my campaign. She made a special point to reach out to let me know how she was doing. I'm so glad she did, because it is through her transformation that I am able to draw hope for the future of this country. She'd felt a calling to divinity school all along, but then she found herself doing what she thought was meaningful and rewarding work, keeping the public informed. Somewhere in there, though, she realized that her gifts were far greater than sorting through hours and hours of campaign footage, looking for inflammatory material to help drive ratings, and so she decided, in the end, to go to Yale Divinity School after all.

Now, it's not as simple or clear-cut as all that, I realize, but it's a sweet and affirming thing to know that the spirit Emily saw at our events factored into her thinking even in the smallest of ways.

"Your words inspired me to be a better person," she said, and I share her story here for the way *her actions* inspired *me*.

# 9.

# Two Paths

On Tuesday, April 12, 2016, I delivered what I believed at the time was the most important speech of my career. Looking back, I still feel this way—and even more important, I think the words I spoke before the Women's National Republican Club in New York City that afternoon offer a healing, hopeful message as we try to get together and fix some of the very real problems facing our country.

In order to communicate what was at stake with this address, it's probably helpful for me to refresh your memory about what was going on in the presidential campaign.

The Republican field had been winnowed to just three candidates, down from the original seventeen: me, Donald Trump, and Texas senator Ted Cruz. You know how every year during the NCAA basketball tournament there's a story about the one-in-a-million fan who correctly picks the Final Four? Every year, it seems, there are all these bracket-busting upsets that upend everybody's pool picks, yet there's always at least one person, out in the heartland, maybe, who through dumb luck or expert analysis manages to correctly predict the semifinal matchups. Well, this was kind of like that. If there were office pools handicapping the 2016 Republican presidential race at the outset, I can't imagine anyone would have filled out their brackets in just this way. Our respective campaign teams would all have backed their own candidate—because, let's face it, we all thought we were in a position to win the nomination. But those other spots would have been up for grabs.

Yet this was how it all shook out.

Trump was all the way out in front in terms of delegates and media coverage, with Cruz a distant second in both areas. And as for me, well, I'd been hanging on and hanging in there for the first couple months of 2016. Other than a strong second-place showing in the New Hampshire primary and a couple solid outings in the early debates, my campaign wasn't able to make a whole lot of noise in the early going. Still, all along we were making just enough noise to offer voters a viable alternative to the leading candidates, and to live to fight another day on the campaign trail.

Meanwhile, former Texas governor Rick Perry, Wisconsin governor Scott Walker, Louisiana governor Bobby Jindal, South Carolina senator Lindsey Graham, and former New York governor George Pataki had all dropped from the race before the first primary.

Former Arkansas governor Mike Huckabee, New Jersey governor Chris Christie, former Virginia governor Jim Gilmore, former Pennsylvania senator Rick Santorum, Kentucky senator Rand Paul, and former CEO of Hewlett-Packard Carly Fiorina withdrew in the first two weeks of February. They were followed later that month by former Florida governor Jeb Bush, who had once been the odds-on favorite to win the nomination. If you remember, it was Bush's candidacy that had me and my team most concerned when I was weighing a presidential run, and now here we were, all those months later, and voters just hadn't responded to his message.

As I've written, the first two months of primary season were tumultuous, and increasingly rancorous. It started out like any other crowded campaign, but it wasn't long before things took a dark, dispiriting turn—in the direction of all that "fear and goading" I talked about previously. The sniping and negativity that had bubbled forth in the first few presidential debates seemed to get uglier each time out, as more and more I found myself standing just outside the line of fire, trying like crazy to bring a measure of sanity and civility to what were starting to feel like shouting matches instead of discussions on the issues. Some of the stuff that was being said was just beyond the pale—and certainly beyond the bounds of decency and polite behavior we had a right to expect from such proceedings. That said, I didn't always get the chance to stand as the voice of reason and calm that I set out to be at first: the moderators didn't throw a whole lot of questions at me, and the only way to make myself heard would have been to yell even louder than the other guys—and I wasn't about to do *that*.

With Bush out of the race after a disappointing showing in South Carolina, there were only five candidates left: me, Trump, Cruz, Rubio, and Dr. Ben Carson, the noted pediatric neurosurgeon who, for a time, had been one of the front-runners. To the folks on our team, it was a remarkable shakeout, a bracket-busting turn of events. For a while, we thought that whatever support Jeb Bush had managed to generate might move over to our side. After all, in terms of our positions, I probably stood as the most moderate candidate in the bunch, appealing to the same base of mainstream conservative voters. Also, as governors of two big states, Jeb and I both checked off a lot of the same boxes for a lot of Republicans. We were driving in the same "lane," to use the language of political analysts.

But that's not exactly how things shook out. Bush veered into another lane entirely and threw his support to Ted Cruz, although his exit didn't really move the needle all that much for me in the polls (or for Senator Cruz, for that matter). So, even without Bush's voters, we just kept at it, in a lane we now appeared to have essentially to ourselves.

Then, in early March, just a couple of days after Super Tuesday, Ben Carson suspended his campaign, saying that he saw "no path forward" to the nomination. About a week later, he announced that he was endorsing Donald Trump, a man whose behavior and temperament seemed to stand in polar opposition to the measured, respectful demeanor of Dr. Carson.

All along, our team had a very clear path in mind as we attempted to steer clear of the infighting among the other three remaining candidates and turned our attention to the Michigan primary, where we expected to do well, and to my home state of Ohio, where we expected to win. At this point, we'd had only that strong second-place showing in New Hampshire, but we were encouraged by the enthusiasm we found at our town hall events, which were getting bigger and more uplifting each time out. I was enormously gratified by the response we were getting from our supporters, and there were even some pundits coming around to our side, pointing to polls that said I stood the best chance of defeating Hillary Clinton in a head-to-head race in the general election, and that voters were beginning to tire of the bad, derisive behavior that continued to pass among the remaining candidates.

Let me tell you, I'd sometimes catch myself at these debates thinking I was at a Friars Club roast instead of a presidential forum, the way these guys were going at each other—and it seemed to be getting worse and worse.

Perhaps the most anticipated date on the primary calendar was March 15, Super Tuesday II, with voting in Illinois, Missouri, North Carolina, Florida, Ohio, and the Northern Mariana Islands. We wanted to do well across the board, naturally, but Ohio was key. (How's that for the understatement of our campaign?) Without a big win on my home turf, my chances of continuing all the way to the convention would be greatly diminished. The same could be said of Marco Rubio on his home turf in Florida. Publicly, I was out there saying that the health of our campaign didn't depend entirely on a primary win in Ohio, but it was clear to all of us on the team that anything short of a convincing victory would make it difficult for us to raise money and push our efforts forward.

But let's not forget, Super Tuesday II wasn't *just* about Ohio. There were 367 delegates at stake, most in winner-take-all states. If anything, there was even more pressure on Marco Rubio to win in Florida than there was on me to win in Ohio. By our math, we could probably have survived a slim margin of victory in my home state, or even a narrow second-place showing, but Rubio was all in. He was going at it with Donald Trump, who despite his New York City roots also considered himself a favorite son of Florida, owing to his Mar-a-Lago residence; the two candidates kept attacking each other in campaign ads that aired in heavy rotation across the state. Rubio even came out at some point and told his supporters to vote for me in Ohio—probably expecting me to come out and encourage my supporters to vote for him in Florida, and while I certainly appreciated the suggestion, I wasn't prepared to return the favor.

Keep in mind, these primaries came around on the calendar the same week as that ugly Trump rally in Chicago I wrote about earlier, which caused me to look for the first time at the incendiary rhetoric of the Republican front-runner—and also, for the first time, to challenge him publicly on it. Up until this time, I had mostly tried to stay out of the line of fire and conduct myself in a manner I thought appropriate to these proceedings, a manner wholly consistent with how I tried to live my life away from the campaign.

But now that I'd spoken out against the hateful tone and bad behavior of my opponents, I felt I had a responsibility to keep doing so.

Clearly, there was a lot at stake on March 15, as the tempers and personalities of the remaining candidates were coming into play like never before in the campaign—mine included.

Happily, we won Ohio in a big way: it was our first primary win, as we pulled in 47 percent of the vote to Trump's 36 percent and Cruz's 13 percent. We took a lot of good-natured ribbing in the press for the way we celebrated that night in Cleveland. I'm told it looked like we'd bought up all the confetti in the state, with the way that stuff came raining down on us from the rafters. No question, it was a big night for us, and in fairness, a lot of staffers had been hard at work for a good long time, so we felt in that moment that there was everything to be thankful for—everything to look forward to, even. (And yeah, there was a whole lot of confetti!)

Things didn't go so well for Marco Rubio in Florida, however. He ended up with just 27 percent of the vote, to Trump's 46 percent, in a state he needed to carry in order for his campaign to remain viable. I can remember sitting in a small room with our team on the night of the primaries, watching the returns, and when the coverage shifted to Rubio headquarters in Florida, where the senator was about to make an appearance, we all flashed each other these looks, because we knew what was coming.

Sure enough, Rubio ended his campaign that night, leaving us in a three-way race for the nomination, which was where things stood for the next month or so leading up to the speech I delivered at the Women's National Republican Club. During this time, as I will detail in the pages ahead, Senator Cruz started calling for me to get out of the race, telling people that a vote for me was a vote for Donald Trump. Meanwhile, Trump himself started attacking me as well, which I took as a sign that he finally saw me as some kind of threat.

So, that was where things stood in the first week or so of April, as we dusted the confetti from our shoulders and looked ahead to big primary votes in Wisconsin, New York, and Pennsylvania, where, again, our campaign expected to do well—especially now that it was a three-person race and I seemed to stand as a clear alternative to the other two remaining candidates. Trump and Cruz were both ahead of me in terms of their delegate counts and in national surveys, but I continued to poll well ahead of them on the all-important question of which one of the remaining Republican candidates stood the best chance of defeating Hillary Clinton in a general election.

(Of course, as we now know, these head-to-head polls were about as meaningful as virtually every other poll taken before Election Day, because Donald Trump did just fine when it came right down to it, defying expectations and so-called expert analysis. After all, what does it matter that I might have been beating Hillary Clinton in a theoretical matchup when Donald Trump would go on to beat her in fact?)

With a win in Ohio in my rearview mirror, and with voting in New York and Pennsylvania on the horizon, I got together with my team and thought about ways we could push our message. Our town halls had been tremendous, and they were getting bigger each time out, but the media had never been able to capture the excitement and energy we all felt at those events, so we determined that the next best thing would be to transpose the upbeat, hopeful notes from a town hall into a major address. That was the impulse behind the "Two Paths" speech, which would highlight the very clear differences among the remaining candidates. I'd already been sounding that great line about refusing to take the low road to the highest office in the land, so we looked to reinforce the high-road/low-road distinction—and from there, I was off and running, determined to make a forceful case for my candidacy and to offer a strongly worded indictment (without naming names) of my opponents' tactics and positions.

What follows, then, are the nuts and bolts of my "Two Paths" speech. Take a look and see what you think:

> I am going to talk today about the choice America faces in this election. It is a choice between two paths—two very different paths. As we make this choice, the world is watching. The world is watching because America is civilization's brightest beacon. Freedom-loving people depend on our leadership for peace and stability. Civilization's enemies only seek our fall.
>
> Presidents come and presidents go, and while the president does really matter, it's the democratic principles that have made us that leader for more than two centuries and that have been sturdy enough to transcend political and ideological differences, a civil war, two world wars, and a century of technological and societal upheaval. Through it all we have remained history's greatest force for good because we have stayed true to who we are—one nation, under God, with liberty and justice for all.
>
> This election may well be one of the most consequential of many generations because the next president will face so many complex pressures—from within and without. [These pressures] will force tough decisions from not only our leaders but from each of us, and we won't always like our options. The issues we confront—from fighting ISIS; handling Russia, China, North Korea, and the Middle East; to addressing displaced workers, civil rights, and the new plague of drug addiction at home, as well as slow economic growth and rising debt, are all critical. The importance of making

the right choices certainly cannot be understated. It can overload us if we let it. But even in the face of this multitude of complex, thorny problems, clarity can emerge.

From the fog of anxiety, the seemingly endless choices can be reduced and then reduced again and reduced again, and they eventually are whittled down to just two. Here they are: Will we turn our backs on the ideals of America that have seen us through for more than two centuries? Or are we going to reaffirm that America is, in Ronald Reagan's words, "This last best hope for man on earth"?

\* \* \*

This is our choice.

For some, the challenges we face, the myriad choices, the potential changes that each decision presents—[they] could give rise to fear or anger. [They] could be paralyzing. The response for some is to retreat into the past—to yearn for "the way things used to be." To these people, today's America is only seen as a broken place, and the people who did the breaking are "the other." People with more money or less money; people with different-sounding last names or different religious beliefs or different-colored skin or life-styles or—whatever. You get the idea.

We have been told that because of all this change, America has become dark, that we have succumbed and that we are no longer strong. We are told that we are no longer respected in the world. In fact, we are even told that foreign governments are actually controlling our destiny because they have become smarter than us and tougher than us.

This picture of America in economic and moral decline is, of course, always followed up with warnings of our impending destruction. For many Americans, these fears and this outlook are as real as the building we are in today. And the anger they cause is real.

It is true, we are fighters in America, but we fight for what is good and what is right—and when we do that we win. Don't let anyone ever tell you otherwise. When we come together, when we unite as a country, America always wins.

For those who are angry or afraid, I want to assure you there is another, better way.

Some who feed off of the fears and anger that are felt by some of us and exploit it feed their own insatiable desire for fame or attention. That could drive America down into a ditch, not make us great again.

Just as disturbing are the solutions they offer. We have heard proposals to create a religious test for immigration, to target neighborhoods for surveillance, impose Draconian tariffs which would crush trade and destroy American jobs. We have heard proposals to drop out of NATO, abandon Europe to Russia, possibly use nuclear weapons in Europe, end our defense partnerships in Asia, and tell our Middle East allies that they have to go it alone. We have been offered hollow promises to impose a value-added tax, balance budgets through simple and whimsical cuts in "fraud, waste and abuse."

We have been promised that unpopular laws shall be repealed simply through the will of a strong man in the White House, and that Supreme Court justices will be empowered with some new extra-Constitutional ability to investigate former public officials.

I have stood on a stage and watched with amazement as candidates wallowed in the mud, viciously attacked one another, called each other liars, and disparaged each other's character.

Those who continuously push that type of behavior are not worthy of the office they are seeking.

And as for me, I will not take the low road to the highest office in the land.

Just as an all-consuming fear of America in decline ends in visions of America's destruction, a political strategy based on exploiting Americans instead of lifting them up inevitably leads to divisions, paranoia, isolation, and promises that can never, ever be fulfilled.

I say to you that this path to darkness is the antithesis of all that America has meant for 240 years.

\* \* \*

Some have a different response to the pressures they see bearing down on America—and themselves. It would never occur to me that America would break, or could break, from challenges to our economy or security. We harden with resolve through ingenuity and coming together. We can't sit by idly and expect fate or destiny to sweep in and rescue us. We always roll up our sleeves and get to work when the going gets tough. We have never seen the American spirit fail.

America's strength is that we are bound by shared ideas, by communities and families and people who are free, creative, and giving.

This is what makes America great, not some politician or some law.

The spirit of our country rests in us. And, notwithstanding all our challenges, America still is great.

Take any measure, whether it's life expectancy, medicine, nutrition, technology, innovation, transportation, or even economic power. America's economy is still the largest and most productive in the world. We're bigger than the next two economies—China and Japan—combined.

America still leads the world in making things.

America is among the largest exporters of goods and services in the world.

America is home to six out of the top ten universities in the world.

America is the world's inventor and leads in intellectual property.

Don't let anybody, particularly a politician, tell you that America is not great. That doesn't mean we aren't capable of drifting. We can—and we have been. And too many Americans are still being left behind, or are making it but feel betrayed by a system that became "too big to fail."

Too many feel that government and politicians have betrayed them.

There are a lot of Americans who ask why no one is speaking for them.

Why is it no one is working for you?

Why is it you hear all these promises from politicians and nothing comes of it?

And you are right. For too long, politicians have been making promises based upon polling or what was politically expedient. That is not leadership. Leadership is the willingness to walk a lonely road with a team of people with their eyes fixed on the horizon, focused on solving problems and healing our country.

Leading is serving.

\* \* \*

There is a better, higher path.

True leadership means pursuing it, even if it is hard. The

sacrifice is part of the job, however, because leaders can't lead unless they are servants first. To run for president, you have to respect the dignity of a job where close to 320 million people are depending on you. Our campaigns should be full of ideas that provide energy and solutions, innovations and excitement, for whatever office we are running for. Because we all have to look our families in the eye and know that we raised the bar.

I want to be able to look my wife and daughters in the eye and know that they're proud of me and the campaign we are running.

American leadership is at its finest when it buckles on that irrepressible can-do spirit that says anything is possible and that everyone can participate in America's blessings. You see, we can restore our economy, rebuild our military, make America safe from terrorism, and reengage as the leader in the world again. We can do this with reasonable and proven solutions rooted in the American ideals that have seen us through tough days before. The proven solutions are right in front of us. We know what needs to be done. There is no better and quicker cure for America's challenges than to grow the economy and stimulate private-sector job creation. To have the resources to solve problems, we need economic strength.

In the '90s, when we balanced the federal budget, paid down the federal debt, cut taxes, and created surpluses, the result was a sustained period of economic growth, lower interest rates, job creation, and national prosperity. Businesses were growing, unemployment was at historic lows, and nearly anyone who wanted a job could have one. In fact, the labor market became a buyer's market for the job seeker.

This was no small feat.

Think for a moment about what we did: for the first time

since Americans walked on the moon, the federal government had a balanced budget. We didn't only balance the budget. We were also able to reform welfare, end generational dependency, reform the Pentagon to strengthen our defenses, cut the capital gains tax, and much more.

You know, I tell younger audiences about this, and they look at me like I'm crazy. They don't believe it ever happened. But we know it did, and it can happen again. It just takes leadership, the will to challenge the status quo, and a willingness to work across the aisle.

Yes, we have to be willing to work with the other party.

I believe that Americans are not only fed up with Washington for what they have not done, but also tired of the partisan bickering. That doesn't mean you compromise your principles. I don't think anyone would accuse Ronald Reagan of compromising his principles, but he did work with the Democratic speaker Tip O'Neill. That's because Ronald Reagan was a leader.

The job of a leader is to first slow down and listen. Then you set an agenda that meets America's needs, and you bring everyone together to make it reality.

There's no place for dividing, polarizing, pointing fingers, or trading on short-term political gain. I hold to this philosophy of leadership because I watched great leaders practice it successfully, and I've seen it work in my own experience. I worked for ten years to pass that balanced budget. It was hard work. When I became chairman of the budget committee, our team was able to get it done—even with a Democrat in the White House. We were proud when we reformed welfare, and as a member of the Armed Services Committee we all came together to reform the Pentagon and realign our military services [in a way] that resulted in a central command structure that allowed the services to work together.

It's the same formula we used in Ohio. We were facing an $8 billion deficit and had lost 350,000 jobs. In a few short years, we turned that deficit into a surplus of $2 billion and gave Ohioans the largest tax cut of any state in the country. We even repealed the death tax.

Ohio has now created 417,000 private-sector jobs. It's working. And we continue to work to make sure that no one is left behind.

This can work for America again as well. This is why I've proposed a 100 Day Agenda for when I am president.

- We will restore our economy with a fiscal plan to balance the budget.
- We will freeze all federal regulations for one year except health and safety, and rebuild our rule-making system to stop crushing small businesses.
- We will simplify and reduce the taxes on individuals so all Americans keep more of what they earn.
- We will reduce taxes on businesses and end double taxation so that they will invest in America and not in Europe.
- We will send welfare, education, Medicaid, highway infrastructure, and job training back to where we live in the states.
- We will protect the border and use common sense on immigration reform that includes a guest worker program.
- And, we will fix Social Security so that we keep the promise to our seniors and future generations.

When we do these things, we will unleash economic growth, which means more jobs, higher wages, and the restoration of the American Dream that our children will inherit a better America than we received from our parents.

With increased stability and strength, America can rebuild its military while at the same time reform the Pentagon to operate like a twenty-first-century enterprise. We will resume leadership of the world and as we do that, we will treat our veterans with respect and lift them to make sure they have what they need, whether it's health care, jobs, or housing.

When America is strong, less dependent on debt, and growing economically, we can reclaim our place as a leader in the world.

Finally, when America is strong and actively engaged in the world, the world is a safer place and America is a safer place.

You know, this is why we do these things. This is about how we want our country to be. You see, economic growth is not an end unto itself. It is a means to make possible everything we want for our nation and our communities and our families.

And, by the way, as we have growth, we have the ability to bring in from the cold those who live in the shadows, those who are forgotten: the poor, the mentally ill, the disabled.

As Americans, we believe that everyone deserves a chance to get ahead. We give them the chance when we give them a hand.

Everyone should have an opportunity to pursue their God-given destiny.

\* \* \*

Yes, there is much to fix in America.

Yes, there are reasons for our anxieties and fears.

Our country has been drifting. Why? Because we have forgotten the formula that makes us strong and [have] caved to political considerations instead. We've seemed to have lost our way. We are stalled. We are at risk of jeopardizing a better future for our children.

I understand why Americans are fearful and distrustful and looking for a reason for the way they feel. I was raised in a small Pennsylvania steel town where if the wind blew the wrong way, people would be out of work. It's awful to feel that insecurity, to feel that circumstances are out of your control, to feel like nobody cares and all the institutions have abandoned you.

But we Americans have overcome challenges before.

Some think that the anger some Americans are expressing is defined by some nostalgic look backward for simpler times. I don't agree. What Americans are looking for is that quality of leadership we are sorely missing from the past to address today's problems. At each moment of crisis in America, we have united as a country and a people. It's always been our secret weapon. It's so simple but it is also invincible.

I spoke earlier about the spirit of our country. But let me say, our strength and spirit do not reside with a president or any politician. Our strength resides within ourselves. The spirit of our country rests in the neighborhoods. It rests in our people. We are the ones with the strength to change the world. The power is within each and every one of us.

A united America is undefeatable. We are an exceptional country. And that's because we are the exception in history— we are not an ethnic group or religion or language. We are that last great hope for earth that Reagan often spoke of, because we have shown that when people from many different backgrounds and ideas and beliefs come together with a common, noble purpose—to be free and just—we are unbeatable.

* * *

Two paths.

One choice—the path that exploits anger, encourages resentment, turns fear into hatred, and divides people. This path solves nothing, demeans our history, weakens our country, and cheapens each of us. It has but one beneficiary and that is the politician who speaks of it.

The other path is the one America has been down before. It is well trod, it is at times steep, but it is solid. It is the same path our forebears took together.

It is from this higher path that we are offered the greater view. And imagine for a moment with me that view. Fear turns to hope because we remember to take strength from each other. Uncertainty turns to peace because we reclaim our faith in the American ideals that have carried us upward before. And America's supposed decline becomes its finest hour because we came together to say no to those who would prey on our human weakness and instead chose leadership that serves, helping us look up, not down.

This is the path I believe in.

This is the America I believe in.

And this is the America I know all Americans want us to be.

Please join me on this higher path. Together, united, we can reclaim the America we love and hold so dear. And lift all of us up to partake in its, and the Lord's, many blessings.

# 10.

# Keeping the Message

As we turned the corner from April into May, I believed we were very much in this thing and that there was a very real possibility we could send the race to the Republican National Convention. Granted, I was no longer in a position to win enough delegates to secure the nomination outright, but it was entirely possible that a consensus front-runner like Donald Trump couldn't win them, either, so we were counting on doing well in the remaining primary states and holding our ground until we could get to Cleveland in July.

Anyway, that was the plan.

So, we pressed on—not because we were out to block my opponents from the nomination, as some were suggesting, but because we continued to believe that we were in the best position to defeat Hillary Clinton in the general election, and that I offered the surest path forward for our party and the nation.

Here again, it helps to set the scene: Following Senator Marco Rubio's exit from the campaign on March 15, Ted Cruz spent the next month or so telling anyone who would listen to him that I should get out of the race. I was in his sights, and Cruz was on the offensive—but I *found* it pretty offensive that he was going after me at this late date with what was essentially a tactical argument. I took it as a sign of a flailing campaign: instead of challenging the clear front-runner, or doubling-down and looking to attract a wider base of support, he was trying to appeal to voters on the basis of strategy. You'd think he would have been out there campaigning on the issues. According to Cruz, the Kasich campaign stood in the way of his ability to compete effectively in the remaining primary states, and he presented himself as the last and best hope of traditional conservative Republicans looking to keep Donald Trump from winning the party's nomination.

I suppose I could have been out there saying the same things about the Cruz campaign, but I just kept doing my town halls, holding fund-raisers, visiting local businesses and civic groups, and trying to build on the momentum we all felt coming out of our primary win in Ohio.

And giving speeches like the "Two Paths" address I shared in the previous chapter.

To be clear, just as I believed that Donald Trump and I were on two separate paths, Ted Cruz and I were also on entirely different roads to a hoped-for nomination.

In order to tell the next part of the story, some additional context is needed. It helps to remind readers that the narrative coming out of the Cruz camp was that I had no business being in the race at this point. They believed I should have dropped out after South Carolina, and they kept pointing out that I'd won only my home state, and had collected a meager number of delegates. Even in a contested convention scenario, they believed they were better positioned to make a run at the nomination, with more than five hundred delegates and a strong base of funds.

However, we saw things a little differently over in the Kasich camp. All along, we'd taken what we believed was a thoughtful and deliberate approach. We stayed on in the race with clear eyes. We had money in our campaign coffers. We never had to lay people off—in fact, one of the reasons we'd managed to keep the lights on in our campaign for as long as we had was because we were so careful at managing our money. Early on, as we looked ahead at the primary calendar, our thinking was that Ted Cruz would have his day in the South, but when the southern primary states came around on that calendar, he wasn't able to close the deal. People just weren't buying whatever he was selling. So, as we looked ahead to the Indiana primary, our feeling was that Cruz's strongest primary states were behind him, while ours (other than New Hampshire and Ohio) were ahead of us.

Quite a different take on where things stood, don't you think?

Admittedly, both Cruz and I were looking to take our campaigns to a contested convention, but even though Cruz was well ahead of me in committed delegates, we did not believe that the count in his favor made a stronger argument for his candidacy over mine—notwithstanding the fact that my team fully expected to be able to close that gap a little bit in the remaining primary contests.

Meanwhile, our polling was showing that if I dropped out of the race, my supporters would largely go to Trump; if Cruz dropped out, the tracking was suggesting that his voters would largely come over to me.

For all these reasons (and a couple more besides), we believed we stood a better chance than Cruz of denying Trump the magic number of 1,237 delegates needed to secure the Republican nomination.

So, that's where we were, as this three-way race took full and final shape.

As you can imagine, there was a lot of backstage drama in the last weeks of the campaign that didn't really get reported. (Or, at least, didn't get reported *accurately*.) One of the most interesting bits of drama had to do with a series of conversations my team had with members of Ted Cruz's team on how to keep Donald Trump from crossing that 1,237-delegate threshold. When word of these conversations got out, it was reported in the media that Senator Cruz and I were somehow colluding. *The New York Times* called it "an alliance . . . formed to deny Donald J. Trump the Republican presidential nomination."

Well, that was hardly accurate. It was an alliance only in the sense that our interests were in alignment for the moment, and our representatives had a brief conversation about it. It's not as if the two of us were teaming up or joining forces in any way. There was no backroom deal or secret negotiations. The story that made headlines was that each of us had agreed not to campaign too, too aggressively in upcoming primary states where we weren't expecting to do well—basically, getting out of each other's way and leaving it to our opponent to go up against Trump in a two-person contest. That's all it was. Our thinking on this had nothing to do with Ted Cruz and everything to do with my team's agenda: with money an increasing concern and the calendar once again working against us, we'd already decided that we weren't going to spend much time in Indiana ahead of the May 3 primary, in the same way that we'd determined early on not to devote too many resources to Iowa ahead of the caucuses there in January. The Cruz camp, it appeared, was having the same internal discussions about upcoming primaries in Oregon and New Mexico, so it just worked out that we had different battlegrounds. Our "two paths" to the Republican convention didn't overlap in some states.

It wasn't even a news story, as far as I was concerned. It was just a reasonable allocation of our available resources, but the Cruz camp wanted to make an announcement about it on Monday, April 25. It got a lot of attention, which I guess was to be expected. And when reporters started asking me about it immediately afterward, I answered honestly, saying it wasn't any kind of big deal. And it wasn't. Even so, Senator Cruz seemed determined to get some press out of the situation, and I now had to answer for it. I told reporters that if people wanted to come out and support me in Indiana, I'd be happy to have their vote.

Well, as you might imagine, this left the journalists covering our campaign scratching their heads and writing articles about the "breakdown" of a supposed alliance between Cruz and me, and left the Cruz team crying foul and saying I'd reneged on our deal.

I heard that and thought, What deal?

As a side note, I want to state for the record that I'm not comfortable writing about these backroom conversations. I believe it takes away from the message I want to bring across to readers— the message I wanted to bring across in the campaign. All I cared about, really, was talking about the very real problems facing the country, and giving people hopeful solutions they could attach to their own lives. I wasn't interested in the *politics* of the campaign; I was interested in the people. Yet, my own people, those folks working with me on my team, found this kind of back-and-forth endlessly fascinating, like a puzzle to be worked over and solved. So, I'm spending some time on it here because I suspect there are some readers who might be wondering what was going on behind the scenes as the campaign wound down.

Here's something worth noting: what was never reported on the so-called "alliance" front was an earlier conversation my team had with the Cruz campaign. What happened was John Weaver got a text from Jeff Roe, his counterpart on the Cruz campaign, asking to meet, so Weaver went to see him. Weaver told me later that Jeff Roe started bashing us as soon as they sat down, saying things like "I don't know why you're still in this" and "There's no way you can win." After a couple minutes of this, Weaver put his hand up and said, "Jeff, you asked for this meeting. Did you call me here just to tell us to get out of the race, or was there something else you wanted to discuss?"

The "something else" was Pennsylvania, which was coming up on the primary calendar. This private "ask" came just a couple weeks after Marco Rubio's very public "ask" that we stand down in Florida, ahead of the March 15 primary there, since he was planning to stand down in Ohio, where we would vote the same day. Keep in mind, Rubio's people had never discussed this with us—their candidate had just put it out there that this was what he was doing and that he expected me to respond in kind. It was bizarre, but such is the nature of presidential politics when the field has taken on meaningful shape, the clock is winding down, and the trailing candidates are running low on campaign funds.

Personally, I found this kind of talk between candidates a little unsettling, a little unprofessional, and more than a little unseemly. Obviously, these other campaigns wouldn't have been reaching out to us if they didn't think there was something in it *for them*. It's not like they woke up one morning and said, "Hmm, I wonder if there's any new strategy we could put in place that might help Governor Kasich." No, sir. Nevertheless, John Weaver agreed to the meeting with Jeff Roe on my behalf, and now that he was there, he wanted to know what Jeff Roe had in mind. If nothing else, he was curious.

What the Cruz campaign wanted, essentially, was for us to concede Pennsylvania. Their message was clear: if we stopped campaigning in Pennsylvania, and pulled all our advertising there, they would do the same in New York.

John Weaver didn't really see the point of agreeing to this, because we certainly didn't want to discourage any of our supporters in Pennsylvania from coming out to vote for me in the primary. But since the Cruz team seemed to be on its heels, John thought it would be amusing to push back just a little. He said to Jeff Roe, "Maryland, too."

He took it to me afterward for my approval, but I didn't really give it a lot of thought. I had to admire this bit of gamesmanship on Weaver's part, carving Maryland into the deal, but I didn't really have the head for this type of maneuvering. Did I sign off on the deal? Sure, but I didn't think anything of it. As I wrote earlier, I'm not a big strategy guy. I'm all about the message, and at that point I was still focused on bringing a message of hope and positivity to the campaign.

I said to Weaver, "Do you think this is something we ought to do?"

And he said, "We're doing it anyway."

That turned out to the first bit of "collusion" between the Cruz and Kasich camps, Pennsylvania for Maryland and New York, well ahead of the soon-to-be-infamous Indiana-for-Oregon-and–New Mexico "alliance." Weaver's first deal never made it into the papers because my guys were able to convince the Cruz guys to keep quiet about it. Truth be told, to announce this approach as any kind of mutually agreed upon strategy would have come across as a Hail Mary pass, when I believed we still had some ground game left, and time enough on the clock to execute that game plan. To put it out there that we were marking our territories in this way would have weakened us in the eyes of our front-running opponent,

Donald Trump, who already seemed to think our campaigns were teetering. We didn't need to give him any reason to confirm that thinking, any ammunition to use against us, and it would have sent a message to voters that we were a little desperate.

Yet, if the Cruz team was offering to step aside and leave Maryland, Oregon, New Mexico, and New York to me, and in return we didn't have to do anything but stick to our strategy and pull out of Pennsylvania and Indiana, leaving our chances there to the fates, why wouldn't we go ahead and agree to that? All we'd be doing under this Cruz-spun setup was what we would have been doing anyway—only, in this scenario, we'd be doing it knowing that one of our two opponents wouldn't put up much of a fight in the states where we hoped to do well.

Jump ahead another couple of weeks, to the California Republican Convention, on Friday, April 26, immediately following a big slate of primaries in the northeastern states of Rhode Island, Delaware, Pennsylvania, Maryland, and Connecticut, where I'd posted a solid second-place showing to Donald Trump in four of those contests. Tellingly, the only state where I trailed Ted Cruz in the balloting was Pennsylvania, with 19 percent of the vote to his 22 percent. That was about the same margin, in the inverse, that we saw in Maryland—so, clearly, that first piece of horse trading had amounted to a whole lot of nothing.

While we were in California, Cruz representatives reached out to arrange another meeting—this time to be attended by Senator Cruz himself. I agreed to meet with him in a hotel room at the San Francisco Grand Hyatt, out by the airport. Cruz was late, which kind of hacked me off, since he was the one who'd asked for the meeting. When he finally arrived, we exchanged a few awkward pleasantries and then he got right to it. He said he thought I should get out of the race.

I'd thought that's where he'd take the conversation, but I'd expected him to be a little subtler about it, maybe finesse his way around the topic. But there it was, in blunt terms: "You should drop out."

I didn't quite know what to say to this, so I flipped the script. I said, "Me? I think you should be the one to drop out."

It was extremely tense in that hotel room, but it was clear soon enough that neither one of us was going anywhere. Then, when Cruz saw that I wasn't about to politely fold up my tent, he wanted to know what our strategy would be going forward if he decided to exit the race after the Indiana primary the following Tuesday.

I couldn't give him an answer—I honestly hadn't thought that far ahead. There were too many eventualities to consider. We'd heard coming into this Hyatt meeting that Cruz was running out of hard dollars to keep his campaign operation going. He might have had a bunch of money in his Super PAC, but that money couldn't keep his campaign going on a day-to-day basis.

So, there we were, in a small hotel room by the airport, at a stalemate—only, I felt that Cruz's position was weakening.

## AND THEN THERE WERE TWO

Something to keep in mind as a backdrop to all this last-minute maneuvering as we leaned into May: in the middle of all this, you had Mitt Romney working to keep Trump from the nomination. He was on a kind of "Anyone but Trump" crusade. This, too, was interesting because Romney had campaigned for me in Ohio, and then had gone out and voted for Cruz in the Utah nominating caucus. It was an odd about-face for a man who'd been his party's presidential nominee the last time out. In a Facebook post announcing his support of Cruz, Romney wrote, "I like Governor Kasich. I have campaigned with him. He has a solid record as governor. I would have voted for him in Ohio. But a vote for Governor Kasich in future contests makes it extremely likely that Trumpism will prevail."

Eventually, Romney would float the idea of an independent presidential run, either for himself or a candidate he would pledge to support. More than any other national figure in the Republican Party, Mitt Romney was out there sounding the alarm against Trump, playing both sides against the middle, and doing whatever he could to send us to a brokered convention in Cleveland in July. He was loud and clear on this; he let it be known that he would do anything and everything in his power to keep Trump from the Republican ticket and, once that seemed like a foregone conclusion, from winning the White House. Alongside all this were a lot of pundits and political insiders speculating that Romney was still hanging back, hoping there'd be an eleventh-hour hue and cry for him to enter the race and save the party. (Although, at this point, it would have been more like a thirteenth-hour conscription, and such a move would have failed to recognize that what a great many Republican voters believed the party needed saving *from* were old-school GOP stalwarts like Mitt Romney.)

That's where we were as we headed into the Indiana primary on Tuesday, May 3—a winner-take-all contest in every sense of the phrase, it turned out, because a Trump victory in the Hoosier state would have made it extremely difficult (but not mathematically impossible) to keep him from the 1,237 delegates needed to secure the nomination. We would have had to run the table going forward, keeping Trump off the board in all future primaries— which, frankly, didn't seem all that likely. Therefore, Indiana loomed large as the primary approached. As I've indicated, we were mostly sitting this one out, but the Cruz campaign was making a full-on push, announcing that week that Carly Fiorina would be the senator's vice-presidential pick and securing the endorsement of Indiana governor Mike Pence. Each of those announcements made headlines for the Cruz campaign for a couple of minutes of the daily news cycle. Yet, despite all this late maneuvering and politicking, Trump won the state handily.

This turned out to be the knockout blow for the Cruz campaign.

I had a phone conversation with Cruz before he announced he was suspending his presidential run. I think he just wanted to feel me out, see what I was planning on doing. It wasn't really clear what he was hoping to hear from me, and he certainly wasn't sharing his own plans, because he didn't let on that he himself was thinking of quitting, even though he threw in the towel only an hour or so later.

Me, I was holding onto that towel for the time being. Trump's Indiana win might have been a knockout blow for our campaign as well, but I wanted to give it some time to sink in. We even put out a press release following the Cruz announcement to reassure voters that we were moving forward. It included the following statement: "Our strategy has been and continues to be one that involves winning the nomination at an open convention."

My thinking that night, as we assessed the result in Indiana, was that we could press on for another week or so. That we *should* press on for another week or so. That we had enough money in hand on the campaign side to keep the organization going for another while. Most of all, I thought we owed it to our tireless volunteers and faithful supporters to play out the clock and hope like crazy we could turn things around. With the field of Republican hopefuls now down to two, we knew there'd be a greater focus on our message, and that the "two paths" to the presidency I'd laid out in my speech before the Women's National Republican Club would stand as a stark reminder of the two decidedly different choices facing Republican voters. There was now spread out before us the high road to the highest office in the land, and the low road to the highest office in the land, and I felt bound to keep walking that high road for as long as I possibly could.

At the same time, I worried about how my thinking might bump against reality—meaning that, at some point, we'd have to make a fund-raising push, all the while knowing that we might have to shut things down at any moment.

Before turning in, I had a late-night conversation with my friend Wilber James, who had a great way of getting me to see a situation as it really was and not as it appeared. We talked about how I might reconcile the sense I was getting from my team that we ought to keep the lights on for the next while with the difficult reality of continuing to ask for money and support, when I knew deep down that it was only a matter of time before we had to suspend our campaign as well.

I said, "How can I go out there and do any kind of fund-raising when I'm not even sure I can stay in the race?"

To which Wilber very reasonably suggested that I sleep on it.

So, I did. I actually went to bed that night trying to convince myself that we were entering an exciting new phase in our campaign—a conviction that didn't last too terribly long, I'm afraid. I woke up the next morning worried that the positive message of our campaign would be lost if Trump started attacking me even more forcefully and started yelling that I had no chance at the nomination.

Once again, I reached out to my friends and advisers—probably what I was doing was gathering as many trusted and valued opinions as I could muster. I remember speaking to Don Thibaut that morning—like me, he was worried I might lose the message of our campaign if I overstayed my welcome. I even spoke to Jai Chabria, who'd left the fold after nearly twenty years as my right-hand guy, but who never lost his concern for me, or for the campaign he'd helped to launch.

He said, "Be careful here, John."

Meanwhile, I should mention that in addition to feeling excited and conflicted, I was also angry—furious, actually—at Republican National Committee chairman Reince Priebus, who, following Ted Cruz's withdrawal, had tweeted that Donald Trump was now the party's presumptive nominee. I thought that was low, and it got my back up.

"What Priebus did was dead wrong," I later told *The Washington Post*, igniting a feud between me and the party chairman that would continue through the general election. "I was still in it," I said of the race, "and I think he dissed me, and I think it's inappropriate. I haven't spoken to him. I don't think there's any point to it. I don't even understand what he was doing. It was amateur hour for him."

(For the record, my daughters appreciated that I was quoted in the paper saying the word *dissed*, and that I had apparently used it correctly.)

As long as I'm setting the record straight, I'll mention here that I had a very civil meeting with Reince Priebus at the Trump Inaugural. He had signed on as the White House chief of staff, and I suppose it was inevitable that we would run into each other, and as we shook hands I realized that there was no room in this scenario for continued bitterness—at least, not on my part. I still thought he'd treated me shabbily toward the end of the campaign, but it was time to move on.

Other than Reince Priebus, though, my main worry following Cruz's exit from the race was money. I found myself thinking about it more and more as we'd set out each day for a full day of events. Remember, all along, I'd kept saying that I would not go into debt to finance the campaign. We still had enough in our account to keep it going for another while, and there was every reason to think that, in my new role as "last man standing" against Donald Trump, it might even be easier to raise the hard dollars we'd need to keep at it all the way to the convention. I could only imagine that there was money on the Super PAC side of things as well, but of course there was no way to know for certain, since I wasn't involved and could therefore only imagine.

Looking back on it, I'd have to say we did a decent job of fundraising, on both sides of the campaign. In all, we probably raised close to $20 million for the campaign and about $29 million for the Super PAC—big numbers when you think about how we started out, with virtually no name recognition outside Ohio, and stuck somewhere in the middle of a crowded field of hopefuls for the first six months or so. True, these fund-raising numbers were relatively small compared to the big bucks some of the other candidates had been able to raise on the Super PAC side: Jeb Bush with roughly $120 million; Marco Rubio, about $50 million; Ted Cruz, between $60 and $80 million.

But here I could only marvel that little Johnny Kasich from McKees Rocks, Pennsylvania, had managed to raise close to $50 million in a run for president of the United States!

It wasn't nearly enough, as it turned out, but at the same time, it was *everything*.

## THE END OF SOMETHING

One of the reasons I wanted to take this wait-and-see approach before I decided whether to continue the campaign was to buy time to see if there would be a significant influx in donations, the kind of money that would allow me to blanket the airwaves in upcoming primary states like Oregon, Washington, California, and even New Mexico. Remember, if I'd stayed in the race, from there on in we would have to make a clean sweep in the remaining contests to keep Donald Trump on the short side of the delegate count. Also, a strong showing in the popular vote in these late-primary states—if we couldn't keep Trump from that 1,237 number—would at least help make my case if we were looking at the prospect of a contested convention.

In the end, it was the money that made the decision for me to pull the plug on my campaign—not because we didn't have it, and not because I didn't think we could raise more of it, but because it didn't feel right to be out there asking people to donate if we knew there was a very real possibility I'd have to call it quits in just a few days. I'd never gone out and raised money for one of my political campaigns without fully and firmly believing I could win. I mean, I couldn't go out there and say, "Let's give it another week, folks, and see how much money we can raise." That would have been disingenuous. Worse, it would have created a kind of "death watch" around our campaign.

Still, I was of two minds on this as I set out on the morning of Wednesday, May 4, for Washington, D.C., for a series of fundraisers and a visit with the editorial board of *USA Today*. We also had two national security adviser briefings, and a press "gaggle" scheduled for our arrival at Dulles Airport. On the one hand, I was energized by the events of the past month—our thrilling primary win in Ohio; the overwhelming response we continued to get from my "Two Paths" speech; Cruz's departure from the race; a growing disenchantment among voters in both parties at the likely outcome of the Republican and Democratic primaries and the choice they would soon face in the general election. On the other hand, I was concerned—by the swift dismissal of my candidacy by GOP chairman Reince Priebus and others; by the prospect of the all-but-certain attacks that would now find me from the media and the Trump campaign; by the idea that by continuing to ask my supporters for money, I was somehow being hypocritical, since I knew deep down that it was likely just a matter of time before we'd have to call it quits.

Mostly, I was worried about losing the message. We'd spent the past year sounding an important message of hope and decency to the American people, and it would have killed me to see that evaporate if I held on too long. So, as I boarded the plane with my team to set off for the nation's capital, I turned to Chris Schrimpf and asked him for his take on this.

I said, "Do you think we might lose the message?"

Chris answered without really stopping to think about it. He said, "Yeah, it's possible."

That really struck me. I figured he'd at least give it some thought—but perhaps he already had. And now that he'd given his opinion on the matter, it was *all* I could think about. By this point, we were settling into our seats and getting ready to take off. There were Doug, Chris, Alex, and Zach, in their usual spots on the plane, and we were joined on this trip by King Mallory, who had relocated from New Orleans to coordinate national security policy for the campaign; and Pat Kellum, of our highway patrol security team. And I just looked at them, and I kind of knew. At the same time, they were looking at me, and I think they kind of knew.

It was at that moment that I knew I'd have to call it. I didn't say anything just yet, but I knew.

We were due to depart Landmark Aviation in Columbus at 9:30, due to meet the national press in Washington at 10:45—all of which presented a bit of a problem. I was firm in my decision, but I didn't want to announce it without giving it some further thought. Preserving the message of my campaign was my overriding concern at this point—and to do that, I believed, the announcement that I was suspending my campaign needed to be handled just right.

When I finally told my guys what I was thinking, it's not like they were shell-shocked or anything. They could see that this was coming, and now that it was here—well, there wasn't a whole lot they could do. There followed a short discussion on how and when to hold a press conference, but we couldn't very well fly to Washington and step off the plane and hold it there. That made no sense. Besides, there were already a bunch of reporters waiting for us at the airport, expecting another story entirely.

One of the first calls I made while we were still on the plane was to Beth Hansen, who was driving from her home to our headquarters, which was just a couple of miles from the airport. I didn't tell her of my decision just yet, but I said we were holding the plane and asked her to meet us at the airport. When she arrived, that's when I told her. I could immediately see a difference in her demeanor—it was if a great weight had been lifted from her shoulders. Oh, she wasn't happy that we were pulling the plug on the campaign; in fact, she was fairly devastated. At the same time, I could tell from her body language that all those rolling waves of the campaign had really been beating down on her.

We gathered in a small office at the airport and started drafting a statement and made a bunch of phone calls, and in the middle of all this activity, I ducked out behind the building to steal a moment for myself. I didn't tell anyone I was going anywhere. I just kind of wandered out to the airfield, and when I looked up, I was standing with my back to the outside wall of the main office, having a little cry. There was no one around, just me and my thoughts.

I wasn't alone, of course, so I wiped the tears from my eyes and offered up a small prayer. I said, "Lord, it just wasn't to be, but I'm okay."

And I was. Really and truly. For months after the campaign, people would ask me how I was doing, if I'd recovered, and they'd wear these looks of genuine concern for my well-being. But the truth was, then and still, I felt very good about the race we ran and the ways we managed to connect with voters. Even as I stood there behind our borrowed office at that airfield, wiping away my tears while my team sat huddled inside, unpacking our campaign, I felt good about it. Not just good: I felt terrific.

Bob Klaffky joined us at the airport as well. He arrived while I was out back stealing this private moment, so when I got back inside, we all sat in a small conference room that was made available to us while we figured out our next moves. Doug Preisse took a moment when the team was all together to make one final pitch for keeping the campaign going; he really thought there was an argument to be made for continuing on to the convention. But I knew we had breathed our last.

It was time.

We called down to Washington and told the people we were due to meet there that we would be delayed, without really offering a good explanation for that delay. The reporters due to meet us at Dulles would figure it out, we felt sure, but we wanted to hold off on making any sort of statement until we knew what, exactly, we wanted to say.

I called Karen and told her I'd decided to suspend the campaign. She was upset, but she'd seen this coming. In fact, we'd talked about the possibility the night before, as I was sorting through the news of the day—with Trump nearing that 1,237 delegate threshold, and Cruz's withdrawal, and that slap in the face from Reince Priebus.

Next thing I knew, I got a text from Reese at school. She'd seen on social media that I was ending the campaign. (What the heck she was doing on social media during the school day, I'll never know—something to discuss with her teachers, I guess.)

It had never occurred to me that my girls would be plugged into breaking news during the school day, and that I wouldn't have a chance to talk to them about all this before they heard it from someone else. So, what did I do? I went straight from the airport to the girls' school. I recruited Doug Preisse to head on over with me, and when we got there we went to see the principal. He called the girls out of class, and the three of us shared a sweet moment together. What was amazing about that visit to the girls' school was that the students and teachers all seemed to know that I was there—more to the point, to know *why* I was there. As I walked through the lobby, they started to applaud. It was a spontaneous show of emotion and appreciation and genuine good feeling, and I was blown away by it. (Really, really.) Here I'd thought we were making this little detour to share a private moment with my girls, only to be blessed with this somewhat larger private moment—a moment with our Worthington Christian family.

When I tell my friends about that little side trip to the girls' school, they're fairly struck by it. Why? Because it's the sort of thing a parent does when there's been a death in the family, an unexpected tragedy. You go get your kids at school and give them a hug and help them realize that everything is going to be all right. And I guess the end of the campaign did feel a little like a death in the family—at least, that's how it felt to me—although maybe I was projecting my own emotions of the moment onto Emma and Reese. Maybe it was *I* who needed a hug from *them*.

We didn't get around to making a formal announcement until later that afternoon, from the Franklin Park Conservatory, where our entire campaign staff was joined by hundreds of friends and supporters and volunteers. Karen and the girls were at my side of course. And the media were out in force, as they had been since I announced my candidacy at Ohio State the previous July. Alas, the world had changed during the year I'd been running for president—*my* world had changed as well—and I could only be grateful and humbled by the fact that people seemed to want to hear what I had to say as I stepped away from the race.

Included in what I had to say was this: "I have always said that the Lord has a purpose for me, as he has for everyone. And as I suspend my campaign today, I have renewed faith, deeper faith that the Lord will show me the way forward and fulfill the purpose of my life."

## WHAT MATTERS

That purpose, in many ways, found me as forcefully in the months following the suspension of my campaign as it did during the campaign itself. Remember how I wrote earlier that I had almost no name recognition when I decided to run for president this time out? How nobody outside Ohio (and maybe Washington, D.C.) seemed to want to hear what I had to say? Well, the campaign changed all that—dramatically. By the time I exited the race in May, I was pretty well known. The message of hope that had attached to our campaign had somehow spread, and now people were stopping me on the street like never before; reporters were asking me for interviews, instead of the other way around.

As a result, I now found myself on the receiving end of a whole lot of attention. This took some getting used to, I'm afraid. A good illustration of this came about one afternoon in late summer of 2016. I was in New York City having lunch with Phil Griffin, the president of MSNBC. Since suspending my campaign, I had been doing my best to avoid any media attention, mostly because I was tired of answering the same questions over and over about why I wouldn't attend the Republican National Convention, why I was refusing to endorse Donald Trump. Plus, I didn't feel I had anything else to say. I'd run my race, given it my best shot, and come up short. Whatever I had say about the future of this country, my hope for this country—well, I'd said it in my town halls and in the debates. Also, I didn't think it was my place to weigh in on the general election—that was for the pundits and prognosticators. Still, the campaign had cast me as a kind of "person of interest" in the election cycle, so I found myself talking to a lot of influential media types behind the scenes.

So, there I was, having lunch with Phil Griffin, and he happened to mention that MSNBC was launching its new show with Brian Williams that night. Phil let me know how important it would be for Brian Williams to have me as a guest on his debut show, and I gave it some thought. If you remember, Brian Williams was dropped as the lead news anchor at NBC News after it was reported that he might have bent the truth in his reporting from the frontlines, and suspended from the network for a time. Now he was back working for NBC's sister station with another nightly news show of his own, *The 11th Hour with Brian Williams.* I asked Doug Preisse, who was with me at the lunch, to get in touch with our media people to see what they thought about it. Almost immediately, word came back that I should continue to keep a low profile. They suggested that, for the time being, I decline the invitation to appear on Brian's show. I told Phil that my people thought it didn't make sense for me to do any interviews at this time, and that I had to agree with them. He said he understood, but he kept pressing me, so I went back to Doug and asked him to check in again to see if we could make it work. Once again, the answer came back that I should avoid doing any media appearances, so I felt I ought to listen to my folks. After all, I'd brought them on board to advise me on this type of stuff, so I trusted their take.

For a second time during that lunch, I declined Phil Griffin's invitation to appear on the show. Then he asked if I would at least come back to the office with him and say hello to Brian and wish him well. Of course, I was happy to do this: I'd always liked Brian, he'd always been fair to me, and I wanted to let him know that I believed in second chances. And sure enough, he seemed happy to see me when I went up to his office with Phil. We talked for a bit, I wished him luck on the new show, and that was that.

Then, on the ride down in the elevator, I started to regret my decision not to appear on Brian's show, and as soon as my feet hit the sidewalk outside the NBC building at 30 Rockefeller Center, I told myself this was just crazy. I thought back to when I had my own debut on the Fox News Channel and how difficult it was to book guests. My very first guest was Harold Ford Jr., the Democratic congressman from Tennessee, and I could remember how grateful I was when he decided to come on the show. So, I told Doug to call our media team and tell them I was doing Brian's show, despite their good counsel. Then I called Phil Griffin and told him there'd been a change of plans and that I would be happy to do an interview with Brian, if they still wanted me.

I couldn't do the show live, because it was a late-night show and I was scheduled to leave the city that evening, so we made arrangements to tape my segment later that afternoon. Phil Griffin was there in the green room to greet me, along with Chris Matthews, the host of one of the network's flagship programs. We talked for a bit, and then we were joined by a third person—an unlikely visitor on this scene.

I recognized him immediately: Academy Award–winning actor Tom Hanks, who was in the building to promote his latest movie, *Sully*, in which he plays the title character, Chesley Sullenberger, the United Airlines pilot who famously landed a passenger plane on New York's Hudson River.

I shook Tom Hanks's hand and needled him a little. I said, "I understand you don't like Republicans or conservatives very much."

He said, "Oh, I like you just fine."

Someone suggested we take a picture together, and as we smiled for the cameras, I turned to Tom Hanks and needled him a little more. I said, "Just do me a favor, will you? Tell them not to put that movie on anymore of you on that island talking to that volleyball."

He laughed and said, "Don't be criticizing that movie, Governor. That's how I put my kids through college."

The exchange was meaningful to me, not just because I'd always admired Tom Hanks's work, but because it gave me an opening to mention this chance meeting in my interview with Brian Williams, and to bring up the heroic landing of that airplane on the Hudson River—putting it out there how important I thought it was to celebrate our true American heroes, especially after this rancorous campaign.

There was a vacuum out there, I was realizing, that the general election wasn't about to fill, and I thought back to that epiphany I wrote about earlier, the one I'd had as I ended my campaign and started thinking how we all live our lives at a kind of base level. What matters, I reminded myself, are the times we manage to rise above that base level and be our best selves. What matters is the way we reach a little further, dig a little deeper, climb a little higher. What matters is drawing from the strength of character from a lifetime of experience to, say, allow yourself to land a plane in the middle of the Hudson River without incident. What matters are the moments when we go above and beyond, when we live outside ourselves for a little bit, beyond ourselves for a little bit—when we go *big*.

What matters are our moments of grace, after all.

## STAND FOR SOMETHING

Once I stepped away from the race, it fell to me to decide whether I could endorse a man like Donald Trump for president of the United States. People started asking me about it straightaway—members of the press, leaders of the Republican Party, friends and family.

For the longest time, I didn't have a definitive answer. In my heart, I knew I could never support or justify or even understand the ways he comported himself during the campaign. But I didn't feel I could come out and say that now. Instead, I left the door open at first, saying that I wasn't prepared to endorse a Trump candidacy just yet, but that I was willing to sit on the sidelines for the next while and take a wait-and-see approach. If Trump demonstrated a change in his demeanor as he assumed this new position on the national stage, then I could be willing to look at the idea of supporting him in a new light.

During this time, Donald Trump Jr. reached out to John Weaver to float the idea of my considering a spot on the Republican ticket, as Trump's vice president. The conversation was widely reported in the press, so I'm not violating any backroom code by sharing the highlights here—and I do so because what was discussed was so revealing (and telling).

According to John Weaver's account, which he shared with me and other senior members of our team almost as soon as he got off the phone, the Trump campaign had called to gauge my interest in being Donald Trump's vice president.

"The governor would be in charge of all domestic and foreign policy," Donald Jr. reportedly said.

It was a remarkable thing to say—if true—and John Weaver told me he couldn't quite think what to say in response. What he finally came up with was "Well, if that's the case, then what would the president be doing?"

"Why, he'll be busy making American great again," came the reply.

Now, it should be noted that Don Jr. later denied that the conversation took place, but I can only take John Weaver at his word on this. John also offered that there was nothing in Don Jr.'s tone to suggest that the comment was being made ironically or with tongue in cheek. "Making America great again," we could only assume, would be Donald Trump's role, if he managed to win the general election in November; he would leave the running of the country to someone else and keep his focus on the smoke-and-mirrors aspects of the job of president, helping Americans *feel* that he was somehow making their lives better just by being at the helm.

Here again, I wasn't on this call, but I'm relying on John Weaver's account. There was, however, a follow-up call sometime later, from Donald Trump himself—this one made directly to me, this time to see if I would at least consider endorsing him. It was a very brief, very civil call.

One of the comments he made during that call that I thought was interesting had to do with the fact that other candidates had come around to endorsing him. He said, "A lot of the people who were attacking me, they're now supporting me."

I asked him why he thought that was, and he said something to the effect that politicians were like levers. I remember thinking that this was a curious analogy.

I said, "Well, Donald. I'm not a politician."

To which he replied, "Then what can I do to earn your support?"

I put my answer to him in business terms. I told him that I thought we had different values, different objectives. I said, "In a business world, with two different corporate cultures, sometimes it's just not possible to do a merger."

We talked for a little bit about how there'd been a lot of similarities to our campaigns. He recognized the anxieties of a great many Americans, as did I, but he went about addressing those anxieties in a very different way, and that's where we parted company. In order to understand that difference, and why I thought it was important, I suggested that he read a copy of my "Two Paths" speech.

I never heard back from him on this.

If you followed the campaign at all, you'll know that I could never have worked with Donald Trump. And if you've read this far in the book, you'll know why I could never have supported him. Yet, more and more, as the general election approached and I remained steadfast in my position, people seemed to be surprised by my unwillingness to fall into line. What I found surprising was the way all these other Republican presidential candidates took turns shedding what I could only imagine were their own deeply held convictions and setting aside their very public differences with their party's presumptive nominee—some of them even angling for positions in a possible Trump administration.

People weren't only surprised by my refusal to endorse Donald Trump; they were *angered* by it. Specifically, leading up to the Republican National Convention, to be held in Cleveland in July, I started to hear from a number of party officials—led in large part by RNC chairman Reince Priebus, to whom I now appeared not just as a thorn in his side but as a forceful argument against party unity. I was getting a lot of pressure to make an appearance, but I didn't think it was appropriate. You know that old line that used to get tossed around in Hollywood, "You'll never work in this town again." The mood was a little like that, as Republican Party leaders in Washington and at home in Ohio lined up to admonish me for my position, telling me that my point had been made and that it was time to stand with our nominee—or else be made to face the consequences.

I'd hear an argument like that and wonder what the heck these people were talking about. *Consequences?* I'd spent my entire political career not caring a whit about how my deeply held convictions or deeply considered positions would be seen by my Republican colleagues. I was used to going my own way. I had thought that other party members would have been used to me by now.

Keep in mind, my administration had been instrumental in bringing the convention to Ohio in the first place. I'd met with RNC officials myself, together with our JobsOhio organization, to make the case for Cleveland, and we were all thrilled when the Quicken Loans Arena was chosen as the venue.

(By the way, a lot of folks were concerned that the arena, home to the Cleveland Cavaliers, might not be fully available to the

RNC if the Cavaliers had to host the NBA Finals—a prospect most people at that meeting didn't think too likely, so it just goes to show you that our supposed strengths as prognosticators ran to the dominance of LeBron James as well as to Donald Trump.)

Now, there I was, sitting out the convention—but my feeling was that I didn't belong there. Not because I hadn't won the nomination and I was a sore loser. Not because I wanted to push my agenda and saw this silent protest as a way to advance my own views. I just didn't want any part of it, in the same way you wouldn't go to a party at the house of someone you don't know or with whom you weren't friendly. It would have made people uncomfortable. It would have made *me* uncomfortable.

During the convention, I had a breakfast meeting with the Ohio delegation at a nearby hotel, and I explained my thinking on this. A lot of those folks weren't happy with me, but I think after hearing me out, some understood where I was coming from. Then, after Ted Cruz showed up at the convention, a lot of that anger went to him, because of the way he took the stage and quite brazenly refused to endorse the Republican candidate.

Why didn't I endorse Donald Trump simply for the good of the Republican Party? Well, to paraphrase John F. Kennedy, sometimes your party asks too much of you. I am an American before I am a member of the Republican Party. I try not to see our country as red or blue. To me, America is red, white, and blue.

It's funny—despite all this pressure, I never really *felt* any pressure. I never waffled, never wavered. I was comfortable with the stand I was taking—which, really, was no stand at all. I simply could not swallow hard and set aside everything I believed for the good of the party. This election was about so much more than that, and it amazed me to flip through the news channels at night and see all these pundits floating my name for this or that position in a

Trump administration. It left me wondering if they'd had even *listened* to a word I'd said during the campaign.

But that's the nature of politics. It's a game to most people. You fight the good fight, but you wear your team colors, and you say what you need to say to keep your job, to keep your position of influence, to keep in the good graces of your friends and colleagues.

In the end, as was widely reported, I cast my vote in early balloting back home in Ohio for my good friend John McCain—a man who'd been famously (and unforgivably) derided by Donald Trump during the campaign, but a man who had always carried himself in public life as someone who said what he thought and stood for his beliefs. I knew full well that a write-in vote for the Arizona senator wouldn't amount to much in the grand scheme of things, but it meant a whole lot to me to be able to cast my vote for a true American hero.

To those who suggest that my vote would have been more meaningful, more impactful if I had cast it for Hillary Clinton, I offer this: I could not have stood with her any more than I could have stood with Trump. I was opposed to her political philosophy: she represented bureaucracy, more taxes, more regulation—all the things that I believed were choking our country. We live in a world of Uber and smartphones and Snapchat, a world of speed and autonomous vehicles and drones. There are exciting innovations all around, but I looked at Hillary Clinton and the people who would likely make up her administration, and all I could see were the slow, tired, worn-out approaches of the past.

As to Hillary Clinton's demeanor during the campaign, I didn't think she was as down and dirty as some of her Republican counterparts, but she was fairly dismissive of Trump's supporters, many of them blue-collar workers like my mother and father. She was dismissive of Trump himself, and she struck me as out of touch with the heart and soul of our country, as if she'd forgotten the very people who'd strengthened her party. Yes, she offered a clear alternative to Donald Trump, but it was an alternative I wasn't buying. And as I thought about the binary choice Americans faced in this election, I tried to imagine what my father would have made of the Clinton campaign—my father, a hardworking mailman who'd been a Democrat all his life, would not have recognized Hillary Clinton's Democratic Party, and he would not have supported it.

Neither could I.

So, I cast my lone vote for my friend John McCain—and in this small, simple act, I believed I'd found just the right grace note to this wild, infuriating, unpredictable, and at times even uplifting presidential campaign.

# 11.

# Let Us Be Clear

Let us be clear: America has voted. Donald Trump is our president. Whatever our views and our differences and our strong feelings during the 2016 presidential election, it is now up to thinking, feeling Americans to come together in support of the Trump administration.

I've got to be honest, I never thought Donald Trump would win the Republican nomination. I never thought he'd be elected president. Most of the people I know in politics didn't give him much of a shot. Yet, here we are—and like him or not, support him or not, agree with him or not, Americans need to know that the future of our country is now tied to President Trump's ability to lead us for the next four years. It's not that we've got no choice but to pull for him, or to simply hope for the best; it's that we must listen to the word of the people and draw upon the lessons of this election cycle so that we might grow as a nation. Democracy has spoken. Set aside all the talk about election hacking and e-mail servers and influence-peddling—the swirl of controversy and suspicion can only divide us and obfuscate the lesson of this campaign. There's a reason Trump was elected, and we ought to listen to it, and try to learn from it.

I, for one, am hopeful that a Trump administration can accomplish great things. There's a lot of good President Trump can do, if we work in support of his presidency. He can cut down on regulation. He can begin to address the complicated issue of health care with a new approach that is not *only* market-driven but manages to meet the many and varied needs of the American people. He can work to strengthen the entitlements that threaten the economic future of our children, and look for ways to streamline or modernize government.

Can a Trump administration figure out a way to deal with poverty? Can his advisers draw lessons from the economic laboratories in our states and work them into the president's agenda? Can we maintain respect in the world without walking away from our global responsibilities? Can we protect our borders and still stand as a beacon of hope and opportunity for people all around the world?

I certainly hope so—and I'm betting, you're hoping so, too. But we're at a moment in our history where a change for the good cannot happen overnight, and it will not happen from the top down. Can we rebuild our neighborhoods and recapture the family values that were once the bulwark of our society? Probably, over time. Can we heal the partisan logjam in Washington and in our state and local governments? Probably, over time. Can we address the very real problems of racism, and build a United States of America that is truly pledged to uphold liberty and justice for all? Probably, over time. Can we create dynamic new jobs and find a way to make higher education affordable to the average American family? Probably, over time. Yes, the pace of our lives has quickened, and we all seem to want change to happen overnight, but we must take a realistic view and concede that a lot of the problems and divisions in our country will be fixed only over time, can be healed only over time. It's a generational thing, in most cases. I've come to think of it like a relay race, and as one generation passes the baton to the next, we can only look on and cheer. We baby boomers are still chugging along, and we have to continue to do our part to help our nation heal. But soon we'll hand things off to Generation X, and then it'll go on to the millennials, and on and on.

Look, I never bought into the slogan at the heart of Donald Trump's campaign, "Make America Great Again." I looked at those bumper stickers, those bright red hats, and the message rankled. America has been great for a long, long time. It will continue to be great for a long, long time. The so-called Greatest Generation of our parents and grandparents should stand as a reminder that each succeeding generation has had its own shot at greatness—so, too, will generations of Americans yet to be born. But let's always remember that we didn't become great overnight, and we will not hand over the baton and expect to fix the various messes we're in on the next trip around the track. It won't happen over four years, either—and if it works out that President Trump seeks and wins a second term, it still won't happen on his watch. This is not a knock on Donald Trump; it's just our new reality. We would have faced the same uphill slog if Hillary Clinton had been elected president—or any of the twenty major-party candidates from the 2016 field, me included.

We're looking at a long race, but we'll be running on fresh legs soon enough.

Those fresh legs were a revelation to me over the course of my campaign. Indeed, one of the all-important takeaways of this campaign for me was the tremendous energy and optimism of our nation's young people, which was very much in evidence as I traveled the country. I saw it on college campuses, and in our twentysomething volunteers, and even in some of the teenagers who signed on to work for us. I saw it in the young parents who came out to our town halls with their children snuggled to their chests. There were engaged, bright-eyed, excited, intelligent young people all around. Sure, some of them seemed a little too consumed with their electronic devices at times, but then I realized that they're just wired a little differently than us old folks. They need the constant bombardment of news and information and social media updates to keep connected, and I was gratified to see that those connections run deep. A lot of the young people I talked to seemed to be searching for a value-driven life, a purpose-driven life, as opposed to a money-driven life. They want to believe. They're idealistic. They want to shape the world and make it a better place—and best of all, they believe they can. And do you want to know something? I believe they can, too. Absolutely, they can.

What worries me, more than a little, is the possibility that these same idealistic young people will come to look on the election just past as the order of the day. For many of them, this presidential election might have been the first campaign to which they paid serious attention, as it was for my teenage daughters. It might have been the first time they got involved—by sharing opinions and ideas on social media, by going door-to-door in support of their chosen candidate, or by simply paying good and close attention. I sure hope it's not the last. I don't think it will be, but as I write these words, as the Trump White House continues to take shape, already I've spent some time worrying about this.

What worries me, too, is that, in the past, people's vote in the presidential election was a general reflection of how they felt things were going. They'd consider the state of the economy, our national security, the impact of social and entitlement programs on their lives. They'd vote yes or no, up or down, red or blue—often on the basis of this candidate's record or that candidate's promise. This time around, though, there were different forces at play. This time around, the motivating factors seemed to be more *personal.* This time around, people voted on the basis of how things were going for them in their lives, in their families, in their communities. This time around, people voted for change. They voted for a strongman who promised them he could fix *all* the problems in this country, *all* the problems in the world, even. He saw that our lives were broken and he said he could fix them.

But, really, the president can't fix these things because our problems reside where we live. *We're* the ones who have to set things right—and here I'm reminded of a town hall we held in Oregon, well along in the campaign. As we arrived at the event, a Little League game across the way from the venue. (All during the campaign, I'd seek out these sweet points of pause, away from my schedule.) For a few moments, I was able to reflect on the familiar rhythms of a baseball game, a welcome relief from the endless bustle of the campaign.

This game was very much on my mind as our town hall got under way and a man raised his hand and asked a question: "If you're elected president," he said, "what are you going to do to fix the drug problem?"

I said, "Let me ask you something. What are *you* doing to fix the drug problem?" I mentioned the baseball game I'd stopped to watch on my way to the event and asked this man if there was an anti-drug message delivered to those kids before the game. I asked if the local schoolteachers were warning kids of the dangers of drugs. I asked if whatever civic or church group this man belonged to was taking on the drug problem as an important part of its mission. I said, "So, what do you think? I'm going to fly in here on

Air Force One and fix your drug problem? *You* have to fix your drug problem."

It might sound in the retelling as if I really lit into this guy, but that wasn't my intent—and I don't think it's how my answer came across. The folks at that town hall seemed to get that the solutions to some of the very real problems facing the country were on them—*and* they got that I was passionate about this.

Another thing I'm passionate about is that we've got to stop making this all about politics. This is about putting food on the table, and keeping ahead of our bills, and looking ahead to a brighter, more hopeful future for our children and grandchildren. What the voters were telling us in this election was that they were angry, that they were feeling that their lives were out of control, that there was a sense of helplessness and hopelessness in the heartland.

We need leaders who will address these concerns with compassion—with an open heart and an open mind.

We need business owners to start looking for reasons to keep their jobs and their factories here in America instead of looking to ship them overseas or across the border.

We need executives at pharmaceutical companies like Mylan, maker of the EpiPen, to look for ways to keep their drugs afford-able so that the people who need them don't have to take out a mortgage to pay for them.

We need the folks who work in the front offices of our favorite sports teams, like the New York Giants, to take a stand and re-lease an athlete who has admitted to abusing his wife, even though the guy's a good field goal kicker and could help them win football games—as opposed to, say, the folks in the New England Patriots front office, who took no stand at all by signing a talented wide receiver just two days following his release by the Arizona Cardinals after being arrested on drunk driving charges and for failure to obey a police officer.

We need our leading entertainers to start modeling good behavior: our children are watching.

We need a kid on the schoolyard who isn't being bullied to stand up for the kid who is being bullied.

Perhaps most of all, we need our leaders across the board to do a better job of setting a good example. No, we cannot look to Washington to fix the ills of society. However, we can look to President Trump to set the tone, and to begin to set things right. His candidacy gave millions of disenfranchised voters a voice. Now it's on him to listen to them, and the rest of us to make sure they're heard.

## WHAT WE LEAVE BEHIND

People ask me all the time about my proudest accomplishments as governor, and I always point to the building of the Ohio Holocaust and Liberators Memorial as an enduring legacy. The way it came about was maddening, however. You see, we always held a ceremony in the state on Yom Hashoah, Holocaust Remembrance Day, but I wanted to do something a little more permanent, a little more meaningful to honor all the lives that were lost. I thought we needed a constant reminder of the horrors that can find us when man's inhumanity to man is on full and terrible display. But when I put it out there that I wanted to erect a memorial inside the State Capitol, I was told it would not be possible, so we looked to build it outside. Yet even here we got a lot of pushback. The statehouse grounds features statues laid out in a kind of Civil War theme, and it was felt that a Holocaust memorial would set a distinctly different tone. It got to where a former state senator who opposed the measure—a man who now chaired the Capitol Square Review and Advisory Board, which had oversight on this issue—put up a bunch of PVC piping to roughly approximate the shape and mass of our design. He even suggested that a Holocaust memorial would be only the first blight on the property: "First, it's a Holocaust memorial," he said, "and next thing you know, it'll be something about Donald Duck."

I was outraged; a lot of people were. So, I doubled down on the effort to get the memorial done, raising the money privately so no one could turn it into a political issue.

At one point, it looked like we'd get the memorial approved, but then we hit another logjam, so we doubled down yet again.

Finally, a dedicated group of volunteers raised close to $2 million and we were able to get it through. We retained the noted architect Daniel Libeskind to design it. He'd created the Jewish Museum in Berlin and the Danish Jewish Museum in Copenhagen, and his work was featured all over the world, so we were beyond fortunate to be able to bring him on board.

When the time came for the unveiling ceremony, we had a giant tarp spread over the memorial. Security was tight, too. There had been signs on social media and elsewhere that various groups, including neo-Nazi organizations and supposed skinheads, were threatening to disrupt our event. Eventually, we had to move the ceremony to a theater across the street, where we had a choir and a number of prominent speakers. My daughter Reese even read a passage from *Anne Frank: The Diary of Young Girl*, and for a moment in there it was possible to set aside all the difficulties we'd faced in getting the memorial built. Then, when it came time for the great reveal, with the folks gathered in the theater watching on the big screen, Daniel Libeskind and I raced outside and across the street to pull off the tarp.

I've got to tell you, it was one of the most remarkable, most impactful moments of my life. People started spilling out of the theater and taking in this soaring memorial up close, the only memorial in the country of its size and scope built on statehouse grounds, and certainly the only one of its kind designed by such a distinguished artist. It's really a magnificent, moving piece, and people were struck by the majesty of it, by the power of the inscription that stands as the focal point of the eighteen-foot-tall bronze monument: IF YOU SAVE ONE LIFE, IT IS AS IF YOU SAVED THE WORLD.

Jump ahead a couple years to the death of Senator John Glenn, the former astronaut, one of Ohio's favorite sons. When he died in December 2016, his body lay in state in the rotunda of the State Capitol, and I went to pay my respects to his widow. As I sat in the Speaker's office while Senator Glenn's family shared a private moment, I was joined by Secretary of State John Kerry, who had come to pay his respects. Through the office window, Secretary Kerry could see the Libeskind memorial, and he was struck by it.

He said, "That's really quite a monument, Governor."

It was just something to say, a way to fill the pause before we were called down to join Mrs. Glenn.

I told Secretary Kerry that we'd hired Daniel Libeskind, how it was the only Holocaust memorial of its kind in the United States, how local school and religious groups had responded to it.

He expressed his surprise that other states hadn't built their own memorials. He said, "I imagine it must've been pretty easy to get a monument like that approved."

I said, "You don't know the half of it."

For a number of reasons, that memorial was very much on my mind in the days leading up to the general election, and now it stands as a chilling reminder of the dark side of power and the evils of prejudice and intolerance. And every time I happen by it, I stop whatever I'm doing and take the time to breathe, to reflect, to consider the challenges we all face as we fill our days and look to leave a mark.

## A LETTER FROM MY DAUGHTER REESE

As you might imagine, I was on the receiving end of a lot of criticism on Election Night, as I was before, and in a lot of ways that criticism continues to find me. Conservative Republicans were upset with me because I refused to endorse Donald Trump. But whenever we talked about it as a family, I told my daughters that I wasn't too concerned about any of the criticism because I'd followed my heart and my conscience. I'd stuck to my principles, and did what I thought was right, and when you do that you find a way to handle whatever disapproval comes your way.

Still, my daughter Reese was a little worried about me, and she sat down and wrote me a letter to tell me that she was thinking of me, and that the Lord had yet to cast His vote to let me know the true purpose of the campaign.

Here's what she wrote:

> Couldn't go to sleep until I told you this . . .
> So you mentioned how a lot of people were mad at you, and yeah it sucks but it's impossible to keep everyone happy. You can't please everyone. At the end of the day, you answer to God, and at the end of the day you're the one who has to deal with your decisions; you obviously would have compromised your integrity if you had supported Trump and I don't think you would have ever forgiven yourself for it. Who

cares who gets mad at you?! You didn't get to where you are by staying quiet and following the crowd.

Everyone tells me how proud they are of you during this whole election, so don't feel as if nobody noticed what you did (and thought of it as a positive thing). Sure, people are upset with you, but as Dr. Seuss said, "Be who you are and say what you feel, because those who mind don't matter, and those who matter don't mind."

Also, all day Tuesday I kept thinking about the book of Job and I couldn't figure out why. When I found out who won the election I was obviously mad and I kept asking God why He let this happen and why He didn't let you win. (Ya know, because you try to live your life the way the Lord tells you to and you genuinely wanted to fix America, and God gave you the skills to be able to . . .)

Job came back into my head and I realized that maybe God was trying to tell me to stop asking because He isn't going to tell me. I think He was telling me to just let things happen and don't worry, because the world is in His hands. We have to trust God and trust His plan for us and the world. I don't know, I thought that was cool.

Love you. Night ♥

Out of the mouths of babes, right? Only, Reese is no longer a child. She and her sister, Emma, are finishing up their junior years in high school. Next thing Karen and I know, they'll be headed off to college. They'll be getting involved in their communities, and working to change the world in their own ways—perhaps using some of the tools their mother and I have given them, perhaps drawing on tools of their own. In fact, I believe Reese was drawing on some of those tools when she wrote that letter, looking to lift what she knew was my heavy heart.

And so it is with great pride and humility that I share Reese's letter here—with her permission, of course, because as every father of teenage daughters knows, you've got to get the go-ahead before you shine a light on your kids in any kind of public way.

It seems only fitting, then, that I let my daughter have the last word in *this* narrative.

After all, if we're going to pass the baton to the next generation and let them lead us to a brighter, more hopeful future, we might as well get started on it, don't you think?

# POSTSCRIPT

## A Letter to My Daughters

Dear Emma and Reese:

I started working on this book when I suspended my campaign for president, but in a lot of ways I was thinking about some of the ideas for this book for a long, long time.

As you know, I've been in public life since I was a young man—very close to your age, in fact. I started in politics when I was twenty-three years old. I was elected to the state senate at twenty-six, and to the Congress at thirty. I was in Washington for eighteen years, and I'm currently serving my second term as governor of Ohio. In all that time, I've gotten to see how the country works, how our political system works, how the business of government works. And I've learned a lot about people.

I guess you could say I wrote this book to share some of the lessons I've taken in over twenty-eight years of public service, to shine a light, I hope, on what it means to run for office, what it means to be a leader, and what it means to stand on principle.

Why do I feel called to write about such things? Well, politics has gotten a bad rap lately, but really, it's a grand and noble profession. I want you girls to always remember that, even when it's not so readily apparent. Most people go into politics to express their ideas, to improve the lives of people in their community, in their state, in their country, and in the wide, wide world. And yet, in the presidential campaign that just ended, you didn't see a whole lot of evidence of that, did you?

I wasn't expecting to write a book about this election when I decided to run for president. No, I was expecting to win the Republican nomination, and to go on to serve this great nation as our forty-fifth president. But that's not what happened, and as I reflected on it, I began to see that I was uniquely qualified to weigh in on what this election might mean for this country, now and in the future. And on what it might mean for the two of you.

This was a very difficult election, not just for our family, but for the country. You were with me on the campaign trail a lot of the time, especially over the summer, when there was no school. You saw in our town halls how people were hurting, how they were feeling isolated and left behind. You heard those single mothers talking about how hard they had to work to get ahead, and keep ahead, of their bills. You listened to those young people, just out of college, worry that they'd never get out from under all that student debt. You looked on when I met with people who couldn't afford the prescription drugs they needed to keep healthy. Your hearts broke along with mine when we'd meet people who were living in the shadows.

And then, when you got back home to Ohio, you followed the campaign on your laptops. You watched the debates on television. You told your mother and me that you couldn't believe some of the language you were hearing, some of the behavior you were seeing, even some of the positions that were being discussed that seemed to stand in direct opposition to the values we've tried to instill in you since you were little girls.

It was tough to look at this election and find anything grand or noble in the pursuit of our nation's highest office. This was troubling to me, for so many reasons, but on a deeply personal level, I was troubled for you girls. Why? Well, this was really the first campaign you followed as young adults, and I hated that this was your introduction to presidential politics. I didn't want you to think this was a typical campaign—that is the farthest thing from the truth. And I certainly didn't want you to feel as though you were looking ahead to a lifetime filled with the hateful, horrible rhetoric that came to characterize our political climate.

Reese, I saved a text from you where you told me how I should try not to yell as much as all those other candidates onstage during the debates. Lord knows, I appreciated the advice because, hey, there was an awful lot of yelling.

Of course, there have been nasty elections before this one—and I'm afraid there are nasty elections still to come. The 1824 campaign, when Andrew Jackson challenged the incumbent John Quincy Adams, is widely regarded by presidential scholars as one of the nastiest in our history—but I'd never seen anything like the 2016 campaign. When I was your age, when people ran for president, their words really meant something. Candidates might have clashed over their vision for this country, but there was a measure of respect and decorum missing from this election cycle.

You probably heard some of the pundits on television saying that this type of behavior was just politics, but I want you to know that it was something else entirely. I want you to remember that we have had some great leaders in this country. There was George Washington, the father of our country, who could probably have been king if that's what he wanted. But he realized that in our new democracy, he needed to stand as a duly elected president. There was Abraham Lincoln, who, through terrible personal sacrifice and harrowing ordeal, helped to lift our country and heal a great divide. In modern times, we've had leaders like Lyndon Johnson, a president you're not likely to hear much about in school, who believed that everyone should be treated equally, regardless of race. And Ronald Reagan, who talked about America being a shining city on a hill.

These great leaders gave voice to big ideas—*great* ideas. But despite all the yelling during the 2016 campaign, we didn't hear too many great ideas. All we heard, a lot of the time, was noise.

Most of all, girls, I want you to recognize that the strength of this country does not reside with the man or woman who sits in the Oval Office. Oh, our leaders matter, you'd better believe it. But one of the things I learned growing up was that the strength of this country resides in each of us as individuals. What I worry about for this country is that people have been conditioned to expect our leaders to fix all our problems. That's not how it works. We all need to take some personal responsibility and address our problems in a ground-up sort of way. We need to find ways to work together. And we need to recognize that we're Americans before we're Republicans or Democrats, conservatives or liberals. We do best when we come together, not when we're being pulled apart. Absolutely, we count on our leaders to set an example, to lead the way, but here it felt like we were only being led to fear and anger and confusion.

Just to be clear, there was confusion and uncertainty when I was growing up, too, but we were blessed with leaders who inspired us to look at our problems and to come together to fix them. We didn't see too much of that this time around, did we?

Mostly, I don't want you to think that this is how things are going to be from here on in. I want you to expect more from our politicians, more from our leaders—from your friends and neighbors, too. I don't know about you, but I don't want to live in a nation where our leaders just shout each other down, and say whatever they think they need to say in order to win election, so we need to hold our politicians to a higher standard. We need to insist that a life devoted to public service can once again stand as a grand and noble calling.

This wasn't how adults were supposed to act. This wasn't how leaders were supposed to act. It must have been so confusing for you, to have to see your own father in the middle of such craziness. To be made aware that there were kids your age (and even much younger) in schools across the country who were being bullied by other kids over this election. Kids would see this kind of bullying on television, and they'd listen to their parents and other adults arguing over the election, and to people fighting at some of these rallies, and it all kind of spilled over into the schoolyard. Students were being teased or taunted because they didn't share the same views, because the tone and tenor of the campaign had let the bullies think it was acceptable to try to intimidate someone on the other side of an issue.

We talked about this whenever we were able to carve out some family time during the campaign, remember? We talked about how the nastiness of some of these candidates was embarrassing for our country, how it sent the wrong message. We talked about how, when you run for president, you ought to be above this type of low behavior and how, as a candidate, you ought to set a good example for your supporters and for the country. You told me how it bothered you that some people in the media would say negative things about me, and that some of the other candidates would say negative things about me, and I told you not to pay any attention to that stuff. People have been saying negative things about me my entire career. I'm used to it by now. It doesn't mean anything.

It should have been a thrilling experience, a blessed thing, to take part in a presidential campaign with your family. It should have been a privilege. And I hope it was, on some level. You girls did a great job, whenever we were interviewed together. Do you remember that Republican presidential town hall we did as a family, with Anderson Cooper on CNN? You girls were terrific. Your mother and I were so proud of the way you handled yourselves in front of the cameras, in front of all those people. During a break in the interview, Emma, I said you should speak up more, and you pointed to your sister and said, "Well, if Reese would ever shut up, I would."

That was a lot of fun, right? But it wasn't just an adventure for our family; it was a meaningful journey. We were out to change the country, to lift people up by creating opportunities for them, empowering them, *acknowledging* them—and you were both a part of that. I'm proud of what we were able to accomplish. But I also know that it must have been a disheartening experience for my family, my friends, my dedicated campaign team, and my tireless volunteers. Frustrating, too. And it pains me to know that you were a part of that as well.

I'll say it again, girls: This was not how elections are supposed to go. This was not how I expected *this* election to go. It became a kind of roller coaster, and I'm sure that when we were on that ride together, it must have felt to you like the whole thing was out of control. There were highs and lows and twists and turns, and sometimes you couldn't help but get a little sick to your stomach. And then, when I ended my campaign, that roller coaster just kept right on going, didn't it? You had one candidate calling his opponent a crook and a liar, while the other candidate was calling her opponent a bigot and a misogynist. There was finger-pointing and name-calling all around. The two paths I'd talked about in my speech weren't so clearly defined as the general election approached. Every day, there was some new horror, some new low—and your mother and I could only look on with the rest of the country and wonder how the heck we could help our kids make sense of it all.

That's really why I wrote this book: to help the two of you make sense of it all, to help the country make sense of it all. But let me tell you, I'm not so sure I understand it myself. Some of the stuff that went on—it's beyond anything I'd ever seen before, beyond anything I'd ever even considered. And now here we are, in the first days of a presidency of a man I refused to endorse, and I hope to find a way to make you understand *that* as well.

With perspective, I hope, we'll be able to put the 2016 presidential election in context. We'll learn from it—and grow from it as a nation. We'll come to see that it was an election built on wild promises designed to make people feel good, and outrageous distortions and complete fabrications designed to make people wary. I suppose I could have gone out there and made a bunch of wild promises myself. I could have promised voters the moon, the stars, and the sky. Instead, I chose to tell them how we should go about solving some of the very complex problems facing America. I suppose I could have been louder, or cooked up some crazy allegations about my opponents, but I wasn't about to change. This wasn't a game to me. I was in it to win it, but not at all costs. Not at the expense of honor and decency. Not at the expense of speaking the truth. Not if it put me down in the ditch with anyone else, on what I believed to be the wrong path, stoking those same fears. All I could do was share my ideas, and offer up some solutions, and hope against hope that enough people would find enough things to like about my platform and my character to send me to Washington.

Now, I'm not able to say everything I want to say in this book. There are even some things I've said to you and to Mommy privately that didn't make it into these pages. That's because the election has passed, and we must look forward instead of backward. That's because this book is an opportunity to lead, to heal, to offer a message of hope to a country that's been divided by the most bitter, most contentious, most polarizing election in American history.

We have a new president, a man I opposed in the primaries, a man I didn't support in the general election, a man I'm now pulling for to succeed. How can that be? Well, I try to answer *that* in this book as well, so I hope you'll finish up your homework and set down your smartphones and take the time to read it. Together, maybe we can figure out a couple things about the election just past and reach for ways we might help unite our divided nation.

If we get it right, we might just be able to look ahead to our *next* presidential election with hope, with a sense of inclusion instead of exclusion, with the certainty that America's best days are ahead of us, not behind us.

One thing you girls will learn as you get older is that every election is talked about as the most important election of your lifetime. That's the way I felt about the 2016 election when we were in the middle of it, and now that's the way I feel about the 2020 election going forward—but in this one instance, that old political saw rings especially true. Do you want to know why? Because the two of you are seventeen years old as I write these words to you, which means that the next time we have an opportunity to come together as a country and elect a president, you'll be old enough to vote, and I want to do everything I possibly can to ensure that when you fill out your first presidential ballots, you can vote for a candidate who inspires you, who challenges you, who encourages all Americans to think freely and to dream bigly and to celebrate our differences.

Now wouldn't that be something?

# ACKNOWLEDGMENTS

First and formost, I want to thank my friend Dan Paisner for his partnership with me, and his great help in capturing my voice and articulating my ideas. Dan and I have completed three books together and these efforts have led to a real friendship between us. It's a joy to work with him and I appreciate his great talent.

Beth Hansen, Bob Klaffky, and Doug Preisse were critical in remembering many moments from the campaign and helping me to express them with clarity and color. They are amazing people and I'm lucky to have them in my life. John Weaver also offered invaluable insight and a key assist in launching the book; he has a great mind and a great heart. Matt Carle weighed in on tone and the core message of the book, while Jeff "The Dude" Polesovsky's "letter from New Hampshire" really captured the life of our volunteers—I'm grateful to them both. Jordan Garcea worked tirelessly to transcribe most of the interviews for this book, with an assist from Rich Reis, R. J. Richmond, Dalton Miller, and AnneMarie Morrissey; Nazar Zhdan and Kevin Bingle sorted through thousands of photos in search of the dozen or so images that would best reflect our time on the campaign trail; and Alex Thomas was always available to answer questions and fill in some of the gaps in my memory—a huge help. My friend Ron Hartman—"Rondo"—has been a kind of guardian angel to me; he always comes through with advice and direction, as he did on this project.

Of course, Jenny Bent is a very special talent and friend who advocates for me, encourages me, and has been with me through all of my books. John Silbersack is an awesome person I greatly respect. He always has my back. Jenny and John were able to bring this project to the attention of Tom Dunne and Sally Richardson at St. Martin's Press, who took a chance on this book and worked tirelessly to improve it. My thanks to the entire publishing team at St. Martin's for their dedication to this effort, beginning with our editor, Stephen S. Power, and extending to David Stanford Burr, Laura Clark, Tracey Guest, Paul Hochman, Cameron Jones, Amelie Littell, Joe Rinaldi, and Michael Storrings—talented and dedicated professionals, all.

On the home front, Karen, Emma, and Reese read the manuscript several times and gave me great advice and some much-needed encouragement. It meant the world to me. Love you♥

# INDEX